The Philadelphia Mummers

The Philadelphia Mummers

Building Community Through Play

PATRICIA ANNE MASTERS

TEMPLE UNIVERSITY PRESS
Philadelphia

Temple University Press
1601 North Broad Street
Philadelphia, PA 19122
www.temple.edu/tempress

Copyright © 2007 by Patricia Anne Masters
Published 2007
Printed in the United States of America

⊚ The paper used in this publication meets the requirements of the American
National Standard for Information Sciences—Permanence of Paper for Printed Library
Materials, ANSI Z39.48-1992

Library of Congress Cataloging-in-Publication Data

Masters, Patricia, 1945–
    The Philadelphia Mummers : building community through play /
Patricia Masters.
        p.   cm.
    Includes bibliographical references and index.
    ISBN-13: 978-1-59213-609-4   ISBN-10: 1-59213-609-5 (hardcover : alk. paper)
    ISBN-13: 978-1-59213-610-0   ISBN-10: 1-59213-610-9 (pbk. : alk. paper)
    1. Philadelphia Mummers (Organization)—History.   2. Parades—Pennsyl-
vania—Philadelphia—History.   3. New Year—Pennsylvania—Philadelphia—
History.   4. Philadelphia (Pa.)—Social life and customs.   I. Title.

    GT4013.P5 M37 2007
    394'.50974811—dc22   2006037508

2 4 6 8 9 7 5 3 1

For my mother,
  Anne Parker Zellefrow
  (1921–1974)
and my husband,
  Hugh

CONTENTS

Photo gallery follows page 94

ACKNOWLEDGMENTS

Ethnographic research always represents a collaboration between the community that is the subject of study and the researcher. This book is the product of the collaboration between the Mummers and myself. Though I take final responsibility for the interpretation of the information gathered throughout this research, I deeply appreciate the assistance and support I received from all of the Mummers who shared their lives and their knowledge with me. I am especially grateful to William (Curly) Conners, whose prodigious memory of Mummers lore and collection of newspaper clippings, beginning with the earliest parades and carefully kept up to date, were the backbone of my research. Bill could be found every Saturday morning at the Mummers Museum, where he worked on the archives in the library. The library is not the same since Bill's death a few years ago. Though he saw my dissertation through to completion and was always available to answer last-minute questions, and to chuckle when I shared elaborate theories of play with him, I am sorry that I cannot present him with a copy of this book as well. In a sense it belongs to both of us.

My research began at the Mummers Museum, where I was initially helped by Joseph Schubert and Robert Finnegan and later came to rely on Palma Lucas, executive director of the museum, and Jack Cohen, archivist and librarian. No request I ever made was denied, and the library became a headquarters where I met and talked with many Mummers. I am indebted to Tom DeNoti, who is the source for many of the oldest clippings the library's files contain; especially useful were his careful annotations within the clipping books, which represented hours of devoted research.

Al Heller, another of the Mummer historians, shared his encyclopedic knowledge of the parade and was especially helpful in my research on the comic division.

Dr. Charles E. Welch Jr., whose study of the folklore of the parade was the first source I read on the Mummers' history, was supportive throughout this research, leading me to many others who were helpful. Though clearly a Mummers enthusiast, Dr. Welch was also a careful scholar who shared his insights on the social significance of the Mummers' tradition.

I am deeply grateful to the members of the Golden Crown Fancy Brigade; marching up the street with them and being a small part of their parade preparations provided a unique perspective on the Mummers' experience. Bill Burke Jr., Golden Crown's captain until his recent retirement (he continues to direct from the sidelines), welcomed me into the club and encouraged everyone to share their experiences and make me feel "at home." They certainly did.

In addition, I am grateful to the following individuals who shared their memories and, often, pictures during what were sometimes very long interviews: Frances and Susan Bauer, Wendell Bright, Bill Burke Jr., Walter Burke, Tom Cloney, Mark Coley, Edward Conner, Daniel F. Creedon, Joseph Foley, Randy Giancaterino, Jacob Hart, William Hudzynsky, James F. Kenney, Alice Koresco, Patricia Lowery, Debbie Mastoianni, Donald M. McGrath, Sonja J. McHale, John Pignotti Jr., Richie Porco, James Sexton, Joseph Shuey, Michael Stermel, Jack Walsh, and William Wayterra. Many others spoke with me less formally, and their contributions are also woven into this tapestry.

Esther N. Chow chaired my dissertation committee, and her patience, enthusiasm, and sage advice were constants throughout the research process. She remains a friend, a mentor, and a role model.

Mark D. Jacobs served on my dissertation committee, and from my undergraduate years to the present he has stimulated my thinking about all things sociological. I am delighted that we are colleagues at George Mason University.

Other faculty at American University who guided my early research include Kenneth Kusterer, Muriel Cantor, and Jurg Seigenthaler.

My colleagues at George Mason University have consistently been supportive and encouraging. I am particularly indebted to Lois E. Horton for her broad perspective on urban history and race relations, and to Susan B. Trencher, who provided an anthropological critique of the manuscript. I appreciate the help of Joseph Scimecca, Rutledge Dennis, and Steven P. Vallas.

Jenny Aley offered her thoughts on organization, structure, and language, as did Mort Rumberg. Neither was familiar with the Mummers or the parade, so they offered a fresh perspective on the material.

Nancy Smith, who typed and formatted my dissertation manuscript and transcribed hours of taped interviews, helped put the finishing touches on the book manuscript. She was calm and patient about dealing with the "small stuff" and provided useful comments on content that reflected her familiarity with the themes of the book.

I am most indebted to Micah Kleit at Temple University Press. Micah was most enthusiastic about my project from the moment he read the first draft and he provided encouragement and support through the review process. Temple's production and marketing staff, including Gary Kramer, have responded patiently to all of my first-time author questions. Lynne Frost oversaw the production of the book, adding visual interest to the pages and working with me to choose historical and contemporary photos of the Mummers at play. I am pleased and grateful that my book found a home at Temple.

My family supported me enthusiastically at every stage in this project. My father, Albert Earl Zellefrow, provided love and encouragement as I worked on my dissertation. I was especially happy that he was present when I received my doctorate at American University, though he died shortly thereafter. My sister, Donna, and my brother-in-law, Tony Martinez, provided a home base in Yardley, Pennsylvania, and videotaped television coverage of the parade when I was either curbside or back in Virginia after completing the early research. They were wonderfully supportive as I embarked on the project of updating the initial research to complete this book. My son, Chris, had the momentous responsibility of carrying Bill Burke Jr.'s alternative backpiece the first year we were marshals with Golden Crown, and I was very proud that he never missed a cue as we headed toward City Hall. My daughter, Jenny, has also been a strong supporter, though we never did get her to march up the street.

My biggest debt is to my husband, Hugh, who for almost forty years has been my partner and friend. His steady encouragement and belief in every project I have undertaken has made it possible for me to combine the multiple roles of wife, mother, and scholar.

The Philadelphia Mummers

INTRODUCTION

*South Second Street, known as Mummers Row, is quiet the day after
"the Parade." The January sky is grey. In the bow windows, where
Christmas decorations were replaced in some row houses by elaborately decorated Mummer dolls[1] as New Year's Day drew near, all
that is evident is the prosaic lamp framed by half-drawn curtains.
The Mummer neighborhood clubhouses are silent. Their members
have returned to the ordinary business of working and catching up
on family chores neglected in the rush to prepare for "going up the
Street." Yet traces of "Two Street"[2] remain in the glitter and stray
sequins that seem embedded in the very concrete of the sidewalks,
or in the occasional piece of trim or plume that the street cleaners
missed the morning after "the Parade." Suspended on the utility wire
above the street, the startling presence of a pair of gilded sneakers,
tossed in the air by an exuberant comic, gives mute testimony to the
boisterous celebrations of the preceding night, when the Mummers
returned from the official city parade to perform in the narrow
streets where their tradition began.*

*The Mummers Parade is over for another year. But the memo-
ries of performing together at City Hall will be replayed in the clubhouses in the weeks and months to come. In January fantasy is put
aside and play suspended, but the Mummer community endures, as
it has for a century. After a brief respite, the Mummers will come
together to begin their preparations for performing again on the
first day of the next new year.*

—Field notes, 2 January 1996

This book is about the community created over the past century and reaffirmed annually by the Philadelphia Mummers.
At the core of this community is the annual Philadelphia
Mummers Parade. In preparing for their performances, the Mummers
enact and re-create traditions, work collaboratively to produce art

and entertainment, and share in one another's lives inside and outside their clubhouses. What binds them together is a passion for playing and performing. Through tracing the emergence of the Mummers from their beginnings in the mid-nineteenth century, it is possible to learn about how communities form, what forces enable them to retain a distinctive identity, and the extent to which they are affected by the larger cultural milieu in which they are embedded. The transformation of many small ethnic celebrations into a public ritual that has occurred for more than a century and a half reveals the way in which play itself is changed as it becomes a performance for the consumption of a broader audience. Communities are not abstract, nor are they static. A community is created through the interactions of individuals, based on their desire to maintain a connection that promises constancy in a rapidly shifting world.

Sociology and anthropology have a rich and varied tradition of ethnographic study. Through their immersion in the lives of ordinary people, ethnographers have challenged popular wisdom and given voice to communities whose stories would otherwise have gone untold.[3] In this considerable body of scholarship, the authors have taken seriously C. Wright Mills's assertion that "no social study that does not come back to the problems of biography, or history, and their intersections within society has completed its intellectual journey" (1959, 6).

In this book I explore the life-world (Schutz 1970) that the Mummers have created: its structures and essential components, its distinguishing features, as well as the characteristics that are common to communities, and the transformations it has undergone over many years. I emphasize the adaptive responses of individuals as they make sense of their world and time and actively seek avenues that strengthen family and community ties. This ethnography focuses on a successful community, though not a perfect one.

The Philadelphia Mummers[4] are the creators and custodians of the longest-running folk parade in the United States. In many respects the Mummers are similar to other communities, and a deeper knowledge of their interactions adds to our understanding of community formation in general. But the bonds they form through play, the most frivolous of human activities, differentiate them from groups whose purposes are instrumental and practical. Their strong ties are based on their desire to re-create what Johan Huizinga (1955, 22) termed "the feeling of being 'apart together' in an exceptional situation, of sharing something important, or mutually withdrawing from the rest of the world and rejecting the usual norms." It is this emotional experience that distinguishes a play community.

Robert Putnam (1993, 17) maintains that community and civic engagement grow out of play, though play is not undertaken for the purpose of creating social capital.[5] He emphasizes that "members of Florentine choral societies participate because they like to sing, not because their participation strengthens the Tuscan social fabric. But it does." Like the choral societies that Putnam observed, the Mummers play not to create community; rather, their community grows spontaneously from their play.

In conducting research for this ethnography, I spent more than five years immersed in the lives and world of the Mummers; since that initial intense involvement, I have observed recent transformations, large and small, in the parade, though at a distance.

From the outset of this research, it was obvious that the Mummers share a worldview. Their shared perspective includes an awareness of their play community's relationship to other communities in Philadelphia, an understanding articulated through rituals and passed on to successive generations through ongoing socialization in the norms and customs that govern their relationships, and practical and technical knowledge of "how we do things" that enhances their distinctive art.

As I interviewed the Mummers, joined their preparations for the parade, and read their history, I focused on understanding their world as they saw it. Like any ethnographic research, this research privileges the view of those whose world is entered. Though I made extensive use of historical documents and newspaper accounts of the parade,[6] it was with the recognition that neither of these sources is objective. It is important to the Mummers to present a positive image to their audiences, and they have been successful in emphasizing their contributions to the larger Philadelphia community. But the Mummers' view, like that of any community, is limited, shaped by mutually reinforced understandings about "what is going on here." The perspective is heavily influenced by their biographical situations and their socioeconomic positions. As I present the Mummers' world, I place their interpretations within a larger sociological framework, which will help readers to apply the research about the Mummers to understanding the broader concept of community formation.

Who Are the Mummers?

The Philadelphia Mummers Parade grew out of nineteenth-century neighborhood celebrations in Southwark and Moyamensing, immigrant settlements on the southern fringes of the Old City of Philadelphia. Today's event is a large-scale spectacle featuring as many as twelve thousand performers and representing an investment of from four to eight million dollars,[7] money raised by dozens of small, neighborhood-based groups that parade under club banners.

The parade is more than a one-day spectacle. The appearance of frivolity is created by the combined efforts of thousands of Philadelphians, not only the performers themselves but all the behind-the-scenes producers and artists who cooperate to bring the parade up the street. The Mummers belong to dozens of clubs that vary in size and resources; they are "the good working people"[8] of the city, the carpenters, bartenders, accountants, government employees, and clerks who call Philadelphia home.

Though the size of the parade has diminished over time, it is still a lavish production. Traditionally, the event unfolded on Broad Street, Philadelphia's main north-south thoroughfare, on New Year's Day (or the first Saturday or Sunday following 1 January, if the weather was inclement). In 2000 the parade route was temporarily changed to Market Street, a more "tourist-friendly" venue. This shift was not a success, and the Mummers and the city returned to Broad Street again in 2004. The Broad Street route was a cherished tradition for most of the parade's history, and many Mummers resisted and resented the change to Market Street. The return to Broad Street was the beginning of what appears to be a resurgence of the group's popularity after several years of lackluster crowds.

The parade has four performing divisions: the comic clubs, the fancy clubs, the string bands, and the fancy brigades. Each division's performance is different, but all the entertainment includes some mixture of music, dance, comedy, and mime, and spectacular or funny costumes, floats, scenery, and special effects. Though it is frequently referred to as "the Philadelphia version of the Mardi Gras," the two events differ in significant ways. Especially important is that the commercial and business sectors of New Orleans support Mardi Gras because it generates millions of dollars in tourist revenue.[9] Philadelphia's parade, in contrast, continues to depend on the support of the working-class neighborhoods where most of the clubs are located and where Mummery began. The City of Philadelphia provides a prize purse for the annual event. However, this modest sum (usually under $300,000, distributed across the four divisions) is important as an acknowledgment of the Mummers' unique contribution to the city's cultural life. The clubs remain independent of the city and, as several of them proudly informed me, "own" the parade, though they are compelled to negotiate many issues related to the event with the city, which "owns" public space. In the past, the Mummers have spoken to other Philadelphians using satire and comedy, and though this seditious element is still present in the parade, it has been overshadowed by the artistic accomplishments of the clubs.

Why Study the Mummers?

My choice to study the Mummers was serendipitous. I have a long-standing interest in the relation between individuals and their communities, but I initially planned to study communities serving instrumental purposes. Visiting Philadelphia over the New Year in 1995, I watched the Mummers perform on television and was captivated by the spectacle of the parade. Initially I viewed the coverage casually, but as the day-long event unfolded, I became mesmerized by the color, the costumes, and the sheer joyfulness of the productions.[10]

Approaching this research, I knew little about the Mummers. I assumed that the parade was funded by the city or commercially underwritten, and that the performing Mummers developed their presentations working with professional costumers, choreographers, music directors, and production designers. (Some, though not all, of the performances had professional polish.) It did not seem possible that presentations as lavish and intricate as the fancy club or the string band entries could be neighborhood-grown. My assumptions were mostly incorrect. Early interviews with the curator of the Mummers Museum revealed that the parade is an event created by people whose lives are in many respects like my own or anyone else's (but perhaps more colorful), with demands of work, family, and myriad everyday tasks. Though some groups have professional costumers, much of the inspiration for themes, and the expertise for executing their ideas, come from within the clubhouses. Each performance represents hundreds of hours of work. To understand the Mummers' dedication to the parade, I began asking every Mummer I encountered: Why do you parade? Their responses revealed four often intertwined reasons for their involvement.

First and most important, fun or play found in performing or creating the folk art unique to their community drew the Mummers to their clubs. Typical of this kind of motivation was the response of a fancy brigade member:

> Performing is a total, joyous release. Because the minute you step into [the performance area at City Hall] and the crowd reacts, the seriousness [of competing] is still there, but now, you're having fun. Now, you're just going to let all the tension you've had in your job, in your family, from getting ready—you just let it go. There's a big smile ten miles wide on your face, and you're out there to have a good time. That's what [parading] is all about. (Sexton, interview, 1996)

This response reveals the seductive pull of fantasy, the fun of taking the spotlight, and the pleasure of suspending identity and assuming a role far removed from the ordinary. The Mummers are, above all else, performers, and many spoke of the satisfaction of having an audience join them in a shared fantasy.

A second motivation many Mummers identified was the desire to continue traditions started by grandparents, or even great-grandparents, or associated with "the neighborhood." For many Mummers, involvement in a club provides a sense of continuity with the past. One member of a fancy club who has moved to Philadelphia's suburbs maintains his linkage to family through parading.

> My father, my family had been in it [the parade]—I wouldn't say from day one, but my family were charter members of what was the old Gallagher Fancy Club [one of the original groups that paraded at the beginning of the century].... I was born in this [South Philadelphia] neighborhood, and at

that time, when you grew up, just about everybody when they were ten years old started going [parading] with the comics. (Conner, interview, 1997)

This story was told over and over in interviews I conducted. For many Mummers, the story of their involvement began with that first march up Broad Street, dressed perhaps as Little Lord Fauntleroy or Tom Thumb. (Many of the older men recalled with a mixture of pride and embarrassment marching up Broad Street as Little Bo Peep; little girls marching in the parade is a recent development.) The tradition they followed was so much a part of the neighborhood and so inextricably linked to what their family "did" for New Year's Day that it had never occurred to them that they would not make the trek up to City Hall with an uncle or father. Nor do they ever foresee a time when they will not be part of the parade.

A third motivation for joining and staying involved with a club is strong friendships that over time become primary ties, turning friends into family. As one string band member explained to me:

I think there's lots of reasons why people initially do it. They . . . do it because it is a lot of fun, no matter how you define fun. Whether it's drinking beer at the club or hanging out [with friends] or traveling [to perform at different places], or whatever. Performing, that's lots of fun. And what happens is you get, you become absorbed in that environment. You get married and all your friends [become closer friends] and their wives become your wife's friends. Then you start raising kids together, and you become very . . . socialized in that environment. It becomes almost entrapping. Everybody you know or everybody you talk to or everybody you socialize with is from that [Mummers] environment. (Creedon, interview, 1997)

Another fancy brigade member, not a Philadelphian but a "Jersey girl," explained the gradual strengthening of ties through working together and added the attraction of having a place where she could be her authentic self. Her answer reflects the comfort and reassurance that membership in a tightly bound group provides:

It's important to [parade] once a year, but it's also important to be able to be in your community, have a place that you know that you can go to, and socialize and be with friends and feel comfortable and enjoy yourself. And . . . you know you have friends and that you're all working together [in preparing for the parade]. You don't have to be working for the same common goal, but you have a camaraderie there that just builds and builds. But it's just like, you're family, this is *your* group. (Lowery, interview, 1997)

The need for connection is part of the human condition. Gerald Suttles has written about the "community as communion." His perspective stresses that the community is a "symbol in people's hopes for a collectivity in which they can *be* rather than *seem*" (Suttles 1972, 264). The Mummer community, as I describe it in Chapter 6, is a world of multiple layers and different types of relationships. It can be envisioned as a series of circles, with levels of intimacy decreasing as the circles grow larger. The innermost circle is composed of family and longtime friends; the next circle is the club itself, which embraces the intimate group; the third circle is other clubs within the divisions that both compete with and provide support to one another; and the fourth, the four divisions of the Mummers—comic clubs, fancy clubs, string bands, and fancy brigades—which make up the Mummers' community. The barriers between the circles are permeable, with competition and cooperation, closeness and separation, depending on specific times and situations.

A fourth recurrent theme throughout this research was the opportunity that preparing for the parade offered for creativity. A comic suggested that he found a special satisfaction in knowing that what he created through his imagination and skill was presented to an enthusiastic audience on parade day. In this case, the pull of performance was less important than the sense of achievement in transforming an idea into a reality. His words are revealing:

We used to do the work, most of our building [of props and floats] for years down on Delaware Avenue [in South Philadelphia]. No heat, no nothing. Your fingertips used to be frozen. . . . And people would say, "How can you enjoy this?"

But if you didn't enjoy it you wouldn't be able to do it. [The fun of it is in] the creation of something and seeing people enjoy . . . [and] appreciate what you've done. (Conner, interview, 1997)

The Mummers are gifted folk artists and performers, and the parade reflects an increasing sophistication and skill in bringing to their audiences the latest trends in popular culture as well as the enduring features of their art. But the Mummers are also highly competitive, and recognition for innovative and creative work, reflected in prizes, drives change in the parade.

This book explores the four themes that Mummers identified as motivating their efforts and unifying their community. But there are other, less often shared motives for participation. The first is prestige. Mummer leaders are looked up to as examples within the community. The flamboyantly dressed club captains are charismatic leaders. The stage on which they enact their roles is a comparatively small one, yet they are the spokesmen for their clubs and for the parade tradition itself. On another level, prestige is implicit in the pride that Mummers display in sharing the clippings about their grandfathers and in the way they confer special honor on community leaders by electing them to a Hall of Fame in the Mummers Museum. It is tempting to look at the comparatively prosaic work that many Mummers engage in day to day and see the prestige within the community as compensation; but this is not the way Mummers themselves are likely to see honors within their clubs and divisions.

Finally, there is competition. The Mummers are ferocious competitors; each club and every performer on Broad Street has his or her eyes on "the prize": first place. Winning is the reward for the hours devoted to preparation, and recognition by judges who are highly respected is proof of being "the best."

The Mummers as an Example of Community

Sociologists define community in many ways: it is "an aggregate of people who share a common interest in a particular locality . . . [ranging in size] from a neighborhood to a town to a medium-sized city"; or it is "a network of social relations marked by mutuality and emotional bonds"; or, in Weberian terms, it is "communal [in the sense that members share] an orientation of social action . . . based on a subjective feeling of the parties, whether affectual or tradition, that they belong together" (Bender 1978, 7–9). Robert Nisbet has observed that "community is founded on man conceived in his wholeness rather than in one or another of the roles, taken separately that he may hold in a social order. . . . Community is a fusion of feeling and thought, of tradition and commitment, of membership and coalition" (Bender 1978, 9).

I have already given cultural historian Johan Huizinga's definition of a "play community." But the Mummers are also bound by a shared history and ethnic roots. In this book I discuss the boundaries of community as well as recent attempts to include new immigrant groups in the parade. Most of the Mummers performing today are from white ethnic neighborhoods. Black Philadelphians have always participated in the parade, though their part in the celebration has changed over time. The first Mummers celebrated the holidays in the neighborhoods as Swedes, British, Germans, Scots-Irish, Irish, or African Americans. The merging of the disparate celebratory customs traced in Chapter 1 became a hybrid form of play and performance that enabled individuals from different nations to see that what they shared—even if only for one day a year—was more important than what separated them from one another.

The Mummers are bound by a set of norms and values that remain traditional and conservative. Multigenerational links within the clubs ensure the transmission of behavioral expectations and values from one generation to the next. Further, membership in a club, and the connection between that club and the more inclusive Mummer community, involves a dense set of obligations. Growing out of the responsibility that Mummers feel for one another within the extended family that comprises clubs and performing groups is the impulse to show concern for other Mummers and the desire to reach out to the neighborhoods where clubs are based. Clubhouses are places for families to gather—from grandparents to small children. Everyone contributes to the parade. Many of the adult Mummers who shared their stories with me went "up the street" on the shoulders of their grandfathers and fathers. Future Mummers will probably remember their first appearance on Broad Street, Philadelphia's main drag, accompanied by grandmothers and mothers as well. Within the play community, individuals learn the rules not only of competitive play but also of living responsibly with others. Through their reliance on one another, they learn how important it is to be trustworthy and to trust.

The Mummers support and nurture each other. They depend on one another, sharing not only the fun of play but also the difficulties of raising children, caring for aging parents, and confronting illness and financial problems. Within the Mummers' play community, the individual often finds a place where he or she can be understood, valued, and accepted, not for what he or she *has* but for what he or she brings to the enterprise of play and is willing to share with others.

Communities are never monolithic, as Lois Horton and James Horton (1997, xi–xii) wrote in their study of African American community. Rather, the members are likely to be fractious and competitive as well as nurturing and supportive. In this respect communities are like large families drawn together by shared joys and sorrows. Play communities like the Mummers demonstrate these contradictions. On parade day, camaraderie gives way to cutthroat competition. Yet many of the individuals I spoke with over five years asserted, "We are all *Mummers*," or, more simply, "We are a family."

The Nature of Play

The uniqueness of the Mummers is that the driving force behind their community is play—not necessity, not tragedy, and not instrumentality. Play is relatively neglected in sociology, but the impact of this elementary social form on the maintenance and formation of bonds among individuals is significant.

Play is a broad term; thus it is important to specify how I defined it for my research. It has the following characteristics:

1. *Freedom:* playing is not obligatory; if it were it would at once lose its attractiveness and joyous quality as a diversion.
2. *Separateness:* play is circumscribed within limits of space and time, defined and fixed in advance.

3. *Uncertainty:* the course of play cannot be determined, nor can the result be attained beforehand, and some latitude for innovations is left to the player's initiative.
4. *Unproductivity:* play creates neither goods, nor wealth, nor new elements of any kind; and, except for the exchange of property among the players, it ends with a situation identical to that prevailing at the beginning of the game.
5. *Governance by rules:* play operates under conventions that suspend ordinary laws and establishes new temporary rules, which alone count.
6. *Make believe:* play is accompanied by a special awareness of a second reality or of a free unreality, as against real life. (Caillois 1961, 9–10)

This general definition focuses on competitive play engaged in by groups, but it applies to expressive and solitary play as well. In Chapter 7, "The Experience of Play," I examine the different forms play assumes in light of theoretical definitions of play.[11] Play generates culture broadly understood. Culture includes both symbolic and normative components, and through play the Mummers have formed a distinctive, enduring subculture that celebrates and reinforces widely held social values.

I do not assert that the Mummers Parade is a panacea for urban decay, or that it solves the complex, intractable problems that Philadelphia's neighborhoods and their inhabitants confront. The Mummers do not play in isolation, and they have been challenged to assume a role in lessening the divisions within their multiethnic, multiracial city. Their attempts have had mixed success. Yet interviews with city leaders led me to conclude that the quality of life in neighborhoods where the Mummers have a strong presence is enhanced as the traditions associated with being a Mummer are enacted. Therefore, to the extent that strong neighborhoods contribute to the overall well-being of the wider community, the play that I study is consequential in strengthening some of Philadelphia's neighborhoods.

The absence of community is a legitimate concern; however, it is also important to recognize those places where community is present and to understand the mechanisms that draw neighbors together not in fear but in fun. Equally evident as I interviewed the Mummers were fissures within the community, though I found that in difficult times the Mummers cooperate and support one another across divisions and across clubs. Because the processes of building community emerge clearly in examining the life-world of the Mummers, this book attempts to enlarge the understanding of an important sociological unit. The Mummer community is a dynamic example of how individuals playing together form creative, generous, and enduring ties.

Organization of the Book

Chapter 1 looks at the early Shooters' processions that emerged from South Philadelphia's multiethnic neighborhoods and examines how disparate groups joined together in playing. For the groups who made their public debut on New Year's Day 1901, the invitation to Philadelphia's symbolic center was an opportunity to present their gift of entertainment to a broader public. In many respects, the invitation to be part of a city celebration represented a provisional acceptance of immigrant communities that had been economically and socially marginalized. Before 1901 the Shooters' processions were unstructured and disorganized; after 1901 the groups coalesced into a play community, aware of their image as "the Mummers" and conscious that through their play they were developing a unique tradition.

Chapter 2 focuses on the increasing elaboration of the parade and describes the Mummers' ongoing efforts to craft a positive image within the city and develop an art that incorporates contemporary themes and traditional artistic categories. If traditions become rigid, shutting out innovation and insisting on the "old ways," their relevance diminishes. By encouraging new approaches and remaining open to contemporary cultural trends, the Mummers continue to draw younger members into their community. Thus the clubs strengthen intergenerational ties. In this chapter I also explore the increasing structure of competition and its impact on the spirit of play. I describe the evolution of the Mummers' "art world" (Becker, 1984) in terms of both increasing complexity in the performances of all four divisions and the division of labor within the parading units. Finally, this chapter examines both the competitive and logistical rules that govern the parade and the forces that produce a more tightly structured event.

Throughout their history, the Mummers have been highly sensitive to their image as a "white-guys-only" parade. Chapter 3 examines the extent to which the parade is exclusionary and looks at the ways in which the Mummers have—with mixed results—attempted to bring blacks, women, and the "new" immigrants into their play community.

As I began my research on the Mummers, I was repeatedly told, "You can't understand the parade unless you are a part of it." Heeding this advice, I "joined" the Golden Crown Fancy Brigade, a family club in South Philadelphia. Chapter 4 is a detailed account of my foray into Mummery.

Chapter 5 examines the traditions and rituals of the Mummer community. From the sacred Mummers Mass to the raucous Two Street celebration, traditions ensure that the Mummers balance structured and free play. I also discuss in this chapter the process of "traditionalizing," so crucial to the continuity of Philadelphia Mummery.

The Mummers are a "family." Chapter 6 looks at the close ties within the clubs and the connections between the play community and the city. It is in the family that we are loved, shaped, and comforted throughout the course of life. This chapter also describes the merging of family and tradition that keeps the Mummers together in a changing world. Yet the familial emphasis is a mixed blessing, and this chapter looks at the ways in which family linkages frequently supersede organizational structures.

From the solitary hours spent by the fancy club member imagining and creating an elaborate suit to the tightly choreographed performances of the string bands, it is possible to see the range of experiences that fall under the heading of "play." Chapter 7 examines the experiences of the Mummers at play.

Chapter 8 reflects on my exploration of this community. Because the parade never stands still, this chapter looks at recent attempts to update the celebration, and the continuing tension between the desire to maintain local a neighborhood tradition and at the same time unlock the potential of this unique event as a tourist attraction.

Because I frequently use ethnographies in teaching and begin discussing each work by looking at the practical challenges of sociological research, I have included an appendix on theories and multiple methods that I used in exploring the Mummers' world. In describing the challenges that writing this book posed, I also hope to convey the fun of learning about a life-world different from one's own.

I will be grateful always for the generosity and graciousness of the Mummers over the years, as they told me about themselves and their world.

From Play to Play Community
The Early Years of the Mummers Parade

Public appreciation of the significance and value of the Mummers great folk festival dawned only slowly. Philadelphia, it was conceded, had never seen such a spectacle. But it was also said of the Mummers: "The city knew them a century ago. Ragamuffins they were about that time, and ragamuffins the half of them looked yesterday. But the city had called them together with an offer of money prizes, and thus Philadelphia saw on the first day of the twentieth century a procession that Momus himself could not have devised."
—Brandt (1930e, 1)

On 1 January 1901, twenty-five hundred exuberant, lavishly—or outlandishly—costumed performers strutted up Philadelphia's Broad Street to City Hall for the first time, accepting an invitation from the city council to perform and preen before a wider public. Though they paraded as the "Shooters," the groups were quite separate, drawn together by the necessity of working with the city.[1] Philadelphia was then and remains today a city divided by class, ethnicity, and race; in the early period of the Mummers' history, the groups that took to the streets for holiday celebrations were ethnically distinctive, though they shared a marginal class position. Yet, as immigrants or sons of immigrants, the Shooters may have seen themselves as ambassadors from their neighborhoods. The city represented the powerful interests of wealthier residents, and it seems likely that the Shooters recognized the significance of the invitation to entertain in public space. Thus it was undoubtedly a heady experience, for the men who celebrated the new millennium with play, to make the long trek from their communities to the symbolic center of Philadelphia to compete for small prizes financed by a special appropriation. They were a novelty that day, but their appearance was hugely successful. A talent for amusing and amazing others with their performances became the wedge the Shooters used to create a place for themselves and their communities in Philadelphia. Their long journey toward acceptance began with that first invitation to join in welcoming the twentieth century.

This chapter focuses on the early development of the Mummers' tradition. Their history has three distinctive stages. The first covers the first half of the nineteenth century, when the newly arrived immigrants of South Philadelphia used the neighborhood streets to stage their celebrations of the holiday season. The second stage began after the Civil War, when the small celebrations expanded into neighborhood processions that attracted the notice of the rest of Philadelphia—not always favorably—and concluded with the Shooters' Broad Street debut. The third stage is discussed in later chapters and encompasses the contemporary period of the Mummers' history.

Though the individual groups marching in 1901 recognized their ethnic and cultural differences, other Philadelphians saw them as an undifferentiated mob of ruffians and rowdies from the southern fringes of the city. This situation is common in urban areas, where an "us" versus "them" dichotomy characterizes relations between established residents and new arrivals. Being an outsider or insider is important in forming and maintaining a collective identity, and through interaction with others, groups come to recognize their status.

As Gerald Suttles (1972, 13) writes, "local communities and neighborhoods, like other groups acquire a corporate identity because they are held jointly responsible by other communities and organizations." Communities, then, are accountable to others for the conduct of their residents and the degree to which they follow established social and legal norms. The residents of Philadelphia's immigrant areas, usually poor and still struggling to stay afloat in their new environment, were all painted with the same broad brush. It was inevitable that they would resent and resist their negative labels, and it was not long before they began to try to change others' perceptions of who they were. But the transformation of their public image took time. To understand their journey toward acceptance, it is useful to examine the early experiences of South Philadelphia's immigrants and their evolving relations with others from the city.

Contemporary Mummers recognize the challenges their ancestors confronted in gaining respect. Thus, they pass along the stories from their great-grandparents and grandparents, often sharing cherished clippings and old photographs preserved in shoeboxes or pasted in family albums.[2] The history[3] of the parade is inextricably linked to the personal struggles and triumphs of present-day Mummer families, whose ancestors wanted so desperately to be accepted in their adopted country.

Johan Huizinga (1955) asserted that play communities arise spontaneously as individuals discover the joy and challenge of performing with others that enhance play. The element of competition, present from the earliest chaotic and rowdy neighborhood processions, provided an extra incentive for the Shooters to organize and cooperate. However, Huizinga qualified his assertion when he wrote that every bridge tournament does *not* spawn a play community. This raises the challenge of explaining why and how the Mummers came together as a play community.

The Two Philadelphias

William Penn's Philadelphia is among the oldest cities in the United States; the religious tolerance of its Quaker founder and the shrewd commercialism of those who joined him made the colonial settlement a magnet for many different nationalities and faiths. As Struthers Burt wrote in a somewhat romanticized history, *Philadelphia: The Holy Experiment* (1945, 37):

> There was nothing haphazard about [the city], at least in design. It did not just take place. If Penn was too wise to think that man could live by bread alone, he also knew that he could not live by the spirit alone, and every detail of his "Holy Experiment" had been considered for . . . months and years; envisioned, amended, and finally fixed upon. . . . He rewrote and revised his [colonial] constitution, his Frame of Government . . . twenty times before it was finished.

Philadelphia was, then, a planned settlement, self-conscious, self-important, and imbued with the Protestant ethic of hard work and earthly rewards as the outward sign of God's favor. Bounded by the

Delaware and Schuylkill rivers on the east and west and by Vine and South streets to the north and south, the City of Brotherly Love was tiny—only two square miles. Even the grid layout of the streets, interspersed with many small public parks, reinforced the appearance of tidiness and order. Prosperous residents lived in multistory townhouses opening directly onto the street, with alleys to the rear. Tucked out of sight in the alleys and cellars, the poor were all but invisible.

In seventeenth- and eighteenth-century Philadelphia, class differences depended on the different economic and social capital that immigrants brought with them from Europe. Those who had wealth consolidated their positions through investments in commercial and manufacturing ventures that opened up in the areas surrounding the port city. Those with nothing to invest entered the community as indentured servants or slaves,[4] who were variously labeled as either the "deserving poor" or "worthless vagabonds" (Alexander, 1973, 10); they found life difficult and lonely.

The settlements to the south of Philadelphia provided a stark contrast to Penn's bustling city. Ironically, Murray Dubin's (1996) history reveals that South Philadelphia (which included Southwark and Moyamensing) was occupied by Europeans and free blacks seven years before William Penn's "Old City" was founded in 1677. The Scots-Irish[5] immigrants settled the waterfront in Southwark by the early part of the eighteenth century, and they were followed by Swedish, German, Dutch, and English immigrants. Other groups flocked to the area in the nineteenth century: Irish Catholics, Italians, Poles, and Jews. Prior to the Civil War, blacks fleeing slavery via the Underground Railroad joined Philadelphia's free black community. Unlike Penn's carefully planned city, South Philadelphia, like Topsy, simply grew. Newcomers, as Dubin (1996, 9–10) writes, "plopped down in the neighborhoods, renting terrible housing in row house communities." These were an improvement over the flimsy shacks that the first arrivals occupied. Residents were desperately poor, having arrived with little more than the clothes on their backs. But they showed a willingness to work hard because of their passionate desire to make a better life than they had left behind. Some, more fortunate than others, came as part of an ethnic chain of relatives or neighbors from the Old Country who provided temporary shelter and help with finding work.

The differences between the two Philadelphias spurred the development of two distinctive public traditions in the 1800s that Susan Davis documented in *Parades and Power: Street Theatre in Nineteenth-Century Philadelphia* (1985). Established Philadelphians developed an array of public performances. Grand processions celebrated historical milestones in the newly independent nation, businesses organized parades to showcase their products and flaunt their economic accomplishments, and volunteer militia paraded in all their finery. The working class was not entirely silent, and city workers organized strike parades to air their grievances. Other groups used public parades to promote explicitly political messages. In the late nineteenth century, for example, temperance associations used the streets to bring their message of self-restraint and piety to the working class.[6] These parades were "respectable."

Meanwhile, in the ethnic enclaves south of the city, immigrants devised their own celebrations, often following the practices of the agrarian lands they had left. The line between respectable and rowdy was clearly drawn: "Disorderly maskings and burlesques were spontaneous performances that encouraged audience participation. [In contrast to the respectable parades,] burlesques did not create distance between audience and performers—they reduced it. Fantasticals circulated in the streets, toured their own neighborhoods, and surprised the crowds. In contrast [to rowdy parades], respectable parades were announced ahead of time to gather audiences, and they followed defined, published routes" (Davis 1985, 161). Burlesque parades, like European fiestas or carnivals, mixed play with socializing throughout the immigrant communities. As they grew increasingly large and visible, these celebrations captured the attention of more staid Philadelphians.

Similar practices occurred in New York, where settled residents saw large immigrant populations as bothersome at best and dangerous at worst. Paul Gilje's (1987) research on New York immigrant celebrations, like Susan Davis's on Philadelphia, reveals the tension between prosperous Philadelphians and their struggling neighbors.

Holidays are celebrated in ways that range from sacred to silly. Consider the contemporary juxtaposition of the sacred celebration of Easter with the appearance of a huge white Easter Bunny who distributes candy and jellybeans at many churches. For immigrants, including barely assimilated immigrants, carnivalesque gatherings provided temporary relief from the stifling requirements imposed by factory labor and gave them an opportunity to vent their frustrations. All over the world, carnival served an important function in maintaining social order by allowing a temporary breaching of the rules about proper behavior, with the understanding on both sides that order would be restored afterward. Philadelphia's authorities, like those in cities elsewhere, rarely attempted to suppress these activities, allowing them to run their course (Turner 1982; Davis 1985). In South Philadelphia the celebrations did get out of hand, occasionally becoming violent and disruptive. There were incidents where holiday celebrations in the neighborhoods were used as a cover by young male gangs who took advantage of the chaotic atmosphere to attack rivals.[7] Unfortunately, those unfamiliar with the neighborhoods made no distinction between the holiday revelers and the street toughs.

Even though the areas outside South Philadelphia prospered in the early 1800s as manufacturing expanded, the city grew northward and westward. South Philadelphia thus remained unstable long after other areas prospered, and it did not develop economically until the middle of the nineteenth century. The constant shifting of populations and jockeying for employment took their toll on the area, and social disorganization characterized the community. Anti-immigrant political groups targeted the Irish Catholic immigrants, and antiblack sentiment was so strong in the nineteenth century that "a list of South Philadelphia's firsts would have to include the city's first race riot" (Dubin 1996, 7).

This disorder influenced the opinion of others about the neighborhoods to the south, which the authorities saw as troublesome at best, dangerous at worst, and badly in need of oversight by authorities. When, in 1854, Southwark, Moyamensing, and other areas surrounding the city were incorporated into Greater Philadelphia (see the map on the next page), professional policing replaced local constables and the neighborhoods grew less fractious. Outbreaks of ethnic violence did not magically disappear, but they did decrease substantially. Yet South Philadelphia's image remained tainted by the area's violent past. This lingering image was one the immigrant communities were eager to overcome.

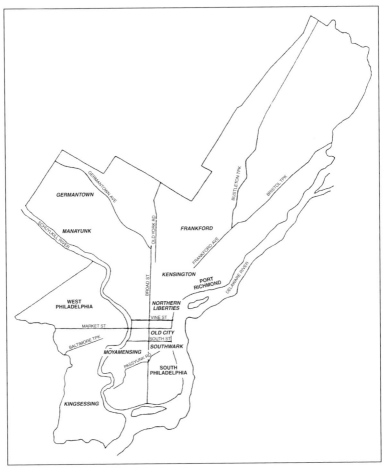

Philadelphia in 1854. *Source:* Davis and Haller (1973).

The image was not entirely accurate, because South Philadelphia's residents, from the time they settled in the area, worked steadily toward building a functioning and secure community. By the early nineteenth century, Irish, Italians, Poles, and Germans had built grand churches, collecting the funds dime by dime and quarter by quarter. These Catholic parishes formed the base of a vast network of parochial schools on which the city remains largely dependent today. Equally important in establishing security in the neighborhoods were the networks of churches, schools, and mutual aid societies that South Philadelphia's black residents formed to promote their well-being.[8]

Schools and churches are essential components of any neighborhood, but the richness of community life depends on more than bricks and mortar. Important also is the successful integration of art and beauty into daily life. Though "poor" in many respects, the immigrant communities showed by their actions that they enjoyed play and valued learning. They were eager creators and consumers of art and entertainment even as disorder erupted around them. Philadelphia's first permanent theater, founded in the eighteenth century, was outside the city limits in South Philadelphia because Quakers disapproved of such frivolity. The first art school in the nation opened in South Philadelphia on Catherine Street. In the settlement houses that reached out to the poor, Shakespearean reading groups indulged their love of language and drama. And nearly everyone played music. This interest in art and enthusiasm for diversion was evident in the evolving neighborhood celebrations as well (Conners, interview, 1995; Heller, interview, 1996).

By the late nineteenth century, the holiday processions mixed music, costumes, and house-to-house entertaining. The bands of entertainers were known as "the Shooters." Though other Philadelphians looked down on the homegrown entertainment, South Philadelphians were drawn out of their small row houses into the streets to join in the general merriment.

Pre-Civil War Celebrations in South Philadelphia

Historian and folklorist Charles Welch (1991, 13) acknowledged that "no one can say for certain what the real beginning of the Philadelphia Mummers Parade was but possibly the Swedes started the Mummers Parade in the Swedish 'Neck' of South Philadelphia not long after Penn laid out his squared green city."

Countless interviews with contemporary Mummers, and research into the history of the Mummers Parade presented in newspaper accounts and books (Welch 1991; Rothberg 1980), emphasize its European roots. Missing from these accounts is discussion of African American participation in and influence on the celebrations.[9] The early celebrations were multiethnic and multiracial. This was inevitable given the heterogeneity of South Philadelphia's neighborhoods, where nationality and race changed from block to block. Blacks, both slave and free, worked and played side by side with the European Americans.

The celebrations of black and white residents in South Philadelphia were strikingly similar, partly because forms of play are similar across cultures. But the parallels are important for another reason: in observing other ethnic and racial groups at play in the neighborhoods, South Philadelphians could see what they shared with those who were "foreign" to them. Examples of these similarities follow.

Among the early settlers in "the Neck" were Swedes. They observed the Feast of St. Lucy on 13 December with traditional holiday visiting. Girls and boys dressed in long robes formed processions and traveled, accompanied by adults, from house to house collecting money or cakes. This ritual, both sacred and social, was transplanted to Philadelphia as early as the eighteenth century. The Swedish customs paralleled German practices such as pre-Lenten Fasching, one of several variants of European carnival, and Christmas celebrations known as "belsnickling" (Heller, interview, 1996).

Irish Christmas Mumming also enlivened South Philadelphia's neighborhoods, particularly after the mid-nineteenth century. The tradition of Mummery in Ireland is centuries old, with the practice continuing to the present. Henry Glassie (1975, 125), in a contemporary ethnography of this custom, explains the attraction of the Mummers' play:

> The mummers' goal [in going from house to house] was gathering money, but their purpose was grander than a full purse. Entertainment was part of this larger purpose. A coddled, dour lot, scholars always underestimate entertainment in their explanations of culture. For people whose days pass in rough work, an occasional break for enjoyment is not a trivial matter. Entertainment makes a hard life endurable.

Yet Mummery serves an enormously important social function. Acting formally, and in disguise, the Mummers could "move outside of the community's conventional distinctions to engage in a transaction with every person living in the area. . . . It was a joint venture in community strength, a monetarily sealed social contract" (Glassie 1975, 127).

The similarities between the Irish tradition and the roaming bands of entertainers in Philadelphia are clear. This excerpt from the memoirs of a nineteenth-century Quaker family describes the mixing of social classes:

> Among the plain folk of Philadelphia . . . New Year's calling, as well as the spirit of the New Year's Carnival, was carried out well into the nineteenth century by the rambling mummers, after the fashion set by the early English, Swedish, and German pioneers. . . . From an old Quaker family has come this interesting record of this earlier time: "It was considered the proper thing in those days to give the leading mummers a few pence or dole, which in the language of the present time, they would 'pool' and buy cakes and beer. It was also regarded as the right thing to do to invite them into the house and [give them] mulled cider . . . and homemade cakes. It was considered a great breach of decorum and of etiquette to address or otherwise recognize the mummer by any name other than the name of the character he was assuming." (Brandt, 1930a)

Holiday visiting was not, however, exclusive to European Americans. William Pierson (1993, 127) described similar practices among blacks. In the coastal South during the late nineteenth century, holiday revelers visited homes to solicit refreshments or gifts; in return, the outlandishly attired participants entertained their hosts with tumbling, "playing antics," and music.

The Irish tradition required that the Mummers remain in character throughout the exchange of entertainment for refreshment. Masking gave the Irish Mummer the privilege of approaching those with whom he would not normally interact. Prior to emancipation, the southern variant of this practice allowed slaves to call on their masters. In both the Irish Mumming and African American visiting, custom demanded that the entertainers be welcomed and rewarded with food, drink, and sometimes money. For both the Irish and the

African Americans in South Philadelphia, then, the tradition of house-to-house entertaining was familiar and fun.

This benign view of the festivities was not universally shared. Others in Philadelphia saw the customs differently, perhaps because of the periodic outbreaks of disorder and intergroup violence associated with South Philadelphia. As Welch (1991, 25) wrote, "The mask was feared and Mumming was identified with the mask and the fear; hence, the custom of Mumming was held with its companion, the masked ball, as responsible for assaulting 'the peace and dignity' of Pennsylvania and was cast out of Pennsylvania."

From 1808 to 1859, masquerades and Mumming were eventually outlawed as "common nuisances"; in a parallel development, New Orleans officials outlawed the Mardi Gras on the grounds that the celebrations undermined civic order. Because local constables rarely enforced the ban, the celebrations continued. After city consolidation, the practices were tolerated, but they occurred under the watchful eyes of professional police.

Minstrelsy and the Shooters

Another major influence on the parade was the minstrel show, so ubiquitous in the nineteenth century. The stock characters of the minstrel show—the "dude" in his white spats and tuxedo, and the "wench" in "her" ruffled dress carrying a parasol—became fixtures of the parade by 1900. The use of minstrel-style makeup was an elaboration of the smeared cork that the Shooters wore in the earliest processions. Then as now, the Mummer entertainers looked to the culture around them for images and ideas. Minstrelsy influenced the parade in the nineteenth century, just as hip-hop music is integrated into present-day performances.[10] Roediger wrote extensively on this connection:

> In the vast Christmas processions of antebellum Philadelphia, blackface spread rapidly to become the "most common" disguise in the festival maskings shortly after its first use in 1829. The revelries of the holiday season were themselves growing during this period, transcending smaller German "belsnickling" and Anglo-American house visiting processions to become huge parades. . . . Not a few young white

toughs took advantage of the season to become blackened *Aunt Sallys,* crossing lines of both gender and race. At first Blacks participated in the expanded celebrations, which much resembled the spectacular, Black-led Jonkunnu . . . festivals held at Christmas time in the Caribbean and just to the south of Philadelphia. . . . Black traditions influenced the expanded Christmas maskings. (Roediger 1996, 105)[11]

Folk practices are complex. They affirm group identity; they express group sentiments and values (Turner 1969); they provide individuals with opportunities to create alternative identities through fantasy (Huizinga 1955); and they provide a framework within which less powerful groups negotiate their place within a diverse community (Davis 1985; Mitchell 1995).

Yet the least-studied motivation for the development and persistence of folk practices is an element that the Mummers identified as the driving force behind their parade: the desire to have fun, to "play together." What brought diverse ethnic groups together in South Philadelphia was the universality of play. Bob Pegg has written, "many customs revolve around basic human requirements and pleasures—eating, drinking, simple enjoyment, and the need for people to examine their identities, both as individuals and as members of a group—and the customs themselves, however strange, provide a framework within which people feel they can legitimately beg for money, get drunk, and entertain or be entertained" (1981, 138).

Pegg's observation should be taken seriously. In the case of the Mummers, the point of the celebrations was fun. The outcomes of play simply happened. The Mummer tradition developed spontaneously and informally over many years, and embedded even in the most reverent aspects of this tradition were elements of play. In the early years, neighborhood celebrations were, quite simply, local fun. The public nature of the holiday celebrations gave the diverse ethnic groups an opportunity to see individuals and their families from other cultures at play and to understand that, as different as their backgrounds were, they could come together as neighbors and friends in the spirit of fun. Playing, then as now, provides a respite from conflicts and problems, and in the context of play, barriers and differences among groups recede—at least temporarily.

The Shooters' Processions:
A Transitional Period

It was not until after the Civil War that the outlines of the contemporary Mummers Parade became apparent. Up until that point, various groups simply adopted play practices that appealed to them, without any attempt at knitting them together. Because no identifiable tradition other than that of the ethnic groups themselves existed, those living in the neighborhoods continued to do what they had always done to celebrate the holidays. As the twentieth century approached, prosperity came to South Philadelphia, helped along by an expanding manufacturing base. Philadelphia's factories in the early 1900s produced all kinds of goods, from textiles, to leather, to machines and tools. In Southwark, a thriving shipbuilding industry employed dockworkers who off-loaded raw materials for these factories. Ethnic groups initially tended to concentrate in specific industries or crafts because information on job availability traveled through the informal networks of kin and friends. However, as employment increased, so did ethnic diversity in the workplace. Thus Philadelphians not only lived but also worked together. Gradually the playful holiday practices became more organized, and the different groups merged their celebrations—all in the interest of having more fun.

Philadelphia was not a major center of immigration by the late 1800s,[12] but the huge influx of Irish Catholic immigrants after the 1840s strongly influenced the neighborhoods.[13] Two-story row houses replaced the dilapidated houses and shacks in South Philadelphia, and many of the immigrants put down roots with the purchase of a home.[14]

The initial steps in building an arena around their play started around 1880, when the Shooters started forming social clubs, sometimes called New Year's Associations. As Claude Fischer has written, immigrants from rural areas often establish formal associations when they put down roots in urban areas; these associations are similar to rural kin-based groups, with their leaders serving the function of village elders. The New Year's Associations followed this pattern. But the organizations' "formal quality" was "usually only a veneer, applied (often for political purposes) to a set of essentially informal relationships based on ethnicity or village background" (Fischer 1976, 106).

Ethnic groups led these culturally distinct holiday celebrations, even as they provided practical assistance to the immigrant groups through their churches and mutual aid societies (Horton and Horton 1997; Sutherland 1973; Clark 1973a).[15] The New Year's Associations, men-only working-class groups,[16] reflected a nationwide increase in fraternal orders (Welch 1991, 31). The clubs met in homes, neighborhood saloons, or buildings owned by ethnic groups. Addresses of the clubs often matched the home addresses of their leaders.

The Irish seemed particularly drawn to joining clubs and were well represented in the Shooters' annual hijinks. Dennis Clark has described the Irish propensity for group play, especially if it included their families: "Pistol firing, dancing, strutting, 'cake walks,' and generally uninhibited frolic were part of the [early Mummers] parade. Such displays were compatible with the Irish propensity for enjoyment. The folksy pantomime, the jingling music, and the ardent defiance of freezing winter weather made the Mummers famous, and the Irish were an eager part of the tradition" (1973a, 127).

The early Shooters' activities began with club fund-raising efforts in the neighborhoods that led to a series of events beginning in early December and continuing through January, when the groups started to raise money to buy costumes for the next New Year (Rothberg 1980). This cycle of activity drew the Shooters together throughout the year and strengthened their links to one another. The New Year's Associations were the core of the emerging play community. The early organizational efforts and the involvement of the communities are illustrated in the activities of the groups that Rothberg presented in her research.

Beginning in early December, the New Year's Associations sent cards to friends and acquaintances announcing a procession in the neighborhoods, most likely on the main streets and always including South Second Street ("Two Street"). Accompanied by hired bands and displaying their names on the canvas of a decorated barouche, the costumed club members were cheered by neighborhood residents and clustered tavern patrons as they trooped from clubhouse to clubhouse.

One spectator's memories of his childhood exposure to these celebrations provide a glimpse of the excitement associated with the club activities:

This parade would be, ah, maybe fifteen minutes or so. It would only be a particular club comin' up paradin' with two bands. A lotta guys dancing out there and the officials of the thing [the club] sitting in the banner car, the barouche, with a high hat and the big rosette. To me that looked like the President comin' up Passyunk Avenue. [On] the advertisement night Mummers would be greeted by shooting off Roman candles. . . . The whole block would use all red lights. Then they'd [individuals in the houses along the street] have Roman candles on both sides of the street and they'd shoot them off. Some of them would have Chinese shootin' crackers, you know. They would have guns, maybe a half dozen of 'em would have them, shoot off the blanks. They'd be at the upstairs windows shootin' up in the air, they'd strike up the band and everybody would dance. (Rothberg 1980, 63)

These events were precursors to the climactic New Year's Eve celebrations. The New Year's Association balls in South Philadelphia began on 31 December at around 9:00 in the evening. At midnight, noise erupted in the neighborhoods as everyone blew on their tin horns and beat on dishpans or tea kettles. Those who had attended the balls joined with other residents crowding the streets. After wishing their families a Happy New Year, the Shooters donned their grand costumes for the New Year's Day processions (Rothberg 1980, 66; Welch 1991). They and their neighborhood friends headed toward Independence Hall to cheer the New Year. Toward the turn of the century the festivities became more elaborate, and the Shooters, who saw themselves as an important presence in their neighborhoods, competed with one another to dazzle onlookers. As Rothberg described the spectacle, "On New Year's Day, Shooters commanded their neighborhood streets. Black-bonneted ladies and girls, frock-coated men, and knickered boys craned their necks to see the procession of richly costumed Shooters pass through the dirt street. Horses, as well as riders, wore latticed sateen or cotton 'capes,' hand-embroidered in floral designs. Caterpillar 'chenille' thread and plumply stuffed sateen 'roses' gave dimension and lushness to the garments. Deep edges of lace trimmed the confection" (1980, 62).

The Shooters were either clowns, "socking" passersby with flour-filled stockings and kissing girls in the streets, or monarchs, dazzling onlookers with their extraordinary costumes. Antebellum Shooters made costumes from whatever materials were at hand, but over time the costumes became more elaborate and imaginative. As the new century approached, the processions were so effective in drawing crowds that neighborhood businesses and individuals offered prizes, which fueled the competition among clubs (*Philadelphia Times* 1893). Competition had merged with play. Prizes had more symbolic than monetary value—silver cups and decorative plates were typically awarded, but—as Huizinga (1955) maintains and as the history of the Mummers Parade indicates—individuals engaged in play seek recognition and acclaim rather than tangible rewards. The Shooters used their prize monies not for personal enrichment but for play for its own sake. The groups competed fiercely, sometimes leading clubs to use knockout drops to kidnap their rivals, at least until prizes were awarded (Shuler 1930d).

Joining the fun, neighborhood saloons enticed the clubs to perform for customers with beer and "free lunches," a practice that considerably slowed and in some cases halted their progress through the community. Bakeries donated prizes to the best clubs, and neighborhood women made cakes to present to the entertainers who stopped at their doors. The Shooters apparently had a sweet tooth, for cakes were also collected after the New Year's celebrations. The annual processions were barely over before the cycle began again. A week or so after the processions, the clubs formed small processions. Horse-drawn wagons, surrounded by Shooters, rolled through the neighborhoods collecting cakes for their annual "cake-cutting balls," which occurred a few days later and included friends and neighbors. The small clubs put aside the money raised on these occasions for use in the next cycle of competitions. To this day, the clubs raise contributions by performing for their communities and collecting money house by house; unfortunately, the sweet tradition of cake wagons seems to have disappeared.

The nineteenth-century Shooters' celebrations, with the New Year's Eve processions as the centerpiece, were consistent with patterns common to agrarian societies that celebrated a season rather than a day. In those communities, such activities filled the void created by winter.

The numbers of marchers in the neighborhoods swelled by the late 1890s. Clubs formed in parts of the city beyond South

Philadelphia, as families left the neighborhoods where their parents and grandparents had settled, transplanting the South Philadelphia traditions to other parts of the city. In 1887 the city started to issue permits for the clubs to march as units between 9:00 A.M. and 5:00 P.M. As the *Philadelphia Times* reported, "until 1893, no permits to parade were required, but it was decided by the city officials that someone should be responsible for good order and that only duly organized clubs should be allowed to parade. This was done to put a stop to increasing rowdyism" (1893). The issuing of permits was a continuation of efforts to contain the celebrations that had begun in 1854 with city consolidation. As Davis puts it, "after the Civil War, Christmas remained a problem of public order, and civil authorities tried a variety of strategies for suppression and control. Suppression proved impossible, but a combination of licensing performers and massive police presence eventually succeeded in turning the wild night into a popular city-sponsored pageant" (1985, 109).

The already established New Year's Associations became official entities with their recognition by municipal authorities. Issuing "permits" was the first overt attempt by Philadelphia's authorities to regulate the Shooters' activities. The families within the associations, eager to gain respectability and acceptance by other Philadelphians, assumed responsibility for monitoring behavior and cooperated with city authorities in exchange for permission to use public space as a playground. Without their cooperation, the attempts to control the celebrations would not have been nearly as successful.

Fragments of news reports provide snapshots of the holiday processions of the late nineteenth and early twentieth centuries. For example, on Monday, 1 January 1900, twenty-eight clubs, now calling themselves New Year's Associations, paraded in Philadelphia.[17] Processions occurred in South Philadelphia, Kensington, Germantown, and Pottsville, and across the river in the New Jersey towns of Trenton and Camden. Welch documented the formation of numerous "fancy" clubs: the Golden Crown, the Bright Star, the Early Risers, the Hardly Ables, the Energetic Hoboes, the Red Onions, the Cucumbers, and the White Turnips. Contemporary Mummer lore holds that the Red Onions, the Cucumbers, the White Turnips, and others with similar names were formed by dockworkers who named their clubs after the products they unloaded. The distinction between the comics and the fancy clubs led to the first unofficial divisional separation among the Shooters.

Though the New Year's celebrations occurred throughout the city, the sentimental and emotional pull of tradition was strongest in South Philadelphia, as Shuler wrote:

> The spirit [of the Shooters], undaunted by weather or elements, remains the same. . . . And counterparts of the black faced comedians who "wisecracked" a generation ago may be found in the comic clubs, who offer horseplay and broad farce and the most subtle satire as they march along thousands strong. . . . Although other sections of the city appear with New Year groups, it is in South Philadelphia that the real spirit of the Shooters is found most alive and most active. The Shooter is a South Philadelphian. He always has been and he always will be. In this locality alone can be found the real history and traditions which help to produce the annual parade—and help somewhat to explain it. (1930a, 1)

By the turn of the century, the attitudes of other Philadelphians had shifted from fearful to encouraging. News accounts emphasized the Shooters' working-class origins, but admiration for the entertainment they provided in their neighborhoods replaced the critical coverage that was typical in the early to mid-1800s. An article published in an 1876 issue of the *Philadelphia Evening Public Ledger* included in an article by Brandt reflected this shift:

> On New Year's Day, the weather was uncomfortable as usual lately, but it seemed to have little effect on the spirits of our citizens who crowded the streets and made the city very lively during the entire day and evening. . . . The Fantasticals, or "Shooters," were out in force during the whole day and caused much boisterous amusement. Indians and squaws, princes and princesses, clowns and harlequins, Negroes of the minstrel-hall type, Chinese and burlesque Dutchman, bears, apes, and other animals promenaded the streets to the music of the Calethumpian [sic] cowbell of the more dignified brass band, and kept up their racket until late at night.

Independence Hall was the grand objective for them all, and the old building received many a cheer and serenade, both burlesque and serious. In the middle of the day, several of these parties united in one grand parade and made quite a striking display. (1930e, 1)

As the neighborhood performers turned their attention to creating sumptuous floats and elaborate capes, they were offered an opportunity to put on a show for the whole city, profoundly changing their play and leading to the creation of a unique Philadelphia institution.

The Mummers on Broad Street

The move to Broad Street marked the initial stage in the development of the Mummers as a community. The informally organized neighborhood processions required little cooperation on the part of the clubs, which operated autonomously. But the invitation to perform as a unit issued by the city encouraged the Mummers to think of themselves as a distinctive group with common interests: performing and competing.

Broad Street is, as any Mummer will brag, "the longest and straightest street in all the world." It is also the main north-south thoroughfare in the city, connecting South Philadelphia's neighborhood streets—Snyder, Girard, Reed, and Mifflin—with Center City. In plain view as Philadelphians come up the street is City Hall, with "Billy" (William, to outsiders) Penn assuming a commanding pose as he looks down on his city. In the early 1900s City Hall was the tallest building in Philadelphia. It was and is a powerful symbol; to perform in this space is to perform for the entire city. It is a grand stage.

Philadelphia's Shooters' processions in the late 1800s remained more rowdy than respectable, but in the midst of all the fun and games, the performers and artists were well on their way to developing distinctive aesthetic and musical forms. The performances showed raw energy and enthusiasm, and the Shooters could never be accused of understatement or subtlety when it came to their "suits" (a term preferred to costumes and still used within the Mummer community). The bright, "predominantly folk colors that were used in . . . the neighborhood performances made them colorful and gay: plush-red, bright yellow, and blue" dazzled the audience and indicated a more sophisticated awareness of presentation (Welch 1991, 140).

Yet another influence affected the Shooters' processions, as it did other city parades. Department store parades provided inspiration to the Shooters, as they did to other parading groups. As Davis has observed, "a new development of commercial culture, the department store, . . . linked festivity, commerce, and spectacle in ways that could redefine public culture . . . by producing parades and festivals, albeit along foreign or exotic lines, to advertise their wares and introduce female customers to commodity consumption" (1985, 170). Commercial parades brought people into the stores and into the city. The city authorities, casting their eyes southward, saw that festivities—properly organized and contained, as they were in the heavily commercial Mardi Gras in New Orleans—offered a potentially lucrative source of revenue and prestige. The minutes of the 4 December city council meeting indicated that Philadelphia's leaders were impressed with the success of commercially sponsored parades (Philadelphia Inquirer 1900b).

Morris Vogel maintains that the impulse behind the early Mummers Parade, from the participants' perspective, was to some extent seditious and defiant:

> Ordinary citizens [wanted to take] one day off from their regular routines each year to mock the pretensions of their presumed betters and to put on airs of their own. This [the late nineteenth century] was a moment of historic change, as an emerging industrial society began to demand ever greater sacrifices of spontaneity and individual autonomy in the name of the discipline necessary for a smoothly functioning interdependent community. The parade offered a fantasy message of license and social equality, a temporary escape from order and discipline, a momentary return to the bliss and hedonism of a lost golden age. (1991, 137)

Davis agrees that groups may use the streets as a venue for asserting independence and autonomy, not necessarily through violence but through humor and mockery of respectable society. She adds that "what Mikhail Bakhtin has called the subverting power of laughter was, in these cases, a way to tug hard at one corner of the emperor's cloak" (1985, 101). Laughter, after all, reduces the distance between social groups.

However, for those who take to the streets, the desire to make their presence stronger within the city and to challenge the powerful are only two possible motives. The lavish processions showcased the artistry and talent of immigrant groups as well. As they became increasingly adept performers and artists, the Mummers courted admiration rather than notoriety.

It is not possible to bring back the nineteenth-century Shooters and learn directly about their motivation. Vogel's and Davis's assessments are undoubtedly accurate, but they are also incomplete. Challenging authority and mocking one's "betters" may have been only one part of what the Shooters hoped to achieve. Similarly, the city's invitation to the Mummers to parade on Broad Street may have reflected a wish to entertain the public. However, given the rowdy history of the neighborhood processions, city leaders also saw the advantage of exerting control over the celebrations by moving them to public space. Whatever forces drew the City of Philadelphia and the Shooters together, more important is what the parade became.

The 1901 Parade

Bart McHugh, a newspaperman, is frequently credited with the idea of inviting the Shooters to be part of Philadelphia's welcome to the twentieth century, when he proposed the idea to J. Hampton Moore, secretary to the mayor (Welch 1991, 42). But contemporary Mummer historians suggest that city council chairman Jacob Seeds initiated the invitation (Conners, interview, 1995). An article appearing in the 15 November 1900 issue of the *Philadelphia Inquirer* is the first mention of the possibility that the Shooters would be invited to perform. As the *Inquirer* reported on 1 December, "The idea of getting all the New Year's Shooters together in one grand display will probably be urged on the Mayor by Chairman [of the city council] Jacob Seeds. The idea of having a grand twentieth-century Mardi Gras is regarded as one of the very best that has ever been suggested."

Other commemorative ideas emerged, including the addition of commercially sponsored floats and military units to the parade. By early December, Seeds was aggressively pursuing the Shooters' clubs, including those based outside the city in Camden, New Jersey. The *Philadelphia Inquirer* (1900b) quoted him:

> I have sent for a man who is well posted on all the New Year Clubs and I have asked him to get up a complete list of all of the Shooter organizations. We will place ourselves in communication with them at once and get down to a practical working basis. I think if these clubs are made to understand that the City of Philadelphia will cooperate with them and will aid them in bearing the big expenditure that they are under that they will join us. If we could get all these clubs together in one line it would make a parade more than an hour and a half long.

Chairman Seeds, though acknowledging the unpredictability of the December weather, also floated the idea that Philadelphia make the Shooters' parade an annual event—if it was well received. His report suggests that the small clubs were sufficiently organized that city officials could identify their leaders. However, as the negotiations continued it became clear that the clubs and their leaders cherished their independence. They were far from a unified community, but they did share a pride in their performances and an awareness of their skills as artists and entertainers. Initial contacts between Seeds and the club "captains" made it clear that arranging an event and gaining the cooperation of the fiercely competitive and independent clubs was going to require not only negotiation, but also prize money.

By 1900 the clubs had competed for neighborhood prizes for at least two decades. Their elaborate costumes and their comparatively modest personal incomes made it necessary for them to recoup at least some expenses involved in entertaining their neighbors. Because they could rely on the support of their neighborhoods, Shooters did not expect the city to give them financial support for what was, after all, local fun. But marching to City Hall, while a great honor, required extra effort that they felt deserved some compensation, even if it did not pay all their bills. Further, they were unwilling to entertain the city on New Year's Eve and insisted on a daytime parade. The city capitulated gracefully. The *Evening Item* reported, "as the New Year's Shooters practically contribute their services, the committee will have to meet their convenience in this matter" (1900).

Just two weeks before the scheduled event, a special parade sub-committee met with about twenty club representatives. On 14 December the *Philadelphia Inquirer* reported with some understatement that subcommittee chairman "Heltzel found as soon as he started to talk business that his post is one that will require the graces of a diplomat. Jealousy between the clubs runs high, and it did not take the green-eyed monster long to make itself manifest. . . . There were many points on which the club captains disagreed, and there were some warm passages at arms between representatives of the Shooters and the Chairman" (1900d).

City officials apparently suggested that the Shooters parade in two "divisions," emphasizing the differentiation of skills and performance that had already taken place in the neighborhoods. The divisions were the "grotesque" or comic clubs and the fancy costume clubs. City prize money—a princely sum of $2,000—was to be divided as the Shooters chose. Wrangling over who would get how much money occupied the clubs for many days. Despite these conflicts, however, the Shooters were excited about the invitation and showed some capacity to negotiate with the city and present a united front. Another indication of their excitement and interest was that clubs that had not paraded in the neighborhoods for several years pulled themselves together and applied for a place in the parade. The desire to "win 'first'" is reflected in the extra investment that many clubs made in this debut at City Hall. Newspapers reported that the Shooters' clubs with enough money were hiring costumers rather than making suits at home.

The 20 December 1900 issue of the *Philadelphia Inquirer* bubbled over with enthusiasm, quoting Heltzel:

> It will be the greatest event of all the celebrations the City has ever seen. There will be one grand demonstration of all the New Year's Shooters, a Philadelphia fixture, which we should hold together for all time. These clubs which have for years been rivals have come together under a common plan in order that the birth of the century may be well remembered. The grandeur of their costumes and their whimsical antics ought to have the effect of arousing Philadelphia to the core. Philadelphia on this occasion as she has always done,

[will] excel, and . . . we will have a New Year's celebration that will be a pleasant memory for a long time to come. (1900e)

The next point to be negotiated was the parade route. The Shooters, most of whom were based in South Philadelphia, managed to convince the city that the parade should begin in their neighborhoods, where they could compete locally for the usual prizes. The 1901 parade route started at Reed Street and wound its way toward City Hall, ending at a reviewing stand at the south plaza. As excitement mounted, dozens of merchants announced their intention to award prizes to the best clubs passing their reviewing stands, located both in the neighborhoods and in commercial areas along the route; these prizes were, of course, one reason that the clubs wanted to have some say in choosing their route. The prizes were impressive.

> The Fifth and Porter Streets committee offers $25 in gold to the best fancy club and $20 in gold to the best comic club passing women judges at 519 Porter Street on New Year's Day from 8 to 5 o'clock. Every club will be presented with a cake.
>
> The businessmen in the neighborhood comprising 15th, 16th, 17th, and 18th Streets and Snyder Avenue and Passyunk Avenue and Jackson Street will offer cash prizes to the extent of $100 for . . . clubs that pass their places of business. The judges have been selected and will sit in Cunningham's Hardware Store.
>
> The residents of Moyamensing Avenue from Moore to McKean Streets offer $30 in gold to clubs passing there between 8 and 6 o'clock. (*Philadelphia Record* 1900)

The local prizes reflected the intense neighborhood involvement in the Shooters' activities; in South Philadelphia families invited their friends to watch the parade, socialize, and sample traditional pepper pot soup, made days in advance so that wives and daughters could join the festivities. Welch described the city's mood:

> The twentieth century dawned clear and cold, and a strong wind swept down Broad Street from the north to greet the

Mummers. Spectators had to bundle up and stamped their feet to keep warm. The marchers were in a merry mood and kept up a rapid pace. The official history of the Mummers Parade dates from this, the first city-sponsored parade. It was small by current standards, as only 2,500 men participated in the four Fancy Clubs and eight Comic Clubs in the parade. (1991, 47)

Captains trailing long capes held by "pages" led the fancy clubs; comic "wenches" and "dudes" carrying parasols and canes cavorted up Broad Street in a bright stream. Some groups, not exhausted by the long trek through the South Philadelphia neighborhoods to Broad Street, headed over to Kensington, north of the city, to compete for more prizes.

Frances Brandt's recounting recognizes the importance of the first Mummers Parade. "The year 1901 proved a red-letter day in the growth of the mummers and a great turning point in their history. . . . The grand plaza about the City Hall and the streets converging were choked with people, a healthy, clean, orderly congregation. The city had put its official seal upon the mummery, the lawmakers were there as sponsors and directors, and from the windows of the courts of justice wives and daughters of the Judges viewed and enjoyed the parade" (1930f).

The Mummers were justifiably proud of themselves; they had favorably impressed their city and begun—on Broad Street—the long march toward respectability and fame. Best of all, they had managed to parade with few restrictions on their play. The city printed the first set of rules for the parade on the back of permits issued to each club. All the rules governed conduct on the public stage of Broad Street. They were:

- Each club or leader of any organization is to have the name of the captain or leader of the association together with the address registered at the police station.
- The captain or leader is to be held responsible for the behavior of each individual member of his organization.
- In case of any complaints lodged at this department of the bureau of police, the [club or association] captain will

give the name and address of the offender to the police authorities.

- It is understood that no firearms are to be carried and that all parades should be conducted in obedience to the law.
- It is also understood that if any member of a club or association, while in line, becomes intoxicated or unruly, he is to be handed over to the police department.
- No personification of the uniform of a policeman will be tolerated as it is understood that it is against the law.[18]

In addition to a parade free of regulation beyond that imposed on *any* group marching up the city's main street, the 1901 parade had only a few prize categories, a situation that was to change as the spectacle expanded and the prize monies increased. In 1901, first, second, third, and fourth prizes were awarded to the "Best Dressed Club"; and first to sixth prizes were awarded to the "Funniest Club."

After 1901 the parades assumed a greater degree of structure, as the number of participants grew steadily, the number of prize categories expanded, and the rules governing competition came into place. The nature of "play" began to change when the groups imposed order on the "free-for-all" celebrations that had enlivened their communities and been inclusive of virtually anyone who wanted to join the processions: young and old, men and women, people of means and those with nothing to invest beyond cork to blacken their faces and a coat turned inside-out. The bar for entering the Shooters' processions was raised as competition became part of play.

The Mummers' play evolved continually in the twentieth century, and the Mummers themselves began consciously to craft an image that they presented to the larger community and a set of traditions that became Philadelphia Mummery.

2 Expanding the Play Community
The Contemporary Parade

*Dancing and prancing to the stirring lilt of numerous bands, the
fancy clubs and brigades filled the wide reaches of Broad Street with
a mile of vivid, moving, and ever-changing pigment, while the comic
clubs struck smartly at the foibles, weaknesses, and follies of the
year just closed.*

—*Philadelphia Evening Bulletin* (1932b)

Three decades of appearing on Broad Street, with cheering
audiences jamming the sidewalks and hanging out the windows of businesses along the parade route, transformed the
Mummers' play into folk art[1] and the Mummers themselves into
gifted entertainers. Like any artistic community, the clubs devoted
their energies to experimenting and innovating, so that each parade
included traditional elements as well as fresh material drawn from
popular culture. Because each performing unit, from the comic
groups, made up of just a few members, to the large clubs, boasting
more than a hundred individuals, wanted recognition and the coveted first prize in their division, competition was fierce. The capes
of the Fancy Brigade captains became longer, spanning a city block,
the string bands added new instruments to their traditional banjos,
violins, and glockenspiels, and the comics sharpened their satire.

From informal, spontaneous entries, often produced by a single
performer, the Mummers' extravaganza now represented the collective work of many individuals, each of whom brought to the enterprise of play specialized skills and talents. In short, the Mummers
had come together in what Howard Becker (1984) calls an "art

world." This art world existed side by side with the Mummers' intensely personal network of family and friends, and within the clubs the ongoing collaboration enhanced the sense of connection and interdependence that cemented the play community. Inevitably, the competition of the Mummers necessitated a codified set of rules, and the judging of entries by outsiders led to aesthetic standards that transformed playful improvisations into respected folk art. But in the move from free play to structured performance, the Mummers retained for the most part the essentially playful character of their enterprise. This chapter describes the evolving parade and examines the changes in organization that became necessary to the process of "going up the street." Major developments are summarized in the box on page 44.

The 1929 Parade

The over-the-top extravagance and carefree exuberance of the Roaring Twenties permeated the 1929 Mummers Parade.[2] The string bands, a novelty in the earliest parades, had become a separate division in 1920, and their paid performances, which raised money for competition throughout the year, had made them the best-known Mummers as well as the best financed. In addition, the traditions of South Philadelphia had moved to other sections of the city and beyond. By 1929 the investments in suits and props had increased enormously. In response to the Mummers' popularity, the prize money allocated by the city increased to the impressive sum of $28,000. But, as in the past, the cost of going up Broad Street far exceeded the appropriation.

Bad weather delayed the parade, but this did not dampen the enthusiasm of a "record crowd" of several hundred thousand Philadelphians of all ages, from bundled-up children to grandparents. Approximately fourteen thousand Mummers strutted the length and breadth of Broad Street. Spectators used wooden peach baskets as makeshift seats, and sometimes umbrellas to protect themselves from the intermittent rain. More fortunate Philadelphians, whose offices lined Broad Street, took turns sitting on window ledges and showering the Mummers with confetti. The light rain transformed the street into "a black mirror" that reflected the colorful suits and backpieces of the kings, queens, devils, and clowns, all taking a star turn

EVOLUTION OF THE CONTEMPORARY PARADE

Pre–Civil War Years	Neighborhood processions, ethnically distinct and informal, with men and women parading through the neighborhoods.
1880s	Emergence of the "Shooters." Formation of "social clubs," with membership reflecting family links and shared race and ethnicity. With rare exceptions, these groups were limited to men. Comics, with makeshift costumes, paraded, but the New Year Associations, which relied on neighborhood fund-raising, began to spend more money on elaborately decorated costumes, transforming the Shooters into "kings for a day."
1900	Shooters were invited to parade on Broad Street on 1 January 1901, with city prizes awarded to two "divisions," the comic or "grotesque" and the "fancy." The comics offered political satire; the fancy clubs featured elaborate costumes and floats built around exotic themes.
1920	The string bands marched as a separate division, adding drills in formation and music to the parade. Prior to this parade, the musical groups had marched as a novelty. Brass bands continued to provide musical accompaniment for the fancy and comic clubs, though these bands did not compete for city prizes.
1978	The fancy brigades split off from the fancy clubs and began marching as a separate division. Their performances included elaborate choreography and brass band accompaniment; by the 1990s the brigades had switched to recorded music.

on Broad Street. Having mastered public relations, the clubs provided the newspapers with previews of their themes and human interest stories. Anticipation was high as the parade director, Bart McHugh, led the parade astride a white horse, followed by twenty-five mounted police. Next in line was the automobile carrying the officials of the parade, underscoring the city's sponsorship of the Mummers' celebration. Following the dignitaries came the Mummer "monarchs," the city's working men, who were "kings for a day."

Patriotic themes were as popular with the Mummers then as they are today. One spectacular entry was the Silver Crown Fancy Club, led by Uncle Sam waving the American flag and wearing a "glistening satin robe with a magnificent train stretching behind him almost a city block. . . . [Following Uncle Sam] was club captain Frank Daily with a train decorated in gold, red, and purple in six sections interwoven with ribbons of roses. The cape was supported by 120 pages in colorful robes that complemented the 'King's' costume" (Welch 1991, 49).

Other Broad Street "monarchs" strutted in equally lavish costumes, each attempting to outdo the others. Without exception, they continued the tradition of splendid wastefulness that made Thomas Duffy famous in Mummer lore. Duffy was immortalized in a series of articles on the parade written by Evelyn Shuler in 1930 for the *Evening Public Ledger.* Based on what some of the old-timers had told her, Shuler reported that in 1904 Thomas Duffy paraded in a cape that cost a year's pay. Wearing sixty-six feet of white satin carried by 130 pages,[3] Duffy was "one of twenty captains whose capes had to be measured by the acre not the yard. He was one of the dazzling heroes trudging happily along. Tomorrow they may be opening oysters in white aprons or planing wood, or painting skyscrapers—but for one day they are gay butterflies, fluttering through an exotic and intoxicating hour of splendor. . . . On that day, they are kings. The next day they become the workers of Philadelphia back in the shops" (1930a).

Shuler was discreetly silent on the subject of what Mrs. Duffy may have thought of Thomas's great display. Yet her series of articles captured the spirit of play that makes Mummery so inexplicable to those who lead sober and careful lives. Over the years, some of Philadelphia's more practical residents have written letters to the editor deploring the amount of money wasted by the working classes, who should be putting their limited funds to "better" use.[4] The Mummers ignore this carping and continue their grand game of "can you top this."

In 1929 female impersonators parading in the fancy costume category brought up the rear of the show.[5] Their ranks were filled with New York entertainers and costume designers who came to Philadelphia to compete for the sheer fun of going up the street, and perhaps also for the freedom of flaunting a decidedly marginal sexual identity in a less tolerant era.

Thousands of comics followed the fancies in 1929. Their ranks were swelled by another category of female impersonator, the garishly attired "wenches," dressed in ruffled dresses, who twirled their multi-tier parasols. They were accompanied by the "dudes" in white spats and tuxedos, keeping alive the minstrel tradition that began in the neighborhood processions.

Political satire in the early years was less respectful, and less respectable, than the comparatively mild jabs that the Mummers aim at politics and politicians today. In the 1929 parade,

> The famous League Island Club, from the heart of "the Neck," traditional home of the Mummers, imitated the Prince of Wales hunting for big game . . . [his shoulders hung] with lions [presumably stuffed], [his hands] clutching smaller but no less ferocious animals. He was surrounded by cotton pickers in black face, flappers, and clowns. "Hoover's Farmer Relief" was parodied; bootlegging was carried on in the City Hall Annex; Chicago bandits robbed banks. Bo Bo Hoff, a local racketeer, was presented as Boo Boo Hoof, and immediately began presenting "gifts" to blindfolded policemen. (Welch 1991, 50–51)[6]

The string bands followed the clowns, providing the finale to the event. Among the bands marching in 1929 was the Octavius V. Catto String Band,[7] "a Negro band" making what turned out to be its farewell appearance. The Catto band styled itself as the "Troubadours of 1929" and marched up Broad Street in suits of red and gold velvet trimmed with sequins.

In the same parade, what was to become one of Philadelphia Mummery's most successful and long-lived performing units, the Ferko String Band, displayed both its musical skills and its showmanship. It was led by a young Joseph A. Ferko, who remains one of Mummery's heroes. Its 1929 performance is emblematic of the increasing complexity and sophistication displayed by the string bands even in the early years of the parade. Bradshaw and Frangicetto (1995, 38) in their history of the band included this description taken from newspaper accounts of that time: "Each man in line represented a star with a costume of sky blue satin. A mammoth float, reported at that time to be one of the largest ever, represented clouds with a large five-pointed star more than five feet in diameter, that was made up of 600 miniature mirrors. It revolved as the float passed in review, throwing flashes of silver reflections against a blue background. In the rear of the float, the planets were painted."

Individual musicians' suits consisted of a "great cape decorated with a silvery moon, surrounded by smaller quarter and half moons. The jacket and trousers of the men . . . were in six colors . . . giving the effect of a great waving rainbow" (Welch 1991, 53). No reports document the music that the Catto and Ferko bands played, leaving the impression that appearance was given as much weight by judges as sound, though the two elements of performance were to become equally important in later years. In 1929 and throughout the early years of the parade, string bands marched up Broad Street in columns, playing their music. Their props were limited to the bouquets of flowers carried by the captains and floral-bedecked floats that carried the club banner. In contrast to the irreverent comics, the string bands showed the respectable face of the Mummers. Their straight lines and serious performances were throwbacks to the older tradition of Philadelphia's elite parades, which featured military-style drills and patriotic floats.

The 1930s and 1940s

Despite the gloom of a nation experiencing economic disaster, the Depression era saw Philadelphia's Mummers gaily performing on Broad Street. With less than $10,000 in prize money (raised by subscription rather than city appropriation) for all three divisions in 1932, ten thousand Mummers performed for the city. The parade was first broadcast on the Columbia (International) Radio Network in 1932, a flattering indication of widespread interest in the efforts of Philadelphia's local heroes and the Mummers' first exposure as media stars.

Drawing special notice was Joe Coyle, who performed with the fancies. The *Philadelphia Evening Bulletin* (1932b) reported in typical detail that "Joe Coyle moved along in a six-section cape of green, gold, and white . . . studded with bright stones and rosettes, suggestive of barbaric pomp. . . . Seventy-five [costumed] page boys carried this huge cape [that stretched] a half a block." Not to be outshone, the comics had shed their turned-out coats and cork-smeared faces. One clown, the *Bulletin* noted, wore a huge "costume of black and white satin, with white designs like greatly magnified snowflakes against its black panels."

Such ostentatious working-class display seems at first glance discordant in an era when newspapers reported men selling apples on street corners to try and feed their families. Yet pride in their tradition and the desire to entertain outweighed practical considerations. For the Mummers, play was not a luxury but a necessity. They may have cut corners in putting their suits together (after all, the suits only had to make it up the street once!), but the clubs pulled off dazzling and imaginative displays, and their entertainment provided badly needed distraction to Philadelphia's residents.

As the Depression deepened, however, raising money to mount the spectacle that Philadelphians had come to expect became more difficult. For a few years the city council was unable to appropriate any prize money, and it was too financially strapped to pay for the administrative expenses, extra police, and sanitation costs associated with the annual celebration. Bowing to the reality of diminished city support, the Mummers returned "home," in 1934, parading only in their neighborhoods. As the *Evening Public Ledger* (1934) reported, "This year for the first time since the united clubs began their annual pilgrimage up Broad Street, the Mummers returned to their original custom. . . . After their big parade in South Philadelphia, the participating clubs went back to their own localities for sectional celebrations."

Because clubs were scattered throughout the city, Broad Street's loss was the communities' gain, as the Mummers "gave the home folks the best treat they have had since 1901" (*Philadelphia Inquirer* 1934). The Mummers managed to have a parade and to welcome the New Year despite bad times, but they yearned to get back to City Hall and their official role as the city's jesters.

They had their wish in 1935 and celebrated on Broad Street with an especially lavish event that drew a half-million spectators. People lined the parade route hours before the Mummers started up Broad Street. Particularly noteworthy about this parade was the move to professional judging. Earlier parades had been "judged" by local politicians (and sometimes their wives), public relations men, and journalists; in 1935 judges included the president of the Moore Institute of Art, Science, and Industry, the managing director of the American Theater Society, and city representative Jacob Seeds (*Philadelphia Inquirer* 1935).

The advent of professional judging was important in the development of the Mummers' play community into an art world. Aestheticians and judges serve two purposes in an art world; their assessments legitimate the creations produced within an artistic community as "art" and certify the artist's (and the art community's) special status within a larger community (Becker 1984). Their institutional affiliations gave the judges in 1929 a special cachet.

External, presumably impartial judging was also important within the highly competitive Mummer community. The clubs were eager to win prizes, and outside judges were ostensibly and credibly unbiased in assessing the performances. The judging process put in place in the mid-1930s survives today, and the four divisions pay experts to judge costume design, staging, music, and choreography for every parade. Judges' comments are taken with utmost seriousness, as is evident from the way in which the string bands use them. Each year, after the parade, the entire club listens to the tape-recorded comments the judges make as they walk through the presentations at City Hall, and they make sure that "mistakes" are never repeated.

Responding to the demand for more sophistication, the string bands moved away from the simple music they had played in the early parades and added complex harmonies and polished arrangements to their repertoire. The most successful bands—Ferko, Fralinger, and Quaker City—depended on talented musical directors and raised the bar for their musicians. In every case they emerged from within the bands, where regular practices and auditions for membership had become the rule rather than the exception (Mayer 1972, Regan 1996, Bradshaw and Frangicetto 1995).

The advent of World War II put a damper on the Mummers' play. Adapting to wartime shortages of the lush fabrics used for their costumes, they refurbished old shows, temporarily suspending the informal rule that every year's presentation had to be totally new. Another ban fell by the wayside in 1945, when women appeared as performers for the first time. As Bradshaw and Frangicetto (1995, 81) wrote, "Due to a shortage of 'manpower,' the ladies were allowed and even encouraged to help out." (Like "Rosie the Riveter," however, Philadelphia's women promptly resumed their behind-the-scenes—or scenery—roles after the war, not to return to Broad Street until the 1970s.)

The 1950s and 1960s: A Time for Change

Even as they changed the art of their performances, the Mummers retained some old traditions, including a full schedule of neighborhood appearances sponsored by local businesses. In mid-January 1955 the Greater Kensington Businessman's Association was the sponsor of a huge parade featuring twenty-eight units—clowns, mimes, string bands, fancy clubs, and business floats—that drew half a million spectators (*Philadelphia Inquirer* 1955). A "little Mummers Parade" entertained the Second Street neighborhood, sponsored by the Girard Avenue Businessman's Club (*Philadelphia Daily News* 1955).

Television coverage had become routine by the 1950s. In 1947 a few hours of the Mummers' performances were broadcast under the sponsorship of Sears and Roebuck; the broadcast, as the press reported somewhat breathlessly, was seen "*as far away as Reading*" (Bradshaw and Frangicetto 1995, 85). But the thrill of performing for a living room audience could never match the enthusiasm of the Broad Street spectators. Frederick McCord, a reporter for the *Sunday Bulletin,* wrote of the strength of the bond between performers and street audiences in his pre-parade story on Mummer traditions:

> It is to the outdoor spectators that the Mummer feels closest akin. For one thing they are demonstrating the hardy stuff of which a Mummer must be made [by lining the street despite wind, snow, and cold]. . . . For another it is from those on the curb that the Mummer gets his reward. This lies in what he hears and sees: the child's look of awe, the mother's gasp of surprise and delight, the father's loud guffaw, the crowd's applause and shouts. It is for them that 10,000 Mummers from 30 clubs "go up the street" tomorrow. (McCord 1956, 1)

The love affair between ordinary Philadelphians and the Mummers continued. Parade attendance figures veer wildly, from as few as two hundred thousand in 1954 to as many as 1.6 million in 1961 (a figure that some Mummers consider a gross exaggeration). Some of these numbers reflect post-television crowds. It is unlikely that television coverage had much impact on attendance in the early years of television because few households had sets. Even after TV sets became ubiquitous, however, attendance levels were high, so assessing the impact of television is difficult. That the parade was an eight-hour event by the 1960s makes attendance statistics even more difficult to interpret. The Mummers became a national attraction when their lavish spectacle was broadcast throughout the country, as it was for many years, and this publicity resulte-d in invitations to give paid performances at various events in the United States and abroad, turning some clubs into world travelers.

Broad Street Becomes Off-Broadway: The Parade in the 1970s and 1980s

For any spectator watching the Mummers' four divisions as they perform on New Year's Day, the mixture of new and the old elements is striking. As Becker (1984, 300) observed, "Art worlds change continuously—sometimes gradually, sometimes quite dramatically. New worlds come into existence, old ones disappear. No art world can protect itself fully or for long against all the impulses for change, whether they arise from external sources or internal tensions."

Because of the multigenerational mix within the clubs, change has been evolutionary rather than revolutionary. Competitiveness drives the desire to innovate and incorporate what is fresh and new in club performances. Another motivator, however, is the need to bring young members into the clubs. So the Mummers work hard to keep up to date, incorporating popular themes and trends in art and entertainment into their shows. As Becker (1984, 301) wrote, "The history of art deals with innovations and innovators that won organizational victories, succeeding in creating around themselves the apparatus of an art world, mobilizing enough people to cooperate in regular ways that sustained and furthered their idea. Only changes that succeed in capturing existing cooperative networks or developing new ones survive." Within the Mummers' clubs, this lesson has been learned well, and because of this openness to new ideas and the recognition that play itself requires periodic redefinition, the community has survived for more than a century.

Although the earliest parades were visually spectacular by the standards of the day, over time the Mummers set higher standards for musicianship, elaborated their themes, and added special effects.

Today, the costume is only one component of a complex whole. The comic division continues to be the most traditional, though now the clowns develop satirical sketches that they present in the two minutes they have before the judges;[8] the fancy division, because it has always relied on stunning visual effects, has changed the least, though entries frequently include multiple pieces related to one theme—for example, a circus with Ferris wheel, carousel, and ticket booth—and those walking the suits up the street use them to present miniskits. In addition, the fancy division entries tend more and more frequently to use motion; one recent entry was a huge green-sequined dragon that raised its head and roared, both terrifying and delighting small children along the performance route.

Within the fancy brigades and the string bands, changes are most striking and competition most fierce. The early string bands marched in drill formation. Over time their costumes grew quite elaborate, and capes were incorporated to give movement to the band as it marched. Huge ostrich-plumed backpieces evolved from the stand-up ruffled collars of the early capes. Typically, today's captain's backpiece is anywhere from six to eight feet wide and extends as high as four or five feet above the top of the captain's head. Throughout the 1960s and into the 1970s, each band member wore a backpiece, but the expense of the plumes and the desire to add variety to the show gradually led to fewer large backpieces and more props and special effects related to the theme. Nevertheless, the string bands frequently come into the viewing area with eight to ten backpieces in the front row serving as a "curtain" on the show. When the music begins, the backpieces peel off to the side, revealing the band members and other elements of the presentation.

In earlier parades, banjos were the most prevalent instruments, and the string bands played mostly what one banjo-playing member referred to as "three-chord numbers." The predominance of banjos and glockenspiels (or "bells") gave the string bands a distinctive sound. Today's bands rely more heavily on other stringed instruments and on saxophones to lend richness of tone to their music,[9] and they are judged not only on the complexity of the music they play but also on its relationship to the selected performance theme. Also taken into account is how smoothly the bands make the transition from one piece of music to the next. One band member described the change in the music as follows: "When it started out in the 1900s . . . the music was very primitive [in comparison to] what we play now. There was never harmony in the beginning when they played. Everyone played in the same key. . . . Over the years, the music has progressed, but that notion [the perception of the type of music Mummers play] is still locked in an [older] time" (Creedon, interview, 1997).

Many bands have taken credit for being the first to dance and perform on Broad Street. However, most Mummer historians identify the Harrowgate String Band as introducing what became the most important innovation of the past fifty years. Vittolino and Conforti (1977), reporting on Harrowgate's second first-place prize, wrote, "Harrowgate has been a trend-setter. Before, [as club captain] Fries said, all the string bands used to do was a few counter-marches and then feature a front-line specialty act. Fries says he believes it was Harrowgate who, in 1974, began 'production-type' numbers with their 'Lullaby of Broadway' theme. That year, the entire band tap-danced and placed seventh. 'Now, there must be 15 bands dancing.'"

By examining the bands' summaries of their performances as they appeared in past editions of the annual *Mummers Magazine* and as they were submitted to television stations covering the parade, the changes become most evident.

The Ferko String Band presented an "Old New York" theme in 1963, with Captain Joseph A. Ferko as the city "Boss." The presentation was described as follows in the *Mummers Magazine* of 1963:

Parading through the Bow'ry, the band halts at an intersection. On the corner is the toughie getting his shoes shined. The newsboys are shooting craps and along comes the "cop" who chases them. The band then presents a group of instrumentalists playing and doing the waltz clog to the tune of "East Side, West Side." Then stepping aside the band plays "Streets of New York" and "Boss" Ferko with his "lady" stroll along the Bow'ry greeting his followers.

Within the four-and-a-half-minute performance, Ferko played eight songs, beginning with "Give My Regards to Broadway" and ending with "Sweet Rosie O'Grady."

In the 1973 *Mummers Magazine* the Trilby String Band described a similarly complex theme:

In their presentation, Trilby portrays a caravan of gypsies camped outside a small Hungarian village. As they approach the town square, they announce themselves as Gypsies, Tramps, and Thieves. Joy mounts in the crowd as the gypsies chant and play their happy music. The King of the Gypsies, "Dark Eyes," appears and the gypsy dancing begins with traditional Czardas, featuring the slow start and fast ending. The tambourines of the Romany accent and the rousing tempo of the Hungarian dance and then the gypsy violin is featured in an emotion-packed moment. Happiness grows as darkness approaches; and after a filling meal, the joyous nomads are off again as Happy Wanderers in their ever-moving caravan. The many crooked roads traveled by the happy gypsies are represented by the staggered position of the musicians.

Necessary to this presentation were props to create the village scene and choreography for gypsy dancing that included authentic rhythms. Music ranged from Brahms's "Hungarian Dance," to "Dark Eyes," to "Happy Wanderers," representing the sophistication and complexity of the arrangements that the string bands performed.

The trend toward elaboration has continued unabated. In 1992 the Quaker City String Band presented a theme that used varied pieces of music, shifting tempo and mood, and props that club marshals moved into place. The description that they provided and the videotape of that year's show demonstrate the impressive performances against which 1990s bands competed. The judging information card provides this summary:

Quaker City's 1992 presentation takes us to the high seas where their marauding band of buccaneers pillage and plunder their way around the world. Ahoy, Matey. Welcome aboard the S.S. Fogbound as Quaker City prepares to go "Sailing, Sailing, Over the Bounding Main," as we hear our pirate captain's challenge to his scurvy crew: "Yo, Ho, Ho, Blow the Man Down." These lusty sailors spend their "Life on the Ocean Waves," as their battered vessel goes seeking new land to conquer as we prepare to go "Over the Sea" looting and robbing anyone who would stand in our way. The wail of

"The Sailors Hornpipe" summons everyone on deck as the Captain asks, "What Do You Do With a Drunken Sailor?" Holding aloft an empty rum bottle, he shouts if "It's a Sailor's Life for Me" now, then "It's a Pirate's Life Forever." With a "Victory at Sea" close at hand, this motley bunch wants the world to know that "We're in the Money" as they turn their attention to lucrative pastimes like treasure-hunting. And what better place to look for this newfound wealth than "Under the Sea." What a haul. A treasure chest of rich jewels, new silk, "Old Spice" and other assorted booty from the ocean depths. As we sail off into the sea, we will always remember the good life, the life of a Quaker City Buccaneer.

Woven into the description are the songs chosen and the scripted action that occurred in four and a half minutes. Equally impressive is the description of the suits, which were as lavish as any Broadway costume. This description, though vivid, fails to capture the beauty of what appeared on Broad Street:

The perimeter of the Band features the traditional Captain Morgan pirate dressed in solid white sequined coat and pants, shiny black boots, red velvet belt and sash, topped off with a feathered hat complementing the entire suit. And what pirate worth his salt would be seen without a multi-colored parrot resting on his shoulder? The backpiece consists of hundreds of white ostrich plumes, interspersed with many red feathers, surrounding a ship's wheel and the skull from the Jolly Roger. The pit band wears a smaller version of the perimeter band suit with a red coat, black pants, and boots and a long, flowing blue cape. The deck hands will be wearing three different types of suits of contrasting-colored pants, shirts, vests and hats. Captain Bob Shannon, as Captain Hook, will be in white sequined pants and tunic coat with accent trim of burgundy, gold, and black. His backpiece, a more elaborate version of the band backpiece, depicts the ocean waves at the bottom with a ghost ship on top representing the skeletons of all dead pirate ship captains. The entire backpiece is circled with thousands of white plumes, also with red accent [feathers].

Captain Bob Shannon, who was still leading his band in the 2004 parade, is six foot ten, so his backpiece dwarfed everything except City Hall. This lavish production relied on a full complement of support personnel, including the music director, the drillmaster who charts the movement of the "pit" and "perimeter" band sections;[10] choreographers, who develop and direct the rehearsals and performances of "scurvy crew members," the captain's dancing, and other actions; the makeup artists, often wives and daughters of the club; marshals, who move the scenery around, whether it is bottles of "rum," "treasure chests," or large pieces of scenery such as the SS *Fogbound*. Other marshals help the captain change costumes and backpieces. This division of labor, Becker (1984) asserts, is characteristic of an art world, and in the case of the Mummers demonstrates how far they had come from their informal neighborhood processions.

A similar evolution from comparatively simple to complex artistic performance occurred within the fancy brigades. The difference between the string bands and the fancy brigades is that the latter have traditionally relied on hired brass bands of African American musicians and (more frequently today) recorded music; the brigade members see themselves as dancers rather than musicians. The descriptions of the brigades published in the 1963 issue of *Mummers Magazine* tell the story; the Jokers New Year Brigade chose as their theme "Land of the Pharaohs."

[The Jokers] will be attired in the dress of Ancient Egyptian rulers. The short-sleeved tunic of gold lamé is set off with a sequined bodice opening at the waist and extending to the ankle. It is highlighted by a collar with an ankle-length panel of green and gold nylon. The pants of jade green will extend to the ankle, cuffed by gold lamé. A cape of gold lamé, set off with a green sequined cobra, will hang from the shoulder. Gold leatherette wrist bands and gloves will accent the bare arms. The headdress, a Pharaoh crown of lamé trimmed in intricate designs, will be topped off with gold plumes tipped in green. The Captain, Joseph Walters, will be attired in a similar, more elaborate costume, trimmed in various jewels and highlighted with a towering pyramid containing hundreds of gold plumes. Co-Captain Bucky Walters, age 10, will be a replica in miniature of the Captain. As a drill, the

Brigade will perform intricate movements to the rhythm of "Caravan," "Hindustan," and the Grand March from the opera, "Aida." Marching directly in front of the Brigade will be the Roche American Legion Color Guard.

Emphasized in this description is the detail and thematic "relevance" of the costumes (70 percent of the score for brigades was based on appearance, 30 percent on theme presentation); not supplied is the name of the group that provided musical accompaniment, though the rules indicate that the fancy division had multiple bands in the line of march. The time limit set on the brigade performance was three minutes.

By 1973 the fancy brigades were emphasizing performance as well as visual appeal, as the following description of the Golden Crown New Year Brigade, with its theme, "Dancing Through the Seasons," illustrates:

Spring brings the showers that grow summer's flowers, autumn leaves glow, and winter means snow. In this area, we can appreciate the changing colors of the four seasons. The brigade, captained by J. Schubert, with costumes and soft shoe dancing, invite you to a review of the seasons. There will be green and white in springtime, with its abundance of flowers and the melody of April Showers. The cerise and white roses and butterflies of summer, with dancing to "Everything's Coming Up Roses." Autumn is noted for its colors of orange, gold, rust, and its leaves, and the melody, "Autumn Leaves." Winter is a contrast [with] white, silver, and blue snowflakes, and the melody, "Walking in a Winter Wonderland." Enjoy the season you like best, the beauty of the costumes, and the spirit of the dancing. (*Mummers Magazine* 1973)

Moving Toward the Twenty-first Century: Lasers and Techno-Music

If the string bands are emblematic of the illustrious past of the Mummer tradition, the brigades in the past decade have led the way to the next century by fully embracing both the music and the popular culture of a younger generation. Though demographics may have had a great influence on the style of the brigades in the 1990s, their membership also includes the Baby Boomers, who not only know the old techniques but are receptive to what is new and exciting. The 1996 parade illustrates the changes that have marked the brigades most recently. In 1996 the South Philly Vikings presented "Battle of the Superpowers, for Gotham's Sake." Building on the interest in the *Batman* movies, which rely on dark themes and the stark contrast between good and evil, the Vikings incorporated many of the characters from that cartoon series, as well as the full complement of characters from D.C. Comics and Marvel Comics, including Batman, Superman, Wonder Woman, Iron Man, Robocop, and, of course, Captain America on the side of "truth, justice, and the American Way." These crusaders battled a decidedly unattractive group of evil-doers, including the Joker, the Riddler, Two-Face, and Catwoman, who took over the Hall of Justice. In the course of four and a half minutes, good overcame evil, as the characters displayed not only their dance skills but also engaged in mock combat. The characters were attired in the costumes of their comic book and movie counterparts, and the Joker arrived in a huge gift-wrapped box like those he generally uses for sending bombs to annihilate Batman. The "Robocops" wore heavy-duty silver-tone plastic and masks with dark eye visors. "Batman" drove out of the portals of the Hall of Justice in his Batmobile.

The scenery used in the show was more than thirty feet high and spanned most of Broad Street; the central section featured the spire of the Hall of Justice and a huge bust of the Goddess of Justice, who rather resembled Miss Liberty. The dark, art-deco style of the *Batman* movies, along with a Batman spotlight, created the mood. Much of the scenery used airbrush techniques rather than conventional painting, a trend that has become increasingly prevalent in the past few years.

The brigade chose techno-music—synthesizer music with the bass pumped up so loud that everything seemed to vibrate in time to "Axis Mundi," the theme song. The entire presentation drew on the cultural symbolism popular with a generation that has grown up with the slick effects and pulsating bass of music videos.

To produce such a spectacular show requires a veritable army of individuals with specialized skills. The scenery was designed so that it was entirely mobile (and could be set up within the time limits specified by the rules), an impressive staging feat; the spotlight was operated from behind the scenery; and when good finally triumphed over evil, confetti and streamers burst out from behind the Hall of Justice, adding dramatic "fireworks" to the finale (real fireworks are forbidden on the parade route).

In 1998 the fancy brigade division moved its performances inside the Convention Center, where it staged a ticketed event; the scenery had outgrown Broad Street. That year the brigades performed at City Hall with their hand props and fully choreographed dances, perhaps giving a hint of future directions as the city attempts to nudge the Mummers toward a tourist-friendly all-weather event.[11]

The Second Century

The Mummers welcomed the New Year in 2001 with a parade that moved from the traditional Broad Street route to Market Street, wending its way through the tourist venues of the city. Over the many years of the parade, interest has waxed and waned, and the years from 1999 to 2004 were a time when interest in the Mummers and the parade itself seemed to diminish. The relocation to Market Street, with its proximity to the city's tourist attractions, was intended to draw larger out-of-town audiences. But the Mummers and their hometown fans missed their traditional route, and attendance was spotty.

In 2004 the Mummers returned to their beloved Broad Street, and the *Philadelphia Daily News* ran a headline exuberantly proclaiming the parade as the "Comeback of the Year." The article reported cheering spectators ten deep along the entire route, and these fans started taking their places as early as 9:30 A.M., when the first comics came up the street. As the *Daily News* (2004, 7) reported:

> Mostly . . . fans and big shots reveled in the return to Broad Street for the first time since New Year's Day 1999 after four mediocre years strutting east and west along Market Street. Crowds gridlocked the sidewalks, filled bleachers, and edged into intersections at . . . performance areas from Methodist Hospital to the Union League. That's a phenomenon missing throughout the 1990s as Broad Street crowds

dwindled and the city stopped estimating numbers mostly
out of embarrassment.

The Mummers who appeared on television after their performances proclaimed that they were "back home" and would never leave
Broad Street and the parade's South Philadelphia roots again. The
synergy between audience and performers was reminiscent of the old
days of the parade, and the units performed all the way up the street
rather than simply putting on a show at the designated performance
sites. String band captain Jerry LaRosa Jr. spoke for all the Mummers
when he said, "It's unbelievable, a fabulous experience. I had goose-
bumps. It's nice to be back here. It's where my heart is. We're united
again" (*Philadelphia Daily News* 2004, 16).

Much about the parade followed tradition, but there were striking differences as well. Within the comic division, there were the traditional contenders in the juvenile category and the best couple category, who are judged at separate stands from the star performers in
the string bands, fancy clubs, and comic brigades. However, the bulk
of the comics, numbering in the thousands, streamed up Broad Street
accompanied by brass bands. Their dresses, parasols, pigtailed wigs,
and strut were all traditional, but a hundred years before their ranks
would not have included little girls as well as little boys, and women
as well as men. Drill teams mostly from black neighborhoods performed with each of the parading clubs, and the East Logan Drill
Team, the first all-black parading unit in the contemporary parade,
celebrated its twenty-fifth year as part of the Mummers Parade.

As in the past, the string bands dazzled the crowds with their
mellow sounds and elaborate themes and costumes. But as one Mummer commentator, Jake Hart, noted, there was a new trend toward
"brigadism" in the 2004 performances. The props, previously carried,
were now wheeled into place, and the bands were given extra time
to set up their productions before the official four-and-a-half minute
show began. Inevitably, the props were larger, and in many performances they provided a substitute for the traditional "curtain" of
plumed backpieces.

Inside the Convention Center the fancy brigades entertained
seven thousand spectators at two sold-out shows. The brigade themes
were elaborate and lived up to their billing as "mini-Broadway"

productions. Based on the spectacular crowds on Broad Street, the brigades began to talk about a return to their street show, though they would have to do a somewhat modified drill. The Mummers were indeed back to their old ways, and once again they felt the warm embrace of the city.

The Art World of the Mummers

Over the first century of the Mummers Parade, it is clear that the Mummers became a highly organized community. Becker has written of artistic work as similar to other human enterprises because it is the "joint activity of a number, often a large number, of people" (1984, 1). In the case of the Mummers, cooperation occurs within the intimate club setting as well as within an expanded community that bears collective responsibility for the parade. What categories of people constitute an art world? Art, of course, begins with the artist. Becker's way of examining what he calls the division of labor relies on screen credits for a movie. A similar technique can be applied to a Mummer performing unit by looking at the television information sheet one of the string bands supplied for the 1992 Mummers Parade. Listed on this sheet are the president of the band, whose role is analogous to that of a chief executive officer; the club captain, who leads the band and is the star performer on the street; the treasurer, whose role is to coordinate fund-raising and manage allocation of resources; the drill director, who develops the charts specifying movement of the different musical sections and dancers within the performance; the choreographer, who directs dances of performers; the music director, who selects music that coordinates with a theme; and the publicity director, who handles the band's public and media relations. Performing each of the tasks related to a performance are committees such as the costume committee. Professional costumers may be hired by a club and can be highly influential in developing a theme.[12]

Not all Mummers are performers. The larger the club, the more the Mummers require administrative and logistical skills. For example, raising money is an ongoing challenge in any performing unit, and planning how to allocate the resources that are raised is crucial to the success of a club over the long term.

In the descriptions of the parade over the twentieth century, it is obvious that many individuals with wide array of skills have collaborated. Every performance begins with an idea, and through a division of labor within the performing unit, the idea becomes a reality. Unlike commercial art, however, there is no direct payoff to the individual who invests his or her time, talent, and in many cases treasure to pull off a performance. The rewards of Mummery are ephemeral rather than concrete: the pleasure of play, the close relations with others, and recognition.

Increased Structure Within the Parade

There's two sets of rules you're looking at. You're looking at administrative rules [developed by the clubs and divisions] and then you're looking at rules [adopted to conform to city requirements]. In ours, the comic division, you'll see where it says no alcoholic beverages [on the parade route], no blackface, no sticks or canes. These are pretty specific. The rules that the comic clubs or the fancy clubs, or fancy brigades, make for their participants are [competitive rules] to streamline so that nobody has an advantage. (Heller, interview, 1996)

The early Shooters' processions did not emerge from an integrated art world; people took to the streets to celebrate. An important difference between spontaneous, unstructured play and competitive play is the operation of a set of rules, initially understood and ultimately codified by permanent structures within the play community.

Rules govern competitive play, and play communities enforce conformity to these rules. The Mummers Parade operates under three sets of rules: competitive, normative, and logistical. Competitive and logistical rules are the focus of this chapter; normative rules are part of Chapter 6.

Although the first two types of rules are not antithetical but complementary to play, logistical rules can and do interrupt the play experience within the parade. With increasing competition came the necessity to codify the rules for the different divisions. A second and equally important function of the rules was the city's desire to contain the play within a limited space and time.

The Positive Face of Rules

Rules govern games, the social form of play.[13] Csikszentmihalyi goes so far as to assert that the structure of games motivates individuals into playing them; "the simplest inducement [to play] is competition" (1975, 41). For humans, few experiences are as satisfying as competing with others and winning. Within communities, however, competitive impulses must be balanced with the necessity for cooperation and collaboration. The Mummers Parade offers the opportunity both to compete and to collaborate. The acceptance of mutually agreed upon rules makes this possible. The following are the functions of rules within the play community.

- Rules specify who may compete, categories of competition, and standards against which entries are judged. For example, only bands with forty-five to sixty-four playing members may compete in the string band division. Their music may not be amplified. They are judged on the basis of musicianship, including choice and performance of selections, development and presentation of a theme, and costumes.
- Rules create, insofar as practical, a level playing field for competitors. Though props are permitted, they must conform to size restrictions, and no professional musicians may perform with the band. Though string band members may dance and perform skits using props, they are required to play an instrument. Such restrictions ensure an emphasis on music, not choreography. Choreography, though, is the basis on which fancy brigades are judged.
- Mechanisms for ensuring adherence to agreed upon rules and penalties for breaking rules are in place prior to competition. This function is self-explanatory. What is important, though, is that mechanisms themselves are designed to be, insofar as possible, neutral in resolving disputes.

Winning on the basis of conforming to rules—"playing fair"—lends prestige to clubs and their members. Within this comparatively small community, reputation is valued as highly as winning. Those respected most in the Mummer community, whose pictures occupy a special place in the Mummers Museum Hall of Fame, are revered not only because they won, but also because they followed the rules of sportsmanship and fairness. In this sense, then, playing by the rules demonstrates an individual's moral qualities. And rituals like the brigade serenade, during which the winning fancy brigade is visited by competitors and "serenaded," resemble the political ritual of the loser conceding defeat and shaking his or her opponent's hand publicly. On these occasions, the rules are reaffirmed. But, as the Mummers say, "There's always next year."

Administrative Rules and Their Impact on Play

From their debut on Broad Street under city sponsorship to the present, the city and the Mummers have negotiated the terms and conditions for parading. Initially, the clubs were subject to the same rules that any group using public space must follow. With the advent of television coverage, the Mummers found themselves constrained by new requirements; there was less time for clowning on the sidelines and interacting with spectators under the tighter time constraints imposed by broadcast schedules. In the years between 1995 and 2000, scheduling rules led to a less spectator-friendly parade, as some clubs simply marched past designated performance spots and disappointed their fans. The Mummers disliked this arrangement as much as the spectators did. This rush to City Hall had not occurred in earlier years.

In fact, the differences between the early and contemporary parades is striking. As a fifty-year veteran of the parade describes it:

> It was different [years ago]. There was like four fancy clubs and each of them had a brigade. There wasn't the comic division that [today] takes three hours to pass by. The comic division must have passed by in about an hour. And the string bands didn't stop and do four-minute drills, and the brigades didn't do four-minute drills. You were judged solely on your music and costume in the string bands, and the [fancy] brigades [who then marched with the fancy division mother clubs] . . . just got judged on the costuming. You did not do drilling, so—naturally so—you just went right by the judges

[playing music]. There wasn't five minutes to get ready and then another five or six minutes before the next band got up [in front of the judging stand] and they got ready to go. If you take this twenty times, you have just added a couple of hours. So a division takes not one hour but three. The parade is getting over now at 7:00 instead of at 4:00 [as in the past]. (Walsh, interview, 1996)

The longer duration of the parade is partially explained by the increased complexity of the club entries. Extra time is required to move the scenery and props up the street, position them, and take them down. On the street, this has led to longer gaps between units, and a less entertaining experience. (Television commentators rely on taped interviews and fill the airwaves with histories of the clubs and the tradition itself, as well as commercials.)[14]

Both the expansion and contraction of the parade due to the demands of the city and television sponsors occurred within the seven years I spent gathering data for this research. The first televised parade lasted almost all day; the 1996 parade was not yet over at 6:30 P.M., though the first comics stepped off at 8:30 A.M. The 1997 parade lasted well into the evening, though it had started later than usual; the fancy brigades did not start performing until early evening. In 2001, however, the last string band had finished by 5:30 P.M., and the fancy brigades had moved to the Convention Center, opting out of performing on the street. This change has occurred because of the stringent rules imposed by the four divisions and the substantial penalties for violations. The Mummers accept these restrictions, though not without some backstage grumbling, because schedules are the "cost" of bringing the parade to the largest audience. And they have created opportunities for unstructured play through backstage rituals that occur throughout the year.

In examining the rules as they have evolved over the past hundred years, what is clear is that rigid time limits have made their way into the parade, and these limits have become part of the competitive rules because points are deducted for noncompliance. To illustrate this point, it is useful to examine the box shown on page 66, an excerpt from the comic club rules adopted in 1992 related to time. The comics were the least structured and least controlled unit

---

EXCERPT FROM COMIC CLUB RULES FOR 1992
RELATED TO TIME LIMITS

5. *Comic Club Time Limits*

   A. The Comic Division will cooperate with the city and with each other to assure the continuous flow of the parade and completion of the Comic Division presentations by 12:00 P.M.

   B. The Comic Division Clubs agree that the entries will be stacked at each judging booth; that is, when the previous club presentations are completed at a particular booth, the next club will bring their entries up to be judged without delay, even if the club banner car has not yet crossed the starting line. This stacking procedure will be used at all three judging booths. [Both the comic and fancy divisions have categories assigned to different judging booths to expedite the parade; thus juveniles competing for prizes are judged at "B" or "C" stands rather than at the "A" stand at City Hall.]

   C. If the Comic Division does not complete their presentation within the 12:00 P.M. time limit, then Rule No. 5, plus further limits on the number of entries per category, may be imposed in the Administrative Rules for 1993.

---

in the parade, so it is logical that their division would be the first to feel the effects of regimentation. Equally rigid are the rules adopted in 1996 by the fancy brigade division, shown in the box on the next page. The draconian nature of these rules is felt in the very heavy penalties for brigades, whose total number of points is two hundred. The comic club rules, though quite specific, are shorter than those for the fancy brigades because the brigade performances are so much more elaborate, with more people and more props. String bands are similar to fancy brigades in their formulation of rules.

Without exception, the Mummers I interviewed recognized the need to keep the parade moving up the street so that spectators have a continuous show to watch. At the same time, they expressed their concern that the rush to City Hall to meet television schedules has decreased the amount of time left for performing and interaction with street audiences. It is a difficult balance to maintain. Further, there is not enough time to dance with the children and pose for pictures with the tourists—all of which makes going to the parade a memorable experience for spectators and performers alike.

An unintended consequence of the increasing complexity of the club performances is that it has become harder for newcomers to

1996 FANCY BRIGADE RULES ON PERFORMANCE TIME, PUBLISHED BY THE FANCY BRIGADE ASSOCIATION

B. Brigades will be limited to a total drilling time of four (4) minutes and thirty (30) seconds.

   A. There will be an additional forty-five (45) minute grace period for all floats to be out of the drilling area. Floats must have continuous forward progress during the grace period.

   B. Any members who are not on the float at the end of the presentation cannot go on the float for the forty-five (45) second grace period to exit the drilling area.

   C. During the forty-five (45) second grace period, there will be no dance or choreographed movements by the members on the float.

   D. The brigades will use the same starting line the comics use. You will have the option of starting further back if you choose, but this will be the starting line.

   E. These lines will be painted either red or blue, so as not to confuse them with the regular strut lines.

   F. There is no set-up time. You cannot set up props, floats, etc., at any time.

   G. From the turn to the starting line, there will be no music.

   H. Once the brigade's starter and the director at the starting line agree that the brigade and its music are set to go, any movement and/or music by the Captain, his band, or his brigade will start their time. The brigade starter must remain with the director from the start throughout the entire performance and indicate when the performance is finished. At this time, the forty-five (45) second grace period goes into effect.

   I. If there is no movement and/or music, the time will start with the first person in costume crosses the starting line. This includes juveniles or marshals in costume and the Captain.

   J. The time will stop when the last person or prop crosses the finish line. The drilling area must be cleared of brigade members and props in a total time of four (4) minutes and thirty (30) seconds. Floats will have an additional forty-five (45) seconds to exit the drilling area. . . .

   M. Any brigade over the four (4) minute and thirty (30) second time limit will be penalized three (3) points per judge for every five (5) seconds over: (1) 4.31 to 4.35 = 24 points; 4.36 to 4.40 = 48 points; 4.41 to 4.45 = 72 points; 4.46 to 4.50 points = 96 points. Any float over the forty-five (45) second grace period will be penalized three (3) points per judge for every five (5) seconds over: (1) 0.46 to 0.50 = 24 points; (2) 0.51 to 0.55 = 48 points; (3) 0.56 to 0.60 = 72 points; (4) 0.61 to 0.65 = 96 points.

   N. Time will be kept at a large clock at City Hall to be provided by the City of Philadelphia. Our directors will notify the City timekeeper when to start and stop the clock.

   O. A banner may be carried, pulled, pushed, or driven through the drilling area before the brigade enters. No one in costume may carry the banner or the time will start.

enter the parade and compete with established clubs. The experience of putting a production together year after year is transmitted within the clubs. Marshaling the financial and human resources needed to be competitive is difficult without this institutional memory. Added to this is the competitiveness of established clubs, who show little inclination to be mentors to newcomers. In some cases new clubs rely on veteran Mummers who have left other groups. These clubs have expertise. However, for groups with no knowledge of Mummery, the learning curve is very steep. In the earliest days of the parade, everyone was learning and everyone was engaged in creating a "tradition." The event was thus a "free-for-all." Over time, boundaries have formed around the play community. That said, the Mummers have been sensitive to the need to broaden participation, and, as discussed in a later chapter, new groups have joined in the annual march up Broad Street.

3 Blacks, Women, and the "New" Immigrants

The Mummers and Diversity

The Mummers Parade is the most populous, unspoiled, energetic, uncorrupted annual folk festival on earth today. Today is the deadline for entries for the New Year's Day 1985 parade. The City Department of Recreation must decide who will march, a difficult task. Some groups have waited years for the opportunity. . . . The character of the Mummers Parade is immensely diverse. It is deeply rooted in history, neighborhood traditions, family life and public and private symbolism throughout the entire Philadelphia region. Yet that character is, in fact though not in rules, flawed by a tradition of exclusion . . . absolutely contrary to the sense of joy, pride, and generosity of spirit that is the rich heart of the festival. Moving slowly and under pressure, in 1964 the city banned blackface, long a traditional mummers style, as intolerably condescending and demeaning to black people. In the last few years, a handful of women have begun to appear in the marching groups. . . . In the late 1920s, nostalgists recall, an all-black string band marched for a year or two. An occasional black marches in regular units. Many of the non-costumed bands that accompany the fancy brigades are partly or entirely black. None of that diminishes the fact of exclusion.
—Philadelphia Inquirer (1984)

Controversies surrounding inclusion, exclusion, race, and gender, have followed the Mummers throughout their long history. The *Inquirer* editorial quoted above is one of many calls for diversity in the annual parade. Few would argue against including all of Philadelphia's ethnic groups in a parade that welcomes the New Year. Yet it may not be fair to accuse the Mummers of a deliberate effort to exclude others from "their" parade. Such criticisms, with their underlying accusations of racism or sexism, fail to take into account the history of the parade.

In one area, the exclusion of blacks, the editorial clearly shows a lack of knowledge about the parade's early history. The "white-guys-only" stereotype overlooks the diversity of the clubs and the roles that other groups have played in creating the spectacle that is Philadelphia Mummery. The Mummers' relationship to others in the community and to those outside their traditional boundaries has changed over the history of the parade, and the processes of accommodation, confrontation, and social change have expanded the definition of who is a Mummer.

A "Lily White" Parade?

Of all the stereotypes that have dogged the Mummers over the years, the "white guys only" is the most persistent. Mummers have always argued vehemently, but unsuccessfully, against this label, and their arguments are valid. Despite the *Inquirer's* offhand dismissal of nostalgic assertions that blacks have historically been part of the tradition, news clippings document that "all-Negro" units competed throughout the first quarter-century of the Broad Street Parade, and it is likely that they were part of the free-for-all neighborhood parades prior to that time.

The evidence is fragmentary but solid. In 1916 the *Philadelphia Record* reported that the hundred-member "all Negro" George A. Persch Club "marched in fantastic, if ragged costumes." Other news clippings document the existence of numerous black clubs, including the Ivy Leaf Club (1901), the Blue Ribbon Club (1901, 1911, 1915, 1924), the James Hancock Club (1910, 1911, 1914), the Golden Eagle Club (1902, 1910, 1911), the Homebreakers String Band (1901, 1914), and Homebreakers 2 (1902). This list may be incomplete; in the early years of the parade, groups formed, disbanded, consolidated, changed their names, and disappeared from the public record, so gaps in participation for all groups is more the rule than the exception. Furthermore, press coverage of the clubs within the parade is not comprehensive, so small groups were not necessarily included in accounts of who marched.

After 1930, the "all-Negro" clubs disappear from the Mummers' stage, at least as competitors for the various prize categories. It seems unlikely that if they had continued to march competitively in the parade their identification as "all Negro" would suddenly have been dropped. This was the 1930s, and distinctions between black and white units would have remained in place. There may be several explanations for their disappearance, though each is speculative. The history of white Mummer clubs is plentiful, but similar accounts of black clubs, apart from the fragments discussed above, were not found when the research for this book was conducted.

By the 1930s the Mummers' clubs in South Philadelphia and around the city were well established. As noted in Chapter 1, the Shooters of the nineteenth century, who became the Mummers of the twentieth, set out to craft an image of themselves as the "good working people of Philadelphia." So they developed from the beginning good public relations skills. They provided detailed descriptions of their themes to the newspapers to ensure favorable coverage, and they touted their heroes and stars by early on setting up a hall of fame to recognize exemplary Mummers.[1] There are no blacks in the Mummers Museum Hall of Fame.

This campaign was effective in drawing press coverage, and that is not surprising given that crowds numbered several hundred thousand in the first half-century of the parade. The lavish and extensive coverage emphasized the white ethnic roots of Mummery. No comparable history of black participation is found in the early clippings from Philadelphia's major newspapers.

The white clubs were active in the neighborhoods, then as now serving the multiple functions of socializing younger members, providing performances throughout the year to raise money for worthy causes and for their own presentations, and entertaining and performing for their neighbors.

The coverage of the clubs created and reinforced the stereotypical image of the Mummers as white and as primarily drawn from Polish, Irish, Italian, and German ethnic communities. After a while, it is possible that the public stopped "seeing" the more diverse groups of individuals who were part of the parade. Judith Lorber (1993, 568) turns the phrase "seeing is believing" on its head with her observation that "believing is seeing." Repetition affirms a version of events that are "true." Sociologist W. I. Thomas's classic theorem asserts that "situations that are defined as real are real in their consequences" (1966, 301). Stereotypes can turn into self-fulfilling prophecies.

The white stereotype associated with the Mummers had at least two consequences. First, it effectively erased the substantial and important contributions of black Philadelphians to the Shooters' traditions.[2] Second, it made the Mummers vulnerable to charges that they were exclusionary and closed at best and racist at worst. A third outcome is plausible, but there is no direct evidence for it—the image may have dampened the enthusiasm of Philadelphia's black communities for joining in the white parade, or at least competing in it.

Finally, the early history of South Philadelphia is not only white but also black. Like the Mummers, numerous groups supported and nurtured black communities, from churches to beneficial and welfare organizations. It may be that the black communities were occupied with other kinds of activities, including their own musical groups. It is logical that the different community associations sponsored some of the early black parading groups, though the affiliation of these clubs is unknown. The tantalizing question that arises is why the black groups stopped competing in the parade, apparently abruptly. This does not mean that blacks left the parade entirely, for in the years after 1930 blacks, as members of brass bands, accompanied the competing comic and fancy clubs and the fancy brigades up Broad Street.

The Octavius V. Catto String Band is the most famous example of a black group that has been associated with the parade through most of its history.[3] Unlike other black groups, the history of this band is "documented" in a 1963 city council resolution honoring its sixty-fifth anniversary appearance in the Mummers Parade. The resolution reads:

> WHEREAS, the O. V. Catto Elks Band was formulated in the 1920s and was originally a String Band in the early 20's and 30's. Due to the Depression, the CATTO String Band became a brass band performing for the Comic Mummers in the Parade(s); and
>
> WHEREAS, They have been pioneers of African-American Mummery; and
>
> WHEREAS, They have been great contributors to the tradition of Mummery for sixty-five years in the City of Philadelphia. Their contributions have helped tremendously in the evolution of this unique Philadelphia event; therefore

Resolved by the Council of the City of Philadelphia, That we hereby honor the O. V. CATTO Elks Band for their many contributions to our community over many years.

The city council resolution mentions "the Depression" as the point when the Catto Band switched from competing as a string band to accompanying other clubs as a brass band. Surely this is no coincidence. This opens up the possibility that the band's incentive for the switch was the money they were paid as accompanists. The Depression was a difficult period for all Americans, and it did force some scaling back of the performances by white Mummers. Although the economic struggles of Philadelphia's black community are well beyond the scope of this book, it undoubtedly was more difficult for blacks to find work during the 1930s and early 1940s than it was for whites, partly owing to their exclusion from unionized jobs. The lack of contemporaneous accounts from black participants in the parade during this period makes it impossible to provide a definitive answer to the question of why blacks no longer competed. In any case, once they stopped competing in the 1930s, blacks remained in their "backstage" role until the late 1970s.

The incentive of getting paid was mentioned quite explicitly in an interview I conducted in 2006 with the leader of the Keystone Dixie Land Band, Wendell Bright. His account of the experiences he had with the Mummers provides insights into the linkage between the Elks Club brass bands and the Mummers' clubs. Bright's band has accompanied numerous comic and fancy clubs up Broad Street over the years, and his involvement with the Mummers dates to the 1950s. "When we found out about the Mummers," he told me,

I was under the direction of a gentleman by the name of Walter J. Robinson, and he had a band in west Philadelphia. There were four bands; O. V. Catto was one of them and Quaker City [a black brass band]... one in North Philadelphia, one in West Philadelphia, and two in South Philadelphia. They were all black bands and they were Elks Club bands. And what they did, they [the directors of the four bands] were called on by the Mummers to produce a band [to play with the clubs], and they took members from the bands that wanted to be involved, and they marched with the

Mummers. That's when the negotiation came up with the money. And they would pay us at the end of the parade. You wouldn't see them [the Mummers] until the next time they had it [the parade], and then they would have you come down and rehearse what they were going to do, inside or outside, and we would play for them. That's what started it, then. And we enjoyed it, and there was no problems. They even had us come back on New Year's Day after the parade to play at the clubhouse. They call for us to do that now.

Bright's account indicates that the Elks Clubs were an integral part of the black community in Philadelphia for many years, certainly from the time he was a youngster. These clubs were fraternal groups, they had women's auxiliaries, and they were major sponsors of musical groups, including brass and marching bands. In some respects they had the same mission as the Mummers' clubs in Philadelphia, though they were not organized around the annual Mummers Parade. (Bright remarked that the Elks have largely disappeared.)

The money paid to the brass bands as a result of the negotiations was substantial. Although Bright's experience started in the 1950s, he speculated on why the black units stopped competing in the 1930s.

I agree that the role of competing and accompanying the clubs is different. You see, there were some difficult times when we had to play in the cold and the route was several miles long. Musicians had to put their horns up against the exhaust pipes of the police cars to open up the valves. It was hard work, but you got paid, and of course the money back then was different [than now] 'cause a hundred dollars back then was like a thousand dollars today. I think that at that point, they [the black bands who marched earlier] got tired of doing it in a competitive way, and they wanted to get paid. When we were out there, we were one of the best [bands] at that time, and so many Mummer groups were trying to get us, and we couldn't play for but one. We recommended other black bands in the city, and [the Mummers] picked them up to play. And that's the only reason I think [the black groups] decided to stop competing.

It must be emphasized that this comment is not based on direct evidence, though Bright grew up in South Philadelphia's black neighborhoods and shared his historical knowledge of the parade and of the organization of black communities. Given the timing of the Catto Band's shift, his is a plausible explanation of what may have happened.

The Blackface Controversy

When debates about racism and racist images escalated during the civil rights era, the Mummers, particularly their portrayal of blacks as "wenches" and "dudes," came under scrutiny. The following account of the controversy over blackface has two distinctive, though intertwined, parts. The first concerns the dispute in the public square, which involved two groups: the Mummers and a coalition of civil rights groups led by city councilman Cecil Moore of North Philadelphia. The second involves the less visible negotiations within the Mummer community between black musicians who had a long history with the clubs and white club leaders.

What became known as the "blackface controversy" erupted in Philadelphia on 16 December 1963, with the announcement by Elias Myers, the parade's director, that participants would no longer be permitted to wear traditional blackface.[4] Welch maintains that the roots of the blackface dispute are traceable to earlier efforts among black civil rights leaders in New Orleans to stop the Zulu parades, which were traditional in the Mardi Gras. The Zulus were blacks paid by white businesses to wander through the streets in drunken bands dressed in "African" costumes and acting like "savages."[5] The group most affected by Elias's decision was the comics, who marched as "wenches" and "dudes" in the parade, though early pictures show that blackface was used by other divisions as well. The comics reacted swiftly, gathering at Myers's house to picket. The city's representatives then attempted a compromise: blackface makeup would be allowed "*if it was used to create a character, but not if it was used to ridicule any ethnic group.*" No one liked this decision, mostly because of its ambiguity. The National Association for the Advancement of Colored People (NAACP) reacted by petitioning the Philadelphia Court of Common Pleas to ban blackface from the parade on the grounds that it was offensive to African Americans.

The decision of the NAACP and Congress of Racial Equality (CORE) (representing the most politically active members of the African American community) to bring suit was based on objections to portrayals of blacks as wenches and dudes. The wench, like "her" predecessor in the minstrel shows of the early 1830s and 1840s, danced up Broad Street in a garish ruffled dress, carrying a brightly colored and lavishly decorated parasol. "She" wore blackface makeup with white around the lips and a wig with braids. Escorting the wench was the dude, attired in a tuxedo with too-short pants and spats, wearing a top hat. He carried a cane and marched up Broad Street in the traditional golden slippers. The least organized and most outrageous of all the performers, wenches and dudes filled Broad Street from curb to curb. In the early years of the parade, their exuberance was fueled by beer carried on the trucks that led the units up the street.

The minstrel show was the most popular form of entertainment for the working classes during the early nineteenth century. Lott suggests that minstrelsy drew on black cultural icons. For blacks, the clown and harlequin are traceable to the slave tradition of the trickster, "frequently . . . champions, heroes, back-door victors for the weak over the strong" (Lott 1993, 23).

Mummers had their own interpretation of the origin of wenches and dudes. They asserted that the wench and dude, with their dandified attire, were derived from black parodies of white plantation owners and their wives. By framing the tradition this way, the Mummers categorized the mocking images as no different from other images of rich and powerful whites whose pretensions burlesque parades parodied.

Other cultural historians interpret the portrayals as more sinister and argue that minstrel shows demeaned blacks by treating them "as little more than a source of public entertainment" (White 1994, 28). The minstrel images were not flattering. Concern about how blacks were presented in public performances emerged at a time when civil rights leaders were campaigning for respect and pushing for legislation to affirm their rights, and brought this issue to the public arena. While blacks could and did satirize themselves in the spirit of play, the appropriation of their celebrations was another matter entirely.[6] Civil rights leaders asserted that white mockery of a marginalized group emphasized the power of white men. To further bolster their case, CORE raised the question of whether it was appropriate for Philadelphia's city council to provide both monetary and symbolic support for mocking images of African American residents. The dispute erupted so suddenly that the Mummers had no opportunity to negotiate or discuss the problems posed by blackface with black leaders. Nor was there any attempt by these groups to resolve the issue amicably. Given their fierce resistance to city authority and limitations on "their" parade, the Mummers resisted the city's ban. They continued to identify blackface as a tradition that was devoid of any other meaning besides having fun.

As the controversy unfolded, the positions of the two sides hardened. Welch (1991, 153) wrote, "Militant African-American groups claimed they would stop the parade with a chain made up of their bodies. Threats to import African-Americans from New York and Washington to 'operate' from the rooftops were made."

Frederick M. Calandra, president of the New Year's Shooters and Mummers Association, responded:

> Moving to another city is one possibility, but we would also consider holding the parade at Philadelphia Stadium or at South 2d Street. If it was held at the Stadium, we would charge admission. . . . [Mummers] don't worry about the prize money. . . . The city doesn't pay our bills. . . . I've had rough estimates from the clubs and the total cost [of parading] came in at $300,000. When we get $70,000 [from city funding for prizes] you're only getting one-fourth of what you put out. (*Philadelphia Evening Bulletin* 1964)

Calandra's comments on this issue reflected an unprecedented unity among the three Mummer divisions, which were equally outraged by what they viewed as interference and a misinterpretation of their tradition. Because of inclement weather, the parade was delayed, giving both sides additional time to posture in public.

On 3 January 1964 the Court of Common Pleas issued a preliminary injunction that represented a partial victory for the Mummers. Blackface was banned on Broad Street only, and CORE was prohibited from picketing on the parade route. In addition, the court rejected the NAACP petition to block television coverage, a decision that was enormously important to the Mummer clubs because of the revenues the broadcast generated. The ruling was intended to placate both sides and forestall violent confrontations. On 4 January, however, when the Mummers started their march up Broad Street, it was not "business as usual." The police in force lined the route, and Philadelphians, fearing trouble, stayed home.

This chronology focuses on the public controversy. What it does not do is give voice to the black and white Philadelphians who were part of the parade. Beneath the controversy, white Mummers showed concern for the blacks who marched up the street as part of their clubs; and some segments of the black community maintained their close personal ties with the Mummers. This is evident in the decision of many of the black brass bands to be part of the 1964 parade. Although I asked most of the people I interviewed about the blackface controversy and race, relatively few of my sources had actually been part of the episode. The discussion that follows is drawn primarily from a lengthy interview with a white comic club president and leader within the Mummer community and with the leader of an all-black band that accompanied the comics in 1964.[7] When younger Mummers were interviewed, they still expressed frustration at being misunderstood and misinterpreted by those outside of their community. They were, however, more politically sensitive to the issues surrounding the use of blackface than their predecessors. Here is the account of a white comic club member of what happened in 1963:

> I'm [probably] the last living person involved [directly] in the blackface episode, and it was something that didn't have to come about in the way it did, but it is part of the history, and so we might as well talk about it. . . . John Kennedy was assassinated two or three weeks before the . . . episode started. This is 1963, November. . . . I think all the personal areas of enjoyment sort of took a temporary holiday. Nobody felt like doing [anything] or really participating in any type of major event. We'd had a very solemn Thanksgiving, and it was a tough time on the country. Vietnam rages on, and people were just disillusioned with the whole system.

What is striking about the way in which this account is framed is the attempt to understand and interpret the controversy in the broadest historical context. But there is no explicit reference to race, surely the "elephant in the room." Like many Mummers at that time, and even today, this man emphasized that the Mummers were not interested in "politics." (To the extent that the struggle was "political" for the Mummers, it focused on the relations between city officials and the clubs. This does not mean that some white Mummers were asserting their political power in the city in pushing for the ban to be lifted.) Nevertheless, this informant insisted on the playful aims of the Mummers: "There were so many things happening, and our event [the parade] is done by participants to bring joy and happiness to others. That's the whole connotation of Mummery—to bring happiness and joy and goodwill to others, and [throughout the country] there just wasn't that feeling at the time."

Most Mummers, including this white informant, believed that the issue of blackface had less to do with the practice itself than with the ambitions of local black politicians. (Philadelphians, in general, view *all* politicians with skepticism.) Also implicit in his comments was the perception that "outsiders" could not be expected to understand the relationships between blacks and whites that had developed over the course of a century. This general perception is exemplified in his comment that "what happened was, we had political people here from the black community. One was Cecil Moore ... [I don't know] whether he was making a statement for the black community or making a statement for himself; I don't want to get into [that]."

His suspicions were buttressed by the timing of the challenges to the Mummers:

> If this was such a pressing issue, number one question I had at the time—and I brought it [up with] the mayor—was why wasn't this brought up in February, March, April [of 1963] for discussion? What was this grandstanding all about? We were not, then, talked to ... there was no discussion, no back-and-forth. The gentlemen [Mr. Moore] went to the press and said, "We're not letting," "They can't do," "We're not allowing," and ... threats of violence if it should come about [the wearing of blackface] were made. Well, of course, the situation ... developed into: "You're not telling me what to do" on the Mummers' part.

A similar perspective was apparent in the black informant's view of the timing of the incident: "[The timing of the protests against blackface] was more of a deliberate thing to take something away from the parade. Because I could understand them coming in July or August to talk about it, but to jam it up that close, it was to destroy what they [the Mummers] were going to do that particular year. That's what I think."

In addition to expressing doubt about the timing of the protest, the black informant volunteered his opinion that, to a large degree, the whole controversy was started by groups from North Philadelphia who had no understanding of the traditions of the parade. A South Philadelphian himself, he commented:

> But, you know, I don't think it was too much of that [sensitivity about degrading images] in the thought of people [raising the issue of blackface] . . . it was the people that didn't understand and had no knowledge of what was going on, just like today. . . . It was the troublemakers that got involved, decent respectable people never got involved in anything like that. Because if you did it, you did it [used blackface], and that was the end of that. Why would you want to come up to somebody and start an argument with somebody and just get in trouble. [Blackface] was a taken-for-granted thing, I believe. . . . Why he [Cecil Moore] brought them [the group of blacks] from North Philadelphia I have no idea, because they were not even associated with the parade. They were so far away. The blacks in the community in South Philadelphia lined the streets to see the parade because from Washington Avenue on up to Lombard Street was a black area, and from there on down, there was a huge number of people who watched the parade every year. You see, North Philadelphia at that time had a lot of problems and a lot of hoodlums, and I think he [Moore] [started the controversy] to start some problems, I really do.

These comments are remarkable for the solidarity that the informant expresses with the Mummers. To him, at least, Cecil Moore and his associates were outsiders. Blacks in South Philadelphia had grown up watching and enjoying the parade just as their white neighbors had, and an accommodation between the groups was reached. This older musician's comments also show a clear divide among black Philadelphians about the best means for resolving issues related to race. No consensus was apparent within the black community as a whole about what issues were worth fighting about and what matters were best left alone.

The differences within Philadelphia's black community were similar to the divisions that existed in New Orleans during the campaign to stop the Zulus from performing in the Mardi Gras celebrations. However, in New Orleans, the civil rights groups did not follow up their denunciations of the Zulus with any legal challenges, probably because they knew differences of opinion existed. One New Orleans resident commented on this schism in the community, "I think the Zulu is a disgrace . . . we're split in so many different ways. We don't have just Negroes. We have our Catholic Negroes, and our Protestant Negroes, our downtown Negroes and our uptown Negroes, our light Negroes and our dark Negroes. And we have too many Negroes who don't think they're Negroes" (Welch 1991, 157).

These different perspectives in Philadelphia led to the decision of some brass bands[8] to continue their relationships with the Mummers based on an understanding that had guided their interactions over time. In the case of the black informant I interviewed, it was not a generational divide, because at the time the controversy erupted, he was a young man.

The parade itself was tense, with the two sides anticipating violence. Welch (1991, 153) describes what happened from an outsider's perspective: "The white marchers paraded silently through the African-American districts in South Philadelphia. The majority of the [string] bands refused to play, and all that could be heard was the sullen sound of muffled drums. A bus filled with police officers followed every unit; many were scanning the rooftops. . . . Few incidents were reported during the early stages."

This account of a "few" incidents diverges from the white Mummer informant's more dramatic recollection of what happened at street level. "Our club," he recalled,

> had hundreds of guys arrested. . . . There was a lot of bad feelings on both sides. And this Cecil Moore brought down all these people from North Philadelphia from the black

community, and they tried to stop the Mummers; it was a mistake on their part because when they're [the Mummer groups, in this case comics] all together, they're not easily dissuaded. There was a big fight and a lot of black people got hurt very bad. We proceeded to go around City Hall.

Welch's (1991, 154) account makes no mention of injuries:

One of the Mummers clubs staged its own "sit-in." Members of [the club] sat down in the middle of the street, some shouting, "Negroes sat down in City Hall, we'll sit down here." A new chant started: "One, two, three, four, we hate Cecil Moore." The police moved in and forced the Mummers to rise. The entire incident lasted about 20 minutes, after which the paraders started up the street.

The incident was experienced differently by the black informant. He did not see any confrontation because the parade was diverted from the area where Moore's supporters, allegedly numbering from five hundred to a thousand people, were gathered.

A more equivocal view of the issue was represented in the interview of a colleague of the black informant included in *Strut!*—a documentary released in 2002:

Around 1968 or 1969,[9] some of the black leaders in the city tried to ban the blackfaces from coming up the street, and they vowed to come anyway. The Afro-Americans just wasn't going to stand for that in the parade. It took a couple of years, to sink in, and, of course, they [the comics] were drinking and when that would happen they would really get unruly in the streets and [long pause] a lot of things would happen. But that doesn't happen anymore.

Though the comments of this man do not exonerate the Mummers, they also do not indicate a strong identification with Cecil Moore and the civil rights advocates. And the blackface controversy is not seen even retrospectively as a watershed event in relations between blacks and whites within the clubs.

In the end, the Mummers paraded in makeup that was barely within the rules—black streaks and "dark blue makeup with kinky hair." They complied with the city's ban, but the seditious clowns of Mummery had the last word: "The later unofficial but traditional march down Second Street was quiet. . . . As they moved below South Street, the relative center of the African-American community, the blackface make-up reappeared. As darkness fell, the cry arose: 'The Democrats own Broad Street; we own Second Street'" (Welch 1991, 154).

These descriptions of the incident are limited to the public confrontation in 1964. But prior to the parade, informal discussions occurred between the white club leaders and the black musicians. The white comic club leader reached out sensitively and tactfully to the blacks who were part of his club, but he maintained his stance that the use of blackface was a time-honored tradition among the Mummers. This is evident in his description of negotiations within his club:

At the time I asked the "higher-ups" [club leaders] what they wanted to do. They said they wanted to go [traditional]. This traditional look that Eddie Cantor and Al Jolson and a host of other people have used for years and years [the minstrel theme] was symbolic with Mummery—the black face, the big white lips, the whiteness around the eyes, and the explosiveness of the Mummers [swarming forward at the judge's stand]. Plantation life [was] the dominant theme through most of the century with the Mummers. The [wench] dress of the female and the dudes [accompanied the "female"]. That's the way I had paraded [as a performing comic]. I still have my cane and all that stuff. And that was a very big part of the parade.

Of all the groups in the Mummers Parade, the comics invest the least money in their costumes and do the least planning for their presentations. Thus, it would have been relatively easy for them to modify their plans. They chose not to do so because the dispute was as much about outsiders interfering in the parade as it was about what they would wear in their performances. Beyond the defense of tradition, the white informant felt it was necessary to give the black band members who were part of his club's performance an opportunity to sidestep the controversy. This is shown by the way he approached them prior to the parade:

> First of all, I told you that it was threats and during that month of December what took place was—I had always had an affiliation in our club with the black band. They [the group who had filed suit and others in the African American community] had got hold of the black band leader and told him he couldn't participate—and he'd been [participating] since the 1920s. When he refused [to go along with them], they beat him up and threw him down the subway steps and broke his hip—which years later, he passed away from cancer of the hip in that very spot where they broke his hip. I asked [the black band members] if they wanted to be released from their obligation to parade and the number two guy told me definitely not. So, I put around them all my biggest guys [in the club], my biggest longshoremen I put around the band. We proceeded to do the parade.

More than forty years after this incident, it is impossible to know for certain the views of all the brass band members who marched in 1964. However, based on the limited evidence provided by the interview with the black band member and in *Strut!* their relationships with the Mummers appear to have been friendly and supportive; they felt they were making a valuable contribution to the parade.

For their part, the Mummers protected the groups who marched with them from the racist confrontations that occurred along the parade route. Two accounts illustrate this. The first is from *Strut!*

> I remember one year we were coming down Broad Street, and I had the same horn [gesturing to his instrument], and somebody threw a firecracker down my horn and busted my lip . . . and the guys in the brigade seen who did it, and they told me, "Don't worry. Just stay here, and we'll take care of it." And they went over to the guy and they took *good* care of him.

Throughout the interview with the black musician, he stressed his comfort with the Mummers and the sense of belonging his band had as they played their music for the clubs. He also cited incidents when spectators would hurl racial slurs, though he inevitably characterized them as "drunk" or "out of control." The Mummers who he marched with would do something about these insults, usually in the alleys out of public view.

And, like the competing Mummers, these groups shared their pleasure in performing. As the musician in *Strut!* commented:

> We were all veterans on Broad Street during the years of the fifties and sixties. We supplied a lot of the music for most of the comic groups of the time [and continue to] even today. All the time I've been playing in the Mummers Parade, I've noticed how people really appreciate what you're doing. And the ones that do appreciate . . . they will actually come up and shake your hand. Some will actually throw money down my horn.

Musing on the blackface incident from a distance of thirty-four years, the Mummer informant sounded regretful:

> It could have been easily avoided. [Cecil Moore] had been around Philadelphia, and he knew that the Mummers did this [used blackface] for all the years he had been alive and for many years before that. And the way to get around it or alter it would have been to come like in the early stages of the parade where things could have been [resolved]. . . . The rules could have been explained, and we could have worked it out [in a sensitive way] rather than on a confrontational basis.

Other Mummers echoed these sentiments during both formal and informal interviews; in retrospect and in a racially sensitive climate, today's Mummers acknowledge the negative connotations associated with blackface, though even today they do not acknowledge that the message they intended was racist. These modified attitudes are not surprising, because control of the Mummers' clubs has shifted to a new generation more attuned to the problems of racial

and ethnic minorities and very well acquainted with "political cor-
rectness." However, to those directly involved in the events of 1964,
blackface was a tradition. As one Mummer commented somewhat
defensively, "Yeah, we weren't trying to mimic the blacks or make
fun of the blacks. It was just a tradition that was there. Like two
hundred years ago, I had nothing to do with what happened then,
I wasn't there [during slavery] two hundred years ago years ago"
(Porco, interview, 1997).

Hobsbawm (1982, 9) maintains that traditions serve multiple
functions. For example, in the early days of the Shooters' processions,
as the Mummers adopted the blackface of minstrelsy, this disguise
functioned symbolically in two ways. The blackface disguise offered
whites an opportunity to play at being "black" and allowed usually
prohibited, less disciplined behavior. It also affirmed the differences
between whites and blacks, especially among the Irish, because
whites had the ability to take the mask off and return to whiteness
(Roediger 1996).

By the 1960s, the early meaning of blackface had shifted, and
the makeup and costumes had become a taken-for-granted, time-
honored tradition. Yet the other two purposes may have lingered
beneath the contemporary explanations of "why we do this." The
descendants of white ethnic immigrants had less need to emphasize
their whiteness. But over many years, blackface as a "tradition"
served as a symbolic link to grandfathers and fathers.

In mid-1964 Mayor Tate, in announcing the rules for the 1965
parade, reiterated the ban on blackface. The city was supported by
a number of organizations not specifically tied to the African American community, among them the Philadelphia Bar Association's
Panel on Community Tensions and the Archbishop's Commission on
Human Relations, which spoke for the Catholic Church. Some Mummers resisted, this time on the grounds that other entertainment was
not "censored." Although dark brown and dark blue makeup was
used in 1965 and a few Mummers were ejected from the parade until
they washed their faces, the clubs for the most part complied with
the ban.

Rules banning blackface were quietly adopted by the string band
division in 1964, the comics in 1968, and the fancy division in 1974.
The issue of race receded, not to be revived until the mid-1980s,
when ethnic and racial diversity reemerged as issues. For the Mum-

mers, the controversy was a learning experience; it may not have changed underlying attitudes, but it did remove the issue from public debate. For their part, blacks continued to participate in the annual trek up Broad Street, providing accompaniment for the clubs as they played music, including jazz that celebrated their own cultural heritage.

Women and the Clubs

The 1970s saw changes in the roles that women assumed in both public and private life, and it was inevitable that this cultural shift would affect the Mummers' clubs. The earliest history of the neighborhood celebrations indicates that play included everyone. With the formation of Shooters' clubs in the late nineteenth century (described in Chapter 1), women retreated to the background. Barred from performing, they nonetheless sewed costumes for their men and for little boys, who marched as "juveniles," cooked the pepper pot soup for New Year's Day, and put on their prettiest dresses for the elegant annual banquets that the clubs organized. Women's roles in the Mummer community reflected the traditional female roles enacted in the wider society. Women's "sphere" did not include full participation in a men's club.

The roles that women did assume followed traditional gender lines. For example, the Joseph A. Ferko String Band successfully organized a ladies auxiliary in 1935. After agreeing to pay dues of ten cents per week, "the girls," according to Dave Bradshaw and Tom Frangicetto (1995, 60–61), set about developing a mission statement:

> The object of the auxiliary is to raise and procure funds for the operation of the band, and to bring together in close friendship the wives, sweethearts, mothers, sisters, brothers, and your friends in general, that they may by such association carry on the activities of the band. The auxiliary is for the purpose of raising money for the band in general, no one certain man or other purpose. [Having been authorized by Joseph A. Ferko] . . . the auxiliary is to [bring members] together in close friendship and oppose and assist in eradicating rudeness and vulgarity in conduct of right thinking. There shall be no separate units of this auxiliary.

Ferko's ladies auxiliary had two roles: they supported the band members in practical ways, and they brought refinement and civility to the Ferko "family," where the mere presence of "ladies" tempered language and behavior. In addition, the "ladies" were apparently quite effective in raising several hundred dollars for the band through their "social affairs."

Ferko was a leader among the string bands, so other groups followed its example of bringing women into club activities, though the traditional "men's club" rules persisted. Even if no formal auxiliary existed in clubs, the women formed groups quite frequently under the leadership of the club captain's or president's wife. In general, they agreed with the separation of the genders. One wife of a club president made it clear in an interview conducted in the mid-1970s that she and others felt that it was not appropriate for women to assume public roles in the parade, though they could "help" behind the scenes (Tumulo, interview, 1975). Both men and their wives agreed that because the clubs had bars—even though every club also had a sergeant at arms designated to handle obstreperous behavior—they were not a place where "ladies" should spend their time. (South Philadelphia, to the present day, retains "ladies' entrances" to many of its corner bars.) Furthermore, the men who still cherish the old tradition commented in interviews for this research that their wives would not want them spending time with "other women."

By the 1970s, some women were reinterpreting their roles throughout society but, for the most part, traditional attitudes prevailed within the Mummer community. With feminism swirling around them, few women seemed interested in protesting the all-male parade. What two reporters found when they talked to women about assuming a visible role were ambivalence and indifference (Greenberg and Shatzman 1974). An interview with the president of the Philadelphia chapter of the Women's Political Caucus dismissed the importance of the issue. "I don't feel terribly offended by it," she said, referring to the Mummers' all-male tradition. "I don't think women have any interest in depriving men of comradeship with members of their own sex." She contrasted the exclusion of women from business clubs, where an all-male policy cuts women off from business contacts and hurts them economically, with the Mummers' clubs, which have a less serious purpose. Implicit in this stance is the assumption that the bonds created by the men in the clubs have no important economic outcomes; thus she seemed to assert that while "elite" clubs offered networking opportunities—even though men only golfed together—"working-class" clubs did not.

Lillian Rubin's (1994) research into working-class marriages revealed that even as women assumed more important financial responsibilities within the family during the 1970s and 1980s, they were careful to be supportive and nonthreatening to their husbands, who were dealing with economic issues such as the stagnation of working-class wages. A few women interviewed in 1974 told a reporter that men needed to have some kind of release from the tension and strain of work. They dismissed dressing up and showing off as harmless fun.

Furthermore, although women were "formally" excluded from parading, Mummer history is not without some accounts of intrepid women pioneers. Edgar Williams's article in the *Philadelphia Inquirer* (1977) repeats one story that has had wide circulation for many years: "In 1920, Laura Lee, a Philadelphia newspaperwoman, put on an Eskimo outfit and came up the Street with a Comic Division group depicting Commander Richard E. Byrd and his party at the South Pole. Unreconstructed Mummers still deny it happened, but there is documentary and photographic evidence that it did."

Laura Lee and other women rumored to have been marchers notwithstanding, the first women to appear "officially" in the Mummers Parade marched with the Dick Crean String Band in 1975. (It is notable that Crean is not one of the original sixteen bands chartered by the Philadelphia New Years Shooters and Mummers Association.) Joining these two young women musicians on Broad Street were two high school girls, who marched with the Liberty Comic Club. The revolution that brought women into the club was remarkably quiet. Crean went to the other string bands to request permission for the women to compete, a request that was granted.

An examination of Mummer rules reveals that until 1975 the all-male "tradition" was followed implicitly; only the string bands found it necessary to codify this restriction by including it in their rules. As Edgar Williams (1979) wrote after the changes had been in place for several years, "The participation of women has been legal since 1975. At that time the Philadelphia New Years Shooters and Mummers Association (PNYSMA), wary of civil suits, officially but without fanfare opened its ranks to women."

By the end of the 1970s, small numbers of women marched with the fancy brigades, five string bands included women, and the comic division had opened its ranks so that at least one all-woman comic brigade, the Liberty Angels, had joined the parade. Initially, string bands recruited women because they needed musicians and did not have enough men applying for openings. The increase in female participation has continued since the mid-1970s, with less resistance as younger men come into the Mummers' ranks. Yet some clubs remain all-male bastions. A fancy brigade member and father of one daughter expressed this view in response to a question about the socialization that occurs for young people involved in the groups:

> Doesn't do it much for daughters . . . but does it for sons. I'm looking at my own [all-male] club, I get aggravated about it. I have a daughter who's four, so it'll be a bigger fight as she gets older. . . . We've lost young women to [other brigades] every year. . . . And they're our kids. The argument was and the argument continues to be—well, there's two facets to the argument. The first is, "This is my club, it's a men's club. I want to be up here, smoke cigars, use foul language, watch a football game." . . . The other argument is more practical in that there is concern about bringing into the club from outside twenty-five- or thirty-five-year-old women who would be interacting with people's husbands when their wives weren't there. My argument is, don't do that. Do it [bring women in] transitionally, so that people's daughters grow up in the club who everybody knows; they become members through attrition as opposed to bringing in women from outside. Allow Johnny's or Bill's daughter or some other guy's daughter to come up through the ranks, then this way, they're naturally members. And they should be members anyway. We pride ourselves on being a family club. Yeah, we're a family club as long as the women make food, do makeup, and help out. (Kenney, interview, 1996)

This member expressed concern about the exclusion of women from his all-male club, and he worked behind the scenes to change this policy. But some clubs have marched up Broad Street as all-women units. In the 1980s an all-women fancy brigade marched for about three years; and in the 1998 parade a second all-women brigade marched at the head of the fancy brigades, following the tradition that the newest club marches first.

Women have gradually gained the respect of male Mummers because, as one Mummer commented, "Mummers respect tradition, but they respect winning more." The women delivered, as the clubs to which they belonged won top prizes. Women's increased visibility as Mummers paralleled their growing visibility in the wider culture, and it occurred quietly. A longtime Mummer observer and brigade member offered these comments:

> To eliminate [the use of blackface], the city initially banned [it]. There have been many attempts to try to incorporate or integrate the parade at all levels, with women, gays, blacks, and other minorities. A lot of times, City Hall would try to incorporate [other groups] into the parade by having certain days to honor these people. Many of the traditions have been broken out of necessity. Because the city held . . . the purse strings, [the Mummers] really have to consider the city's [views] seriously. And part of that is just that women got incorporated in the parade, not so much out of a sincerity [about responding to change], but because [without women members] the band or brigade might fold. (Kenney, interview, 1996)

The blackface controversy was a learning experience for the Mummers, tarnishing their image and distracting them from their play. The quiet incorporation of women demonstrated that their leaders decided to make a virtue out of necessity. Women were needed, though not by the "top-tier" bands, which had more male applicants than they could accept. Once ensconced in the clubs, women performers proved to be a tremendous asset because they are talented performers.

Diversity and Inclusion in the Late 1980s

Although the question of women's participation was largely resolved by the late 1980s, the ideal of a parade that included representatives from all the neighborhoods was far from realized, as the *Inquirer* editorial that opens this chapter suggests. Periodically, the city's Department of Recreation received applications from new groups interested in joining the Mummers' celebration, and in 1984 the deputy recreation commissioner announced that he was reviewing six applications. One of the groups applying was the all-black East Logan Drill Team based in North Philadelphia; a second was the Goodtimers Club of North Philadelphia, also exclusively black; and a third was from the Metropolitan Community Church, a ministry to the lesbian and gay community. The city held a lottery to determine whether the third group could join the fancy brigades, because there was a cap on the number of competing clubs; it is not clear what happened in the case of this group, but it appears that the Metropolitan Community Church withdrew its application (Goldwyn 1984b).

The Goodtimers were accepted into the comic division, becoming a sixth club. The president of the Goodtimers at its founding was George E. Hawkins, leader of the O. V. Catto Elks Lodge Brass Band. His group had accompanied the Hammond Comic Club up Broad Street for many years. Hawkins had been a "mascot" with the original O. V. Catto String Band in 1929. The club became an integrated unit as they recruited from different neighborhoods (Goldwyn 1984c).

Also brought into the parade was the all-black East Logan Drill Team. These young people from North Philadelphia were similar in many respects to other Mummer groups; they performed under the watchful eye and with the encouragement of their parents and a group of neighborhood leaders. Their appearance was filled with the joyful exuberance that characterizes Philadelphia Mummery.

The acceptance of these groups garnered a flurry of publicity, and once again the Mummers challenged the implicit assumption of black exclusion. As one newspaper article reported, Hawkins confirmed black participation in the comic clubs: "Mr. Hammond [the president of the Hammond Comics] had a few blacks that went with him, but a lot of people didn't know it because they were under their costumes" (Goldwyn 1984a). This report is consistent with the history of black participation given above.

Philadelphia's population continued to become more diverse toward the end of the century, as Hispanics and Asians moved into the small communities; but few of them indicated an interest in participating in the parade. In 1992, however, the Golden Sunrise Fancy Club made a concerted effort to draw a Cambodian Temple group, located next door to the clubhouse, into the parade. As journalist Laurie Hollman (1992) wrote, "The inclusion of this group into the Parade is an attempt to demonstrate that the Mummers are not so parochial that they can't be responsive to changes within the City's population." The same story stressed what united the Mummers with the Temple group, quoting Palma Lucas, a member of the Golden Sunrise Fancy Club, as saying, "We found out our mission is the same. We try to involve our children, so that we can teach them our traditions and keep those traditions going."

Unfortunately, the Cambodians did not march after this first appearance, because the Temple leaders questioned the appropriateness of their involvement in the parade. But the Mummers had displayed a willingness to open the parade. Yet the problem may be intractable, not because of prejudice but because of the ways in which individuals come into the clubs. One longtime Mummer familiar with the politics of the city as well as the politics of the parade identified the most important barrier to widening participation:

These clubs have grown up recruiting from the neighborhood that they are in. And when that neighborhood is predominately white, predominately Polish, predominately Irish, predominately Italian, the people that are going to join that [club] are going to be from that group. You can't, without a lot of gnashing of teeth and stamping of feet . . . have the city or the Recreation Department require that six black members play with the [all-white] Polish American group. And that's the reason why it happens [as it does]. (Creedon, interview, 1997)

Philadelphia's neighborhoods remain racially divided; the distance between groups may be only a block or two, but that small geographic divide has profound implications for relations between races and ethnic groups. The challenge facing the Mummers as the city grows even more diverse does not lend itself to easy solutions. Chapter 6 describes paths to membership and the networks and formal organizations that have developed over the past century. As the parade has become more elaborate, the cost of participation has escalated sharply, and the expertise for raising funds is crucial to the success of groups. New immigrant groups and distressed neighborhoods that lack both a tradition of parading and the organizations required to raise money may see the barriers to joining the Mummers as insurmountable. They are also likely to share the perception that the Mummers are a closed community. The Mummers themselves profess a willingness to broaden the representation within their celebration, but they have yet to take on the responsibility for sharing their expertise in organizing and performing with other groups.

Yet contradictions exist. The Mummers' anthem is "Oh, Dem Golden Slippers," a song written in the 1800s by black composer James Bland. Although one local leader reported that he had received complaints that the use of this song by the Mummers was "promoting a bygone era of minstrel shows and was offensive to blacks," it is a yearly custom for a group of Mummers from the fancy brigades to visit Bland's grave. And there is a special exhibit to Bland's contribution to the Mummers' tradition in the Mummers Museum on Second Street. This illustrates, as did reactions to the blackface controversy, how important it is to look at individual relations to uncover the realities of racial harmony or discord. The Mummers appear to be open to change. It is up to the larger community of Philadelphia to judge how far they have come toward fulfilling an ideal that reflects "the generosity of spirit that is the rich heart of the festival."

Classic Clown

A prototypical clown from the late 1930s performs the Mummers Street with the traditional three-tiered parasol. (*Photo courtesy of Mummers Museum*)

Comics and Kids

Family is a fundamental link within the Mummers and among spectators whose traditions include bundling everyone up to see the parade. Until recently, performing in the parade was an all-male occupation. Little boys joined their fathers and grandfathers from the time they could toddle their way up the street. Many comics now in their sixties and seventies tell stories of competing as juveniles dressed as girls. This lovely Bo Peep character was actually a boy. The infant firmly secured in a peach basket will probably not remember her first parade, but the toddler receiving a parasol at curbside may recall the warmth and generosity of the comic who shared the fun of Mummery with him. *(Photos courtesy of the Mummers Museum)*

String Bands

Black Philadelphians have been part of the Mummers tradition from the earliest days of the parade. The Octavius V. Catto Band shown in this photo taken in 1920 marched in the string band division until 1929. Today the O. V. Catto Brass Band accompanies the comics up Broad Street and is only one of many black performing units adding to the gaiety of the annual event. The Fralinger String Band entry featuring a Caribbean theme, complete with Carmen Miranda and lots of tropical fruit, is typical of contemporary string band performances. Even with their elaborate choreography and spectacular props, the string bands still focus on flawless musicianship. (*Above, Catto photo courtesy of Mummers Museum; below, Fralinger photo courtesy of the Fralinger String Band*)

Fancy Brigades

Fancy brigade productions have grown so elaborate that they can no longer be taken up to City Hall. Relying on spectacular scenery and energetic choreography, the brigades now compete in the Convention Center. After a brief absence from the parade, the fancy brigades have returned to dance partway up the route with small props to entertain spectators. *(Upper, "Battle of the Super-powers, for Gotham's Sake," performed by the South Philly Vikings in 1996; lower, "The Kingdom of Fire and Ice," performed by the Golden Crown Fancy Brigade in 2007; both photos by the author)*

Fancy Clubs

Long capes interconnected by floats were used by the Fancy Clubs in the first quarter century of the parade. Frame suits, carried by one individual at the center, tested the strength and endurance of fancy club marchers. Only recently were wheels added to these entries. Fancy costumes, which are almost as bulky and heavy as the frame suits and are *not* on wheels, present quite a challenge on a windy day. Yet the fancy club performer still dances for the judges at City Hall. *(Upper, snowflake frame suit, photo by the author; lower, cape float, photo courtesy of Mummers Museum)*

The Next Generation of Mummers

From the earliest days of the Parade, children were involved in the fun on New Year's Day. This 2007 photo of a mother and her two little boys, in clown costumes and facepaint, demonstrates the growing involvement of mothers in introducing their children to the Mummers tradition. *(Photo by the author)*

4 "Going Up the Street"
The Experience of the Parade

There was a tremendous crowd noise. The music blared and the performance began. It was an amazing transformation. The brigade stepped into the blinding light. . . . The fire dancers burst through the curtain, and the capes on the club suits were switched flawlessly from the "ice" side to the "fire" side. The phoenix rose from behind the curtain, the children danced, while the skaters wove in between the other performers. The mirrors and glitter picked up the television lights.

—Field notes, 2 January 1996

From my first contacts with the Mummers, I was told that "you can't understand the parade unless you are a part of it." By 1995 I had begun looking at the history of the parade and questioning the Mummers about their experiences, the first steps in any research about a community. Clearly, however, my understanding of why thousands of people march up Broad Street in funny costumes year after year would be incomplete without some level of participation in one of the clubs; firsthand experience lies at the heart of ethnographic research. So I accepted the invitation of Bill Burke,[1] captain of the Golden Crown Fancy Brigade, to visit their club and learn about Mummery at street level.

In April 1995 I made my first visit to the brigade's clubhouse. I explained my interest in the Mummers and offered to help with parade preparations. The brigade members were uniformly welcoming and pleased, they said, to have "a professor" hanging out with them; I was as "exotic" to them as they were to me. My involvement in the club was irregular; yet I traveled from my home in Virginia to Philadelphia as often as possible so that I could be part of various activities scheduled throughout the year. Because so much of the work for the parade, excluding the fund-raising that requires year-round attention in all the clubs, begins in the late summer and intensifies as 1 January approaches, I increased my time in Philadelphia in the fall. During my first year with the club, I helped finish suits, took pictures, and listened to the Mummers' stories as we worked together. I became quite handy with a glue gun—though not without acquiring some blisters in the process—and learned that there is no such thing as "too many mirrors" on a suit. Through this brigade and through the Mummers Museum, I was able to make a number of contacts with other Mummers, including members of fancy clubs, comic clubs, and string bands. This chapter recounts my experiences with Golden Crown and elucidates in concrete form the themes that I develop in the remainder of this book. Though I focus on performance, it was not only play and fun that I found in the brigade, but also family and tradition.

The Brigade

The Golden Crown Fancy Brigade, like many of the other brigades, was established in 1959 under another name. In 1970 the name was changed, and what members consider its "history" began. Over the past twenty-eight years, the brigade has had three captains, the current captain having been elected in 1976.

Golden Crown moved into a clubhouse in 1984, after meeting in various rented facilities before that. The move to a permanent location on Mummers Row is a testament to its stability and provides a base for fund-raising activities. In addition to the clubhouse, the brigade has a garage space in the Fishtown neighborhood of Philadelphia, where members build most of the scenery and large floats. The clubhouse is a three-story row house located at the upper end of Second Street where it curves into Third Street. In 1996 a none-too-sturdy ladder led to the upstairs and basement, somewhat inhibiting my ability to see everything; I could not quite overcome a longtime fear of heights, so I tended to stay on the main floor. Fortunately, stairs were built in 1997.

Walking toward the clubhouse, I regularly passed many other clubs. The Quaker City String Band headquarters is about a half-block away from Golden Crown, the Hegeman String Band is located at the lower end of the street, and the Woodland String Band is just around the corner. Virtually all of the fancy brigades are located along the Second Street corridor, and interspersed among them are the comic associations.

The clubhouse is the hub of brigade activity; the top floor and the basement are used for constructing backpieces and completing suits that arrive from the costumer in "not quite finished" form.[2] The top floor has a double glass door through which large backpieces are lowered to the street. On the first floor are a long bar, a tiny kitchen, and meeting space. The walls are filled with pictures of the brigade in full costume on Broad Street, as well as plaques reflecting its winning record and that of its captains. A television sits in brackets on the wall, and a pinball machine is usually surrounded with players—though not during the week before the parade.

Golden Crown is in many respects a typical club; it is of medium size, with a core membership of sixty-five, including a women's auxiliary.[3] The 1996 members' list includes seven father-son-grandson listings, and father-daughter(s) and mother-daughter(s) combinations are equally common; Golden Crown is a family club. Several members told me that the family is the building block for all the clubs. As one of them commented, "Without family involvement, the clubs don't survive." Interviews with Mummers across all the divisions—comics, fancy clubs, string bands, and fancy brigades—confirmed that the family is the basic unit of the club.

Children and youths from the families associated with the club also frequent the clubhouse, and many perform in the parade. Most of the children have been part of the brigade since they were quite small; in 1995, nineteen little children marched in bright orange, sequin-trimmed sweat suits and masks. My impressions of Golden Crown were captured in field notes, and as I got to know this brigade, it became clear that what I learned was confirmed through other attempts at "knowing" Mummery.

The 1996 Parade: The Week Before

In December 1995 I traveled to Philadelphia to watch the preparations for the 1996 Broad Street appearance. I had learned of the brigade's theme in the spring, when I first spoke with the captain. Themes are the starting point for developing a presentation, from the smallest comic skit to the most elaborate string band or brigade show. Golden

Crown's 1996 theme committee had chosen "Kingdom of Fire and Ice" as its theme. In early spring Bill Burke had shared with me a preliminary vision of how this abstract theme might be made concrete:

> I see a story. . . . Ice suits that are soft and free, with a soft, almost floating "la-la" opening. Not a lot of that, just a minute or so. And then we get into this more—a little more jazzy. Then the theme turns into "fire" and the fire and ice come together in a strong finale. . . . I said to Bob [the club's costumer] that I wanted to do something where it looks like there's people inside and they're either in it or part of the costume when you first start up. You know, maybe they're behind plexiglass, like they're frozen in it. That's how I see the ice dancers in the beginning. . . . I want a suit that will be [both] fire and ice.

In consultation with the club, the designer suggested costumes, half fire and half ice, and reversible capes with blue and silver on one side and orange and red on the other. Headpieces and masks for the club suits (the largest, most elaborate suits) were half ice and half fire; the female ice dancers were to dress in silver and blue and the in-line skaters and male dancers appeared in red, orange, and gold. Mirrors and trim added visual impact to the costumes, following the conventional wisdom that "more is better." In the days just before the parade, the suits were finished by club members who did most of the trim as they talked and socialized.

My conversations with the brigade members indicated that they had been practicing since early fall with the club choreographer for their various parts of the "drill" (the term used to refer to the performance), but even at this late stage, the week before the parade, they had not been through a rehearsal that included the entire club and all the elements of the performance. Therefore, everyone was excited about the dress rehearsal at a neighborhood school gymnasium scheduled for 28 December, just a few days before the parade. I was somewhat surprised that the presentation was not further along than this, so close to the day when the brigade would perform, but no one in the clubhouse was particularly concerned.

The rehearsal started at 8:30 on Thursday evening. After the chaos of getting people and suits assembled, we arrived at the school gymnasium, which the club had rented for the evening, carefully picking our way over icy streets and sidewalks. Everyone was dressed in the sweatpants and T-shirts that were to be worn under the suits on New Year's Day.

A little after nine o'clock, the music was cued and the camcorder loaded, and the rehearsal began. I watched as the group practiced the drill five times. The choreographer and captain consulted about changes after each take, and brigade members clustered in the rear of the gym so that they could discuss the changes from what they had rehearsed as small groups and how the different groups were to be integrated.

The rehearsal seemed to help smooth out the rough edges of the performance, and everyone got accustomed to moving in their suits. No props were available (they were not yet completed), but the men pretended to have something in their hands (I later learned that these were round, decorated mirrors). By 11:00 P.M., everyone was tired (most of them had worked a full day). But overall, the group was feeling exhilarated at their success in combining the elements of the drill and working out some of the kinks.

Throughout the remainder of the week, everyone's life revolved around the clubhouse and garage. I found myself gluing mirrors, cutting capes for the children from cardboard templates, and then gluing the fabric to a buckram backing so that it would be stiff. In the background, above the hubbub and barely controlled chaos, a sound system blared the taped music for the presentation.

On the Saturday before the parade, some members of the brigade attended the annual Fancy Brigade Mummers Mass at St. Peter the Apostle Church on Girard Avenue, an event I describe in Chapter 5. Although the emotional bonding that occurs within a ritual is a source of solidarity, what I witnessed at the clubhouse was the interaction of a group coming together as its members worked toward a common goal: a performance that would bring them first place on 1 January.

New Year's Day: "Going Up the Street"

New Year's Day fell on a Monday in 1996. The parade got a delayed start because of uncertain weather; the comics who traditionally lead the event had been scheduled to step off at 7:45 A.M., but did not actually start until 9:30. It was chilly, with sunshine periodically breaking through an overcast sky. Experienced paraders pronounced the weather "okay," observing that the rain would probably hold off. Because the brigades are the last units to march and Golden Crown was in the middle of the brigades, there was extra time for rehearsal in a parking lot near the neighborhood Caldor Store on Oregon Avenue four blocks from the clubhouse.

Second Street was buzzing with activity by 9:00 A.M. Just a block from Golden Crown is the Furness High School. As we walked toward the clubhouse, we noticed dozens of rental trucks parked all the way up and down the street.[4] Marshals loaded the trucks and checked out the sound systems placed on the flatbed trailers that provide brigades with their music. Also on the trucks were props, pieces of scenery, and supplies for repairing scenery and suits. The neighbors were out enjoying the hubbub, and at the Furness School playground the Quaker City String Band was practicing its music before a cheering audience.

The beautiful feathers and mirrors and rhinestones on the costumes worn by the clubs reflected the intermittent sunshine, giving me a sense of how they would shine under the lights at City Hall. We moved toward Golden Crown's clubhouse, where the process of loading their truck was under way. Performing brigade members were going back and forth between the clubhouse and the caterers across the street, where they were getting their makeup applied by two men who are close to the club and help with scenery design. Everyone was calm, but there was a noticeable tension, too. Today was "the day."

By 10:30 some of the comic clubs began to return to Second Street, and they marched the length of the street, performing and celebrating before returning to their clubhouses—for more celebrating. Quaker City's bus arrived, and they headed up to the staging area off Broad Street a little after noon. Other clubs either marched off to the staging areas or boarded buses throughout the day. All kinds of exotic characters walked the street, from plush-costumed alligators to knights with helmets and swords.

Inside Golden Crown's clubhouse, work was still under way on the captain's second backpiece (one was for the fire portion of the drill, the other for the ice). Children were being dressed in their suits, and repairs were being made with glue and staple guns as they ran around and chased one another. The young women dancers already had their hair elaborately dressed, their makeup on, and their fingernails manicured, including ice blue nail polish to coordinate with their costumes. They carried marabou bracelets and leg bands to add to their outfits later in the parade. Half-masks were either in blue and silver or orange and gold. I noticed all of the small details that needed to come together as the club prepared to compete.

It was a big production getting the huge backpieces, with their curved iron rods, moved from upstairs. The men designated to wear the "club suits" that included the largest backpieces were wearing special leather-and-canvas harnesses under their suits into which the backpieces would fit. A clean trash can contained long gold-and-silver Mylar streamers that marshals attached to the backpieces as they came down from the top floor of the clubhouse. By the time the brigades reach City Hall, they are under television lights; I could imagine the color and movement that the costumes would have under the lights. The suits zipped up so that when the backpieces were not worn, the suit had a seam.

Watching all of the materials coming out of the second-story opening was like watching one of those tiny circus clown cars that holds an endless stream of clowns. I did not notice the other provisions that were loaded onto the truck: sandwiches and drinks, for which I was later grateful. Like an army, a brigade travels on its stomach. My husband was pressed into service loading the trucks and adding the streamers, and my nineteen-year-old son was fitted with a harness because he was assigned the role of carrying the captain's second backpiece.

At noon, with everyone in their suits and makeup, the brigade walked a few blocks to the parking lot of a shopping center on Snyder Avenue, which merchants had cleared for the clubs to use as a rehearsal site. Along the way we could see the scenery of other clubs stored under Interstate 95. Sequins and glitter were scattered all over the streets around Second Street.

This rehearsal was the first chance brigade members had to work with the large props they had moved overnight from the garage in Fishtown. Props included a curtain, several "ice" floats (on which the children traveled), and a "phoenix" in glittering gold and red sequins with a wingspan of about twenty-five feet. The phoenix was mounted on a forklift so that it could "rise out of the ashes" at the end of the performance. The flatbed truck, with holders for back-pieces, arrived, and the music played through several rehearsals of the drill as the scenery was tested and everyone learned to coordinate their movements around it.

It was amazing to watch the almost professional approach to the production of this show, especially given the time constraints and the number of people and props required. Little conversation occurred; rather, the club members were so accustomed to working with one another that they seemed to just know what to do. Everyone encouraged everyone else, and the anticipation was obvious as they talked about winning "number one."

By late afternoon everything was once again loaded in the large truck and on the flatbed. The women performers and children got on buses for the brief trip to Oregon Avenue at the spot designated for Golden Crown by the city, and the men performers and marshals moved the scenery through the narrow streets to the staging site.

All fifteen fancy brigades were lined up and ready to go at Broad Street and Oregon Avenue. Ahead of Golden Crown were the Downtowners, and following them were the Shooting Stars. The suits and props were spectacular, a gaudy counterpoint to the ordinary stores and businesses that occupy Oregon Avenue. The clubs have traditionally fed onto the Broad Street route from the narrow neighborhood streets, where the residents who aren't going to the parade cheer everyone on and gawk at the brightly clothed "kings for a day."

In contrast to the camaraderie I had observed at the Mummers Mass, where club members shook hands and wished each other luck, I noticed no mixing between the members of different brigades. I asked about this, and was told, "This is competition. We'll be friends *after* the parade." Some Golden Crown marchers walked a short distance up Oregon Avenue to see what the competition looked like, but mostly everyone stuck close together. Sandwiches and drinks were distributed to those who were hungry. I have no idea how long the brigade waited on Oregon Avenue, but the sunshine of earlier in the day was replaced by clouds, and it got colder. There was a sense of time suspended, enormous anticipation, and excitement barely contained.

It was close to 5:00 P.M. by the time the brigade began the trek up to City Hall. Billy Penn's statue atop City Hall and the lights around the performance area got closer and closer as the brigade performed at the various designated spots along the route.

My notes taken during and immediately after the parade tell this story:

> Performances at Methodist Hospital, Pine Street at the University of the Arts, the intersection of Spruce and Broad at the Doubletree Hotel, and finally City Hall.
> Lots of people at each of the four sites, all cheering for Golden Crown. The crowds between performance sites were disappointingly sparse, though. Just before we turned up Broad Street, the club captain had reminded everyone to "smile and wave; after all, they're our audience. Remember, when we're through we all say, 'Happy New Year from Golden Crown.'" The brigade remembered and was greeted with more cheers.
> The performing seemed to go better than the staging, though. At one stop, the curtain stopped functioning, so the brigade members didn't have all of those streamers to burst through. Everyone put their heads together and decided that a piece of fabric on the truck could be used to improvise a curtain, and this was no sooner decided than done. The dancers adjusted. Unforeseen problems occurred with the curved backpieces, with the plumes and streamers seeming to fall off at every stop. This improvisation and all the other repairs occurred as the brigade progressed toward City Hall. There wasn't any panic, probably because the club members had memories of other times when the unanticipated occurred. The performers kept performing—and they kept smiling, too. In the meantime, in the few blocks between the performing sites, the marshals and prop specialists pieced everything together for the next stop.

These notes document the constant improvisation and on-the-spot responses to difficulties with props. One clear difference between the Mummers' performances and those of groups whose productions are mounted for more than one day is that the Mummers' props and scenery, as spectacular as they are, are not built to last. This presents special challenges to the marshals who are responsible for moving and maintaining props as the performance moves up Broad Street.

In describing the categories of play, Roger Caillois (1961) notes that there is frequently an element of chance, of tempting and overcoming fate or circumstances, within the play experience. My observations of the brigade indicated that overcoming the problems that seemed to crop up constantly provided a challenge; it was like jousting with fate. Though I did not see this element emerge until we began to head toward City Hall, it seems to be a part of the challenge of mounting the show. Members of other clubs whom I asked about this after the parade confirmed that "you expect to have problems—that's part of 'going up the street.'" As an outsider, I was amazed at the skill the marshals showed in handling the various problems.

The performance at Pine Street was less effective than at the other two performance sites, and the club captain reacted to this by drawing everyone around him and giving them a combination scolding and pep talk. As I wrote in my notes:

> There was little conversation after Bill's talk. But everyone took a deep breath and glanced at the others; they all looked up toward City Hall. We were at the Doubletree Hotel when the captain came up to my husband and me and asked if we would mind releasing the balloons at the hall. The balloons were held in a net and formed a huge arch that floated above the street. Like many small props, the mirrors, extra sparkling bands that the dancers added to their costumes as they neared the hall, these small elements elaborated the performance as we neared the finale. Handed the balloons (and feeling a huge responsibility for this small part in the show), I kept thinking, How do you do this right? We have to do it right, we wouldn't want to hurt the performance. The performance at that hotel is a blur, but we were finally just a block away from City Hall.
>
> There were last-minute instructions. By this point, we had lost several of the large backpieces, but the men who carried them just moved to the inside of the group so that the remaining backpieces could frame the show. When the tubular framing that held the curtain came disassembled, an older

man who had marshaled for the club for years stepped forward and adjusted it.

The captain talked to the fire dancers. "Remember, you're supposed to just pop out of there [from behind the curtain]. It'll be a great surprise." Half a dozen of the fire dancers placed their hands on the seam of the balloons (I hadn't even had the presence of mind to notice that there *was* a seam!). We reached the intersection outside of City Hall and waited for what seemed an eternity. Downtowners had cleared the area, and there was a pause. As we waited, the brigade members reached out to touch one another and wish each other good luck. There were last-minute whispered instructions and reminders to the little kids. The scenery was brought into place just behind the line designating the performance area. It was really dark. Then the announcer said, "Here they are: Let's welcome Golden Crown."

What were these moments like for the performers? I asked one brigade member to recall the time just before City Hall. He said:

It's the big spot, number one. You know when you go into City Hall, not only for months of rehearsal, but the entire year of breaking your back raising money and arguing over suit design, music selection, prop design and locations, the whole year of . . . worrying and working is gonna turn out right or not. Because you're down there and you have . . . only four and a half minutes to do your thing. . . . It's a funny thing, you know? I'll go up there, and I'll stand behind City Hall like we did this year and start working myself up for it. I'll actually start pacing, and I won't want to talk to anybody. . . . I feel like I'm going into a sporting event where I have to get myself very psyched up to go in there and perform. When we get to the line, I forget everything I'm supposed to do. I forget the drill. It happens every year; I have a mind blank. I don't notice the crowd, I don't notice the judges. I don't even notice the lights anymore. I'm in my own little zone. . . . It's time. Then, the music starts and everything just floods back. It's like [practicing] under the bridge on Sunday morning. It happens. You know what you have to do, and you know where you have to be, and I can usually tell within the first half minute how well the drill is going. (Sexton, interview, 1996)

Standing somewhat outside of the experience, my notes reflected an awareness that was quite different from his:

There was a tremendous crowd noise. The music blared and the performance began. It was an amazing transformation. The brigade stepped into the blinding light. We released the balloons just after the ice dancers started their performance in front of the makeshift curtain. The fire dancers burst through the curtain, and the capes on the club suits were switched flawlessly from the ice side to the fire side. The phoenix rose from behind the curtain, the children danced, while the skaters wove in between the other performers. The mirrors and glitter picked up the television lights.

After releasing our balloons, my husband and I moved toward the barriers lining the performance area and watched the drill and the crowd reaction. It was, for the first time, "perfect." It was magical. Everyone smiled; and *every* prop worked. The captain even managed to make all of his back-piece changes; and he performed like a person inspired. Golden Crown was not separate individuals—but one performing unit.

Looked at retrospectively, it is clear that the parade as a ritual began outside of the lights at City Hall, and the appearances all the way up the street were preparatory to that moment when the group moved into City Hall Plaza and the lights signaled that it was time to show the world how good they were.

After the parade, I conducted several interviews during which I asked about City Hall, some with other division performers. Individual recollections support the definition that Johan Huizinga (1955, 10–11) offered of play as decidedly apart from the ordinary: "Play begins, and ends [and] at a certain moment, it is over. While it is in progress, it is change, alternation, succession, association, separation."

One steps into the light and play begins; it ends in the darkness outside the play arena. But within that timeframe, there is also fun, as the performer enters into a fantasy, a world apart. As one veteran comic told me:

> Then you get up there and you're at the line and you say, "in four minutes, it's over," but for those four minutes you can be Eddie Cantor, you can be Jimmy Durante, you can be the greatest soprano that ever sang at the Metropolitan Opera. And you get the whole judging area to perform. And if you want to be the best bird on Broad Street, the greatest Indian chief, whatever you want to be, you have that opportunity. You have it there, and it's up to you to do it. And the only satisfaction that you have when you're all done is to say, "Boy, we were good." (Walsh, interview, 1996)

Another comic I interviewed reflected on the City Hall experience, providing an especially perceptive analysis of the ritual aspects:

> There is a spiritual aspect. It's very ritualistic. The hall's a symbol. It means something to go up in front of the hall. . . . You see, when you're marching up the street, you can see it from a distance, and you get closer and closer to it. And you know when you're there that this is the performing area. Everything that you've done throughout the year hangs on the success of this one performance—there's anxiety, and you feel the tension. And you can feel, I think, that the performance you gave—afterward, you know—that "This was good; everything connected, we hit it. . . ." The hall represents, well, it's a magnificent structure, and at night when it's illuminated, and you can see the clock and the hall from all angles. It really is symbolic. (Heller, interview, 1996)

The strong traditional feelings that are bound up with the parade led to my asking this longtime comic club member and historian about the impact City Hall may have had on past Mummers. He replied:

> There is a really the concept of why the big cathedrals were created. In creating City Hall to be that [monumental], this had great impact. The common folk making it up here [he gestured to City Hall, which was visible from his office

window], feeling like this was their day, the spotlight was on you [the working person] for a change. . . . [Adding to the awesomeness of the experience was that] the [nineteenth-century Shooters] lived in their communities. They didn't have much contact with center city. No reason to go there unless you had to. Even when the trolleys came, there was no reason to venture there. So there is a feeling of great ambivalence that you made it to the City Hall. That you've reached the pinnacle of the city's power, and you were actually able to stand there without being whisked away.

The parallels between the setting of City Hall and St. Peter's Church, the site of the Mummers Mass discussed in Chapter 5, are quite striking. In the church, the focus is on the Mass, which occurs within an illuminated setting and has vaulted, arched ceilings that force the eyes upward to the central stained-glass window and the crucifix; similarly, the spires of City Hall, and the lighting on William Penn's statue at the tip of the cupola, are so startling against the dark sky (and even, I suspect, against the daylight sky) that while you are waiting to perform, your eyes are drawn to them. In addition, the performance stage is approached up Broad Street, which becomes, effectively, an aisle. Finally, the performance area is surrounded by buildings, and thus bounded—as is the altar at St. Peter's—giving performers the sense of being on stage. So City Hall provides a ritual-like setting.

My notes from after the parade recorded that impression as well as the euphoria that swept over the brigade after we marched out of the light and around to Market Street.

The audience shouted and clapped and cheered as the brigade yelled, "Happy New Year from Golden Crown," right on cue. We moved out of the lighted square into almost blackness (but it was only the contrast that made it seem so). Everyone was still so elated; several people started to cry. They hugged one another and started talking all at once, reliving the performance, praising and reassuring one another. I think they knew they had been good. The tension was gone.
We walked up Market Street, to the buses on Tenth Street. The marshals loaded the backpieces on the truck, and the

scenery was stored in a building underground garage. Market Street was almost as crowded with trucks, buses, and marshals loading props and scenery as Two Street had been that morning. As soon as people were seated—and somebody counted the kids—a case of beer arrived and was promptly distributed. Everyone was delighted with the performance and the day.

What I did not realize was that another kind of experience waited for us on Two Street. After Broad Street, I really thought "it" was over.

Two Street: Coming Home

As we rode the bus through the narrow streets, I listened to the brigade members as they teased one another and relived the experience; they were still so exhilarated that no one seemed the least bit tired. One member told me that we were going to "party" on Two Street. I had heard about the Two Street fun from others I encountered in the process of getting acquainted with the Mummers' play community, but I had no idea of exactly what kind of celebration would occur, so I waited to be surprised.

At about 9:00 P.M., we arrived at Washington Avenue and Two Street. The area surrounding the Mummers Museum was packed with cheering, drinking people, many still in their suits and makeup, others in street clothes. Golden Crown's members grabbed something to drink, and the children were picked up by family members. My notes recorded some of the details of this experience, but even now—years later—I can recall it vividly.

> Everyone got off the buses and waded into the mob. The captain made it a special point to come up and thank my husband, my son, and me for "all your help." His son, also a very active member of the brigade, did the same. It was extraordinarily thoughtful.
>
> One of the men came up to me and said, "Stay in the middle of the street as we go up to the clubhouse; the curbs get a little wild." He had a talent for understatement. Other brigade members came up and talked with us, and several said, "Now you know what it's like, don't you?" We did, but not in the same way that they did.

Our captain, after seeing that the truck with the sound system was lined up, came back and gathered the laughing, drinking brigade members together. They had shed their backpieces, but the captain had not. Their makeup was a little smeared and the sparkles from their masks were embedded in everyone's faces. Some kept their masks on, others carried them. Clustered around the brigade captain, still in his most elaborate backpiece, they bunched together to get some instructions, but it was clearly not the intense, serious group that had gone up Broad Street earlier in the day. The captain was clearly high—but not from beer—it was from the thrill of leading his group up the street and the enthusiasm that he felt at the City Hall performance.

Looking up Two Street, Bill Burke said, "Okay, people, we're home now, and we're gonna put on a show for our friends and our families. Let's do it!" These words had special meaning, for I knew that he had grown up in the neighborhood, and his parents still lived there. This was true, as well, for at least three-quarters of the brigade's members.

People from the neighborhood and other clubs were jammed up several deep along the curbs. Laws about littering were clearly suspended, and aluminum cans crunched under my feet. People hung out of their windows, and the neighborhood streetlights cast a bright glow over the entire street. I noticed some gold-painted sneakers draped over the utility lines on one side of the street—Mummery's "golden slippers." The police practically hugged the walls, staying out of the fun and turning a blind eye to the rowdy behavior.

A "Lady Sumo Wrestler" (whom I'd seen marching up Two Street early in the day)—all 250 pounds of "her"—came up to one of our brigade men and "admired" his fire suit. He laughed and patted "her" on the stomach, saying, "I think you're pretty cute, too, honey." The comic wenches, still in costume, wished everyone a Happy New Year. They appeared to have been celebrating most of the day.

The brigade started up Two Street, sound system blaring. It was incredible; the brigade danced and strutted, performing their "drill." In between the five drills (which brigade members refer to as "serenading" other clubs), they danced with people lining the streets and shouted out to everyone they knew. And every time they reached the end, they shouted, "Happy New Year from Golden Crown." No one held back, and they seemed to pick up steam from the crowd and from each other. Finally we reached the block where the clubhouse was located. The brigade members lined up on either side of the street, like an honor guard, and someone shouted, "Let's hear it for the 'winning-est' captain on Broad Street—Captain Bill Burke Junior!" Everyone cheered and shouted, and Bill performed the drill alone for his club and his neighborhood.

The performances ended about two blocks beyond the clubhouse (though many brigade members left the group to go either to their houses or inside the clubhouse to change clothes when we reached the clubhouse). The captain went to his mother's house and returned to the club later, when the results were reported.

My notes stop at this point. The parade was over, but the party continued far into the night. Traditional vegetable soup and hot roast beef in gravy with hard rolls (for sandwiches) waited in the clubhouse. The television was on, with reruns from the parade, which had by this time ended, but everyone was too busy talking to really watch. The Two Street performance was clearly "fiesta" or "carnival," with fun as its "ideology."

Golden Crown came in second in 1996, half a point behind the first-prize winner. The club's captain, Bill Burke Jr., won his fifth first prize. The brigade was disappointed but still pleased with themselves; and immediately planning started for the next year, when they would once again aim for first prize.

Beyond Street Level

Participation in the club broadened my understanding of the Mummers' world. During this observation, the four motivations for pursuing Mummery were apparent. The multigenerational linkages within Golden Crown were obvious, but the club also drew new members who sought friendships and developed ties that were as strong as those found within a family. Within the club, too, individuals had numerous opportunities to create and to collaborate in the enterprise of producing art. Finally, the club offered a chance to perform for others and in that process step outside of everyday lives and create an alternative vision of personal identity. The following chapters, on the experience of play, the nature of family within the Mummers' play community, and the centrality of rituals, will elaborate on these themes.

While watching the Mummers both prepare for their appearance on Broad Street and perform at City Hall, I also gained a greater understanding of how they resolve the central problem of maintaining the spirit of play even as they follow the rules that govern their performances. Throughout the weeks preceding the New Year's Day celebration, they spent countless hours at the club attending to the details of costumes, floats, backpieces, and choreography. Scraps of material and strips of mirrors filled all the corners of the room; the music for the performance was played and replayed. As artists, they understood that all this work was part of the process of going up the street and competing for recognition. The chance to perform was, for many of them, the real prize. They shared their experiences of past parades as they worked, and in their imaginations they saw themselves once again under the bright lights.

Golden Crown is, by all accounts, a typical club. It shares with other clubs the understanding of what it means to be a Mummer. The forms of play vary, but the experience of performing strengthens bonds across clubs and divisions. It is typified in the oft-repeated statement, "We are all Mummers." The play community is like a large, colorful quilt, each club a square that is connected to others to form the whole. It is noteworthy that few of the Mummers ever see the parade in the same way that the spectator who watches all four divisions perform during the one-day event does.[5] As the comics make their appearance, the fancy clubs are lining up behind them. As the string bands get on their buses, the fancy brigades are occupied with last-minute rehearsals and loading their trucks. Despite this limited exposure to other divisions, however, the individual club members perceive their connection to the whole Mummer community. This larger sense of community is based on a sense that others play as they do, and it is reinforced through engagement in numerous small rituals and the universal experience of the parade itself, which is the central ritual of the community.

Golden Crown has numerous other rituals that bind them as a group throughout the year: the annual brigade serenade, which occurs about a week after the New Year's Parade, when the brigades all march in South Philadelphia, with the last-place club leading off and the first-place club performing last, as a tribute to the winning club; the annual brigade banquet, where special recognition is given to those whose contributions the previous year were "exceptional"; and an invitation-only parade in New Jersey in May that is extended into a weekend of fun and parties. I made it a point to come to many of these events, which, like the New Year's Day performances, mix socializing and performing.

In the years following this first march up Broad Street, I interviewed dozens of Mummers and shared many experiences with Golden Crown's members. My husband and I served as marshals in later years. Yet it was this singular event that introduced me to the richness of the Mummers' world, and it was this experience that I believe is central to the emotional attachment that members of this community have in common. Clearly, the Mummers were right when they told me, "You can't understand the parade unless you are a part of it."

5 Rituals and the Play Community

You can have your Trooping Colors
You can have a fancy ball
But the big thrill for a Mummer
Is "Goin' Round the Hall."

Billy Penn looks down upon us
Does he wonder 'bout it all?
For the big thrill for the Shooter
Is "Goin' Round the Hall."

We've been doing it for years now
We hope we never stall
For what would New Year's Day be like
Without "Goin' Round the Hall"?

Wouldn't it be wonderful
To just send out the call
And have the whole world join us
In "Goin' Round the Hall."
—William "Curly" Conners (1978)[1]

Traditions and rituals, from formal to informal, reverent to rowdy, long-standing to newly minted, link the Mummers to one another, to their clubs, to their play community, and to their past. For the Mummers in all divisions, rituals commemorate their history and express and reinforce cherished values. The traditions most widely practiced by contemporary Mummers combine the continuation of activities from the early history of the parade with adaptations or changes consistent with the present. The Mummers interviewed for this research made frequent references to "our tradition." But the way in which they used the term "tradition" reflected an ongoing incorporation of activities that they simply enjoyed into their repertoire of Mummer traditions. For example, the anthem of the Mummers community, "Oh, Dem Golden Slippers" is a spiritual written by James Bland, an African American composer. On parade day, the Mummers evoke the metaphoric golden slippers that carried one to heaven by spray-painting their Nike or Adidas (or K-Mart special) running shoes with gold paint. This tradition is both true to Mummer history and practical for the several-mile hike that performers take on New Year's Day.

Another Mummer tradition is a visit to James Bland's grave, which occurs near the date of the annual parade. The purpose of the visit is to pay tribute to the composer's contribution to Mummery. Initially, I thought that this practice dated back to the earliest days of the parade, but I learned that it was a relatively new practice, perhaps beginning sometime in the 1980s, when a group of Mummers sitting around the clubhouse decided on the spur of the moment that it would be fun to visit Bland's grave.[2] The group of four or five men scaled the walls of the cemetery (the gates were closed to discourage such nocturnal goings-on) and gathered around the grave site, perhaps (depending on who told the story) singing a couple of choruses of the composer's song. In the years that followed, the group drew other club members into the visit, and some embellishments were added to the tradition, including a few of "the guys" bringing along their instruments to play Bland's tune. At some point, they decided that their visit should involve more of a tribute to the composer in the form of tidying up the grave. Always on the lookout for some new human interest story to supplement media coverage of the Mummers, a reporter who learned about the visit decided to join the Mummers and take some pictures of the "tradition," and eventually the coverage extended to videotaping the visit. What began as a midnight prank hatched over a few beers in the clubhouse was transformed over the course of a few years into a tradition, embellished with specific actions repeated each year and assigned a special meaning retrospectively. It is not coincidental that the ritual included an explicit acknowledgment of African American contributions to the parade, given the Mummers' desire to shed the racist label, though it is doubtful that the original group thought about anything beyond having fun.

The process of merging old and new Mummer traditions is best understood as "traditionalization" or "traditionalizing." Catherine Bell (1997, 145) defines this as "the attempt to make a set of activities appear identical to or consistent with older cultural precedents." These terms capture the dynamic, rather than static, nature of practices identified as traditions. Traditionalization is an important part of rituals. For members of a community, the opportunity to embellish or update a ritual activity adds meaning to what they are doing—they assume an active role in formulating the ceremonies of their group.

Rituals are secular as well as religious, and participation in them generates what Emile Durkheim (1965) termed "effervescence" or what Victor Turner (1969) called "vivacity." Meaning is created during rituals through the use of symbols important to the community. Rituals rely on visual imagery, dramatic sounds such as music, singing, or chanting, and sometimes tactile stimulation or touching.

Three rituals central to the Mummers' play community are the two Mummers masses held at two locations the week before the parade, the formal parade, and the "Two Street" celebration, a burlesque of the formal parade.

The Characteristics of Ritual and Tradition

Rituals incorporate several elements. The first is invariance (Bell, 1997, 150–53). Invariance is not necessarily an exact replication of a past activity. Rather, a ritual can be choreographed or orchestrated repetition of a set of actions that unite past and future. Replication can be partial and modified by changing circumstances.

An example of invariance is the route the parade takes on New Year's Day. Initially, the parade began in South Philadelphia and fed from the side streets onto Broad Street. Over the century, the parade route was shortened, partly in response to changes in South Philadelphia's neighborhoods, where businesses displaced homes and the ethnicity of the communities shifted. What remains invariant, however, is the appearance at City Hall, which continues to serve as a symbolic anchor to the early days of the parade.

The appearance at City Hall is part of another element constitutive of ritual, "sacral symbolism." The appearance before the Hall was and is fraught with emotional associations for the Mummers. City Hall was the most significant performance site for the earliest parades, as it is for contemporary parades.

A parallel is present between "theatrical performances, dramatic spectacles, and public events," all of which are "the deliberate, self-conscious 'doing' of highly symbolic actions in public." The Mummers Parade has much in common with historical pageants that communities used to "create images of a past that gave form to a particular sense of history and tradition" (Bell 1997, 159–61). The move to Broad Street was intensely negotiated by city authorities and the Mummers, as was the timing of the Mummers' first performance, with the city acceding to the wishes of the small clubs. In their initial appearance in 1901, the Mummers agreed to a set of conditions, however minimal. They also began to construct a public persona for their community that acknowledged the demands of the city for respectability and reflected their own image of themselves as hard-working citizens committed to mainstream American values.

Finally, rituals are governed by rules.[3] Implicit in the rules that govern play is the understanding that by defining actions as play, rules can be suspended and social roles inverted, as less powerful individuals ridicule those who are their social betters. Clearly, however, in the breaking of rules, ritualized play reinforces and clarifies social norms and positions (Bell 1997, 154). Put more simply, in consciously breaking the rules in performances such as the Two Street parade, described later in this chapter, the Mummers' play community both reinforces and defies the rules about how things should be.

Durkheim (1965) identified four ritual categories.[4] The Mummers' rituals are representative rites that "commemorate the group's continuity with past and future—emphasizing through sacred observances the links each individual has with both history and posterity" (Nisbet 1974, 183). Initially closely tied with religious observances, representative rites have become transformed into secular celebrations that nevertheless use cherished moral values as their touchstones.

Occurring before and after the city parade, the masses and the Two Street celebration on which this chapter focuses are part of a larger festival. Falassi (1987, 2) defines a festival as *a periodically recurrent social occasion in which, through a multiplicity of forms and a series of coordinated events, participate directly or indirectly and to various degrees, all members of a whole community, united by ethnic, linguistic, religious [and/or] historical bonds and sharing a worldview.* Both the social function and the symbolic meaning of the festival are [closely related to] a series of overt values that the community recognizes as essential to its ideology and worldview, to its social identity, its historical continuity, and to its physical survival, which is ultimately what the festival celebrates.

Falassi (1987, 3–6) identifies the following building blocks of festivals, all of which are ritual acts or rites and all of which are present in the Mummer rituals I describe:

- Valorization rites, the purpose of which is to set aside an area, for example, the plaza in front of Philadelphia's City Hall, as the stage for a festive event. By extension, Broad Street is also set aside.
- Rites of reversal, in which the normal roles are inverted. In the parade, the "working people" of Philadelphia take over its center.
- Rites of conspicuous display, during which the symbolic elements of a community are placed on view. The Mummers' symbols include the traditional golden slippers, the multitiered parasol, and the plumed backpieces, which in various forms appear in all parades.
- Rites of conspicuous consumption, usually involving abundant, even excessive, amounts of food and drink, to be consumed during the festival. Such rites are part of the Two Street processions and can be traced back to the tradition of open houses with plentiful food and drink that were part of the ethnic processions to welcome the New Year.
- Rites of competition. As Falassi notes, "The logic of festival is concerned with the competition and the awards for the winner; the rules of the game are canonic, and its paradigm is ritual. The parts or roles are assigned at the beginning to the personae as equals and undifferentiated 'con-

testants,' 'hopefuls,' 'candidates.' Then the development and the result of the game create among them a 'final' hierarchical order—either binary (winners and losers) or by rank—(from first to last)" (5).

- Rites of exchange, expressing "the abstract equality of community members, their theoretical status as equal members of a '*communitas*,' a community of equals under certain shared laws of reciprocity" (5).

- Rites of devalorization "mark the end of festive activities and return to normal spatial and temporal dimensions of daily life" (5). At the conclusion of the festival the rules of behavior are reinstated.

The Mummers Mass: The Fancy Clubs and Brigades

Among the best examples of the way in which play rites, traditions, and religion are merged in the Mummers' play community are the annual memorial masses held the week prior to the Broad Street Parade. Two masses are part of the annual cycle of Mummer activities. One is held at St. Peter the Apostle Church, attended primarily by members of the fancy clubs and fancy brigades, and the other at Our Lady of Mt. Carmel Church, mostly associated with the string bands. There are elements common to each.

The Roman Catholic Mass is the solemn ritual through which individuals proclaim their belief in Jesus Christ and their connections to God and to one another.[5] Embedded in this framework are sacrificial and imitative rites. The Mass contains all of the characteristics of ritual identified by Bell (1997): formality, invariance, and sacral symbolism and location. Changes in the church liturgy since Pope John XXIII have modified the Mass, but the core elements of the ritual remain as they were hundreds of years ago: readings from the scriptures, a homily, the offertory, the peace, the thanksgiving and consecration, and the blessing and dismissal. Each of these components of the service offers an opportunity to refer to the group present and the community to which they belong. The Mass held for the Mummers is a "High" Mass, the most elaborate form of this ritual (Catholics refer to "smells and bells"), which includes the use of incense and bells at Communion.

I was able to attend three of the masses held by the fancy clubs and fancy brigades at St. Peter's. String bands and comics conduct a similar service at Our Lady of Mt. Carmel Parish in South Philadelphia just before the parade.

St. Peter the Apostle Church is a huge old grey stone building, with a soaring bell tower built in 1854 by the German-speaking Catholic community. The neighborhood surrounding St. Peter's on Girard Avenue is somewhat down at the heels, but a growing trend toward gentrification is evident in some of the streets that branch off from this major Philadelphia artery.

St. Peter's is the National Shrine of St. John Neumann. Bishop Neumann ministered to the immigrant Catholic neighborhoods of Philadelphia and is revered as the patron saint of the Mummers. So the location has symbolic meaning that neighborhood parishes lack.

The interior has the vaulted ceilings typical of older churches; and three stained-glass windows depicting religious themes, centered over the altar, provide color and add drama to the setting. The marble altar is intricately carved and ornamented in gold. Prior to Vatican II, the Mass was celebrated with the priest's back to the congregants, but contemporary Catholic churches have altars that enable him to face forward. To accommodate this change, St. Peter's has a smaller altar about three steps down from its magnificent main altar.

The pulpit is placed to the right of the altar and is approximately seven feet from floor level; thus pronouncements from the priest seem to come from "on high." On the right side of the altar are smaller altars to the "Blessed Mother" and St. Joseph, with votive candles available to those asking for special intercessions to light. A marble altar railing separates this consecrated area from the pews.

Decorated for the Christmas season, St. Peter's is particularly beautiful; banks of poinsettias, seasonal greens, and small Christmas trees, all interspersed with tiny lights and combined with white candles, emphasize the festivity that is associated with this liturgical season. Inside the altar railing is a small table, and on either side are folding chairs for about eighteen people, and a lectern for the lay scripture readers. At the rear of the church is a choir loft with a huge and very old pipe organ.

The service began at 7:30 P.M., but the brigade and fancy club members started to gather outside the church and in the lower-level chapel by about 7:00. They all wore their club jackets. These down-filled short jackets display the club's name on the back, and the individual's full name (sometimes a nickname) is embroidered on the front left side, slightly above the heart; they are worn on virtually every occasion when club members are in public, including the "Hat Day" or "Soup Day" celebration held the Sunday before the parade, when the Two Street club members visit one another to convey good wishes for the holidays and good luck in the upcoming parade. By the time Mass is held, parade badges have been distributed and attached to the jackets. The badges usually proclaim the performance theme for the fancy brigades and string bands and are in the costume colors. Beyond the jackets, dress tends toward jeans and running shoes rather than formal clothing. (Of course, one rarely dresses up for church services in the neighborhoods, so the jeans and jackets are not out of the ordinary.) Providing the music for the Mass was the all-male Mummers Choir, directed by a former fancy brigade captain; in addition to organ music, a few instrumentalists played brass and reed instruments.

At 7:30 P.M., the members of the clubs joined one another and formed a procession behind the priest and other celebrants. At the head of this procession was a satin banner with a silhouette of St. John Neumann and the words, "Patron Saint of the Mummers" appliquéd around the image. Immediately following the priest and celebrants were the captains of the clubs, who all took their places inside the altar rail, where chairs had been placed. The procession of several hundred moved up the aisle, and as the club members entered the pews, the choir sang "O Come, All Ye Faithful."

The use of the banner and the representation of the clubs by the captains inside the sacred space added another layer of valorization to the already sacred proceedings; in this case, it was clear that what was offered was not a general Mass but a Mummers Mass.

The celebrant in 1995 (and in 1996 and 1997) was a priest known to the Mummer community who is associated with a parish in Wildwood, New Jersey, a favorite summer resort area for many Mummer families. Immediately after the opening acclamation, the priest announced that the names of those Mummers who had died in the previous year would be read by the club captains. As the names were read, the families brought lighted votive candles that were placed on the table inside the railing. The linkage between past and present Mummers was thus affirmed. As the lists were read, the choir sang "As the Saints Come Marching In," quite softly at first, but rising to a crescendo. The sounds of the choir and the soaring notes of the trumpet eventually changed the song from a dirge to a joyous, and quite jazzy, rendition of what is a Mummer standard. Prayers were offered for the souls of the departed members.

The scriptural selections related to family (but they are invariant because they are assigned for the day by a liturgical calendar); the gospel reading in 1995 was about Christ preaching at the temple in Jerusalem. The priest used these scriptures as the theme of his homily, which covered these points:

- Although the modern family is not identical to the traditional family into which Christ was born, the Mummers value family ties.
- The value of family is exemplified in the involvement of children and grandparents, with their parents, in the great enterprise of creating a parade.
- Further, the "club" family members are loyal to one another, work together, and play together—all "family values" that the society surrounding this group should emulate and admire.
- The "impulse to make laughter, to give love and joy to the city of Philadelphia, is a gift of entertainment and a gift of self from the Mummers and their families"; it requires long hours of hard work and commitment from all of the Mummers and the communities that support them.
- The parade creates a bond that brings everyone together to greet the New Year in peace and love.

Interspersed within the homily were many jokes about the Mummers' propensity to party and celebrate all year, thus "consecrating" fun and play.

After the homily, the most spiritually significant segment of the Mass began with the offertory, preparatory to the consecration of the bread and wine. However, in addition to the traditional "gifts" of bread and wine, the Mummers brought symbols of their "gifts" to the altar. These were an elaborately decorated Mummer parasol (representing the comics and the oldest traditions of the parade), a plumed backpiece for the fancy brigades and the fancy clubs, an elaborately costumed Mummer doll, and a pair of gilded shoes or "golden slippers." These were accepted by the priest and blessed. Following Holy Communion, the priest blessed the congregation with the traditional Catholic blessing and dismissal: "May the peace of God, which passeth all understanding, keep your hearts and minds in the knowledge and love of God, and of his Son Jesus Christ our Lord; and the blessing of God Almighty, the Father, the Son, and the Holy Spirit, be amongst you and remain with you always. Amen."

The priest then turned to the congregation and asked them to join hands across the aisle as they sang the hymn "Let There Be Peace on Earth," a hymn that stresses community and love and that echoes the Mummers' own values. Before beginning the hymn, everyone turned to his or her neighbors all around and hugged or shook hands. In singing together within the sanctified space of St. Peter's, the Mummers shared an experience that was visual, aural, and tactile. Slough (1996, 181), in an extensive exploration of hymn-singing events, maintains that these activities are "mystical, transcendent, religious, cosmic," in the following senses:

> Hymn-singing events can expand the singers' sense of self and increase their awareness that "the sum is greater than its parts." There is far more going on than meets the eye or ear. This experience has something to do with how the physical properties of sound create a sense of being; how various voices create different qualities of sound; how the singers share some basic beliefs, values, and/or commitments (religious or otherwise); or how camaraderie is experienced through knowledge and practice of similar skills, facts, operations, and processes.

Both the experience of singing together, then, and the selection of hymns strengthen the effervescence of the ritual. After the priest's dismissal of the group, the Mummers filed out of the service behind the Mummers banner.

In 1996 the homily focused on St. John Neumann, his life and background. Bishop Neumann spoke, the priest said, seven languages, communicating with all the ethnic groups in their own language. In this way, the priest linked this Philadelphia saint to the multiethnic

origins of the Mummer tradition and to the Mummers' own practices of generosity to the larger community.

Outside the church the Mummers took the opportunity to greet
one another and to wish each other success in the parade, a ritual of
sportsmanship that is repeated throughout the cycle of activities surrounding the parade. Most then returned to their clubhouses, where
the frantic last-minute preparations continued far into the night.

The String Band Mass

The string bands also hold a Mass, described by one Mummer more
as a celebration than as a memorial, at Our Lady of Mt. Carmel in
South Philadelphia. I did not have an opportunity to attend this ritual, so in describing it I rely on news accounts (Chicoine 1993),
interviews, and video footage.[6] The string band Mass was started in
1990. A parish priest described its purpose as "to celebrate the spirit
of Mummery, the spirit of neighborhood, and the spirit of the season. . . . With all the spirit of Mummers, so many people who experience the . . . Parade, they're able to catch on to that spirit and put
a smile on their face, or just get a sense of hope about the goodness
of people. The members [of the performing groups] experience that,
and it extends out [to the community]" (Chicoine 1993, 10).

Like its fancy club and fancy brigade counterpart, the Mass
includes the requisite liturgical elements, combined with traditional
hymns and string band selections. Playing the music is a group of
musicians drawn from several bands. The string bands use a special backpiece for this ritual; its elements include a star to represent
the Star of Bethlehem and a crucifix to represent Christ; blue and
white plumes and smaller feathers encompass the crucifix, as blue
and white are the colors associated with the Virgin Mary, whose
feast day is 1 January. White plumes also represent God and "his
presence in Jesus," and the dove at the top of the crucifix represents
the Holy Spirit.

The gifts presented prior to the consecration are similar to those
used at the St. Peter's service: a banjo, golden slippers, a decorated
parasol, and a Mummer doll. Unlike the memorial rite at St. Peter's,
the Mummers all come to the front of the church, where the priest
gives them a special blessing and sprinkles the group with holy water.

Like their brigade and fancy club counterparts, the congregants wear club jackets and enter as parading units. Thus, this event stresses club unity as well as the bonds of the Mummer community. After the Mass, the combined string band marches around the corner to Wolf Street, where the musicians perform for the neighborhood.

The Meaning of the Mass

The Mummers' masses are a ritual within a ritual. The merging of symbols of play with the sacred symbolism present in the traditional Mass blurs the line between the sacred and secular. The highly decorated parasol, for example, represents not the hilarious performance of the comic on Broad Street, but his or her gift of entertainment. The same transformation of meaning occurs with the other objects from the Mummers' play.

On a more profound level, however, the Mummers' deliberate social structuring of this experience, their choice to merge play with religious rituals, suggests that they recognize what social theorists assert: that play is constitutive and reflective of the bonds present within their community.

The Mummers Parade

The experience that all Mummers, past and present, share, from comics to fancy brigade dancers, is "Goin' Round the Hall." Every activity in which club members participate throughout the year is related in some way to this single, thrilling appearance under the towering spire of Philadelphia's City Hall.[7] Though "Goin' Round the Hall" occurs in the present, the way in which individuals interpret it is affected by the meanings this experience had for their predecessors; in a life-world where traditions are strong, the individual's experience is inevitably informed by the past.

The Broad Street Parade is identified as the centerpiece of a series of events that make up a festival. Fiesta and carnival are equivalent designations for these events. Brandes (1988) writes that fiestas, though strongly connected to religious observances, have an equally strong connection to revelry and merrymaking. Carnival, which occurs in various parts of the world, including Europe,

Trinidad, and Brazil, has the same religious-secular character. As Abner Cohen (1982, 34) has noted, carnival "occasions release from constraints of the social order, generates relationships of amity even among strangers, and allows forbidden excesses. . . . [It] connotes sensuousness, freedom, frivolity, expressivity, merrymaking, and the development of what Turner calls 'communitas,' as contrasted with structure."

On Broad Street, the carnival spirit of the Mummers is disciplined by competitive rites; it reemerges during the Two Street celebrations. Though audiences for the two events are different, the connection that is formed by those who play and those who enjoy their play is spontaneous and temporarily intense.

Preparatory to the parade, the space where it occurs is set aside through a variety of steps. The city's Department of Recreation barricades Broad Street from Oregon Avenue to City Hall using sawhorses, and in the space around City Hall Plaza bleachers are set up for spectators. Starting lines are painted, designating where the performance will begin. Taken together, these concrete actions are valorization rites. By taking such steps, the city annually invites the Mummers to appear "before the whole city," setting aside a special place for their performances.

The parade begins early in the morning, with the comic division marching at 8:30 A.M. Though the comics compete for prizes, their primary purpose is to emphasize the reversal of roles that occurs in the parade; they represent the ordinary citizen, whose views they present in their satirical sketches of city life and politics. In the early days of the parade, city officials marched ahead of the first performing units; today, the mayor leads the string bands, reflecting a more cynical desire to appear before the largest number of people and thus maximize political gain. (The string bands draw the largest crowds.)

Rites of conspicuous display are apparent in the presentations of the fancy clubs, the string bands, and the fancy brigades. The creation of floats that serve no purpose beyond aesthetic display, and the expense represented in the elaborate costumes of the string bands and the brigades, are frivolous; like Thomas Duffy's cape, which cost a year's salary, a legend in the Mummer community, these expenditures represent the desire to show off, regardless of practical constraints.

For the Mummers who participated in the earliest parades, the appearance on Broad Street was an exchange; clearly, the structuring of their activities through the ongoing negotiations with the city and among themselves involved an exchange of free play for the opportunity to perform as artists, musicians, and clowns. Beyond this exchange, however, the Mummers also gave to their city a "gift of fun," as the celebrant pointed out during the Mass at St. Peter's. For immigrants who gradually achieved assimilation, giving fun to other residents may well have been an opportunity to repay their adopted country.

Finally, the city devalorizes the play space in a surprisingly practical way; the bleachers are removed, the traffic patterns return to normal, and the city sanitation crews prepare Broad Street for the next day's traffic. The painted lines at City Hall fade away during the year and are painted again when the cycle resumes.

The Two Street Celebration

Second Street, known in South Philadelphia as "Two Street," is the spiritual home and geographical center of the Mummer play community. Close family-neighborhood-club links exist within the Two Street corridor, as Chapter 6 emphasizes. Clubhouses are literally next-door neighbors to families. The presence of the Mummer clubs adds to the liveliness of the neighborhood, and the residents are the most enthusiastic supporters of the clubs and their activities. It is to this neighborhood, to their "home," that many of the Mummers return after the Broad Street performance; they return as "heroes" who have represented their neighborhoods on a stage "sacred" to the city. From mid-morning until after midnight on New Year's Day the Mummers return to the tradition of performing for their friends and families; no valorization of the area is necessary for this street celebration. It is, after all, Two Street. But preparations are made for the evening parade. The streets are blocked to normal traffic when the string bands begin to come home, and police are present, though they do their best to be inconspicuous and merely watch the fun. (Occasions have arisen in the early morning hours when it was necessary to encourage what some Mummers call "the rowdy element" to clear the street.)

Both the Mass and the Broad Street Parade include formal ritual elements; the Two Street celebration is, in contrast, a counter-ritual, a burlesque of the disciplined performance that the Mummers present to the city. In interviewing some older Mummers, I asked if the Two Street celebration was similar to their memories of the earlier Broad Street Parades; they replied that it was like the "old days," particularly the open house tradition of New Year's Day. The doors to houses are open, and people visit neighbors and entertain family and friends who may be making a return visit to their South Philadelphia roots.

Some contrasts are obvious. For example, the audience for the Broad Street Parade remains on its side of the barriers, but on Two Street the spectators and the performers dance in the streets together. The Broad Street Parade is linear, with performers marching up the street on schedule with performances—these days—at scheduled points that are announced by the city in advance; clubs appearing on Two Street perform all the way up the street, with no time constraints. The Philadelphia Department of Recreation makes an effort to discourage alcohol consumption both in the stands (not always successfully) and within the marchers' ranks (quite successfully, because the ban is enforced by the marching clubs themselves). As the Mummers point out, with the time and money they have invested in their performance, they would hardly want to parade drunk. Broad Street audiences typically flout the no-alcohol rules. On Two Street the beer flows freely for performers and their fans; and the celebration is rowdy and boisterous. On another level, however, my own impression of the Two Street celebration is that it is a "ritual" in that the spirit is one of a victory parade or a heroes' welcome. My experience as a participant-observer within a fancy brigade confirmed that this was the case.

The contrast between the experiences on Broad Street and Two Street is important for another reason as well. The Two Street parade is a means through which the Mummers can revisit what was initially the impetus for the Shooters' processions—unrestrained, unrestricted play and fun. Though they freely take on the obligation to present a public face as performers who are skilled and disciplined and community members who are respectable and sober, they make room "backstage" for freedom, improvisation, and fun. Though Two Street is a public venue, it is also, as the home of the Shooters, seen as private and intimate. Thus the Two Street parade is a return "home."

Ritual, Tradition, and Community

Huizinga (1955) asserts that a sense of community is born in playing together. The community exists prior to and survives beyond the individual's lifespan, and the rituals of the Mummer community are both spiritual and temporal. The close connection between these two realms in the early history of humankind accounts for the strong bonds that are forged in the experience of play. The effervescence of religion and the vivacity of play are socially constructed around the multisensory elements of play and ritual; both rely heavily on the presence of others who share common values, beliefs, and definitions of the situation.

Play, whether spontaneous or structured, strengthens the bonds individuals feel to their group. Play is not one experience but a number of different experiences, depending upon the setting in which it occurs. Different emotions are elicited in each of the events described. In the setting of the Mummers Mass, the dominant themes are community and family, generosity and sharing; "community" and "family" are understood in the broadest sense. Thus the Mass stresses the bonds that link all Mummers to one another, regardless of club affiliation or divisional membership. The Mummer "family" is counterpoised to the city. During the Mass, the individual affirms his or her bonds to others and to the sacred (whether God or society). In the Broad Street Parade, the "family" is smaller, consisting of the club as a cohesive competitive unit. The dominant themes are competition, discipline and skill, and fairness. The individual bonds with his or her club, collaborating to produce a performance that represents the best that he or she has to offer in terms of skill and artistry; it is not individual acclaim that is the goal, but collective glory. No longer a group of individuals, the club members recognize that to be successful they must function as one. For the brief time that they perform, nothing outside that lighted stage is relevant. On Two Street, the Mummers return triumphantly to their families and friends. They perform, repaying a debt to the neighborhood whose loyalty and support enables them to compete;

but in that setting where family and friends are literally within arm's reach, there is paradoxically "room" to lose inhibitions and return to the experience of fun.

Though appearing separate and distinct from one another, the play rituals described are different faces of the overwhelming and compelling experience of play. The Mummers preserve the spirit of playfulness in their community by balancing structured and disciplined rituals with spontaneous, liberating play activities that have ritual elements embedded in them. By oscillating between seriousness and fun and mixing seriousness with fun, they carelessly—and carefully—broaden the definition of play that sustains them as a community. And in this playing together, they generate a culture that includes the most important of human values: family, tradition, community—and fun.

6 Family, Club, and Neighborhood

It is said that hot soup from 2nd Street flows through the veins of anyone christened with the name Joseph T. Tyler. A newborn member is fitted for his golden slippers long before he gets a pair of Buster Browns, and when it comes time to retire, those same golden slippers go nicely with a pipe and robe.

—Richman (1974, 8)

The Tylers exemplify the strong linkage between family and tradition that permeates the Mummer play community. Participation in the parade runs in families like red hair or blue eyes. Writ small, the Mummer family is kin; writ large, "family" embraces the wider community and indeed the entire city. When the Mummers talk about their tradition, they consistently stress the overlap between their commitment to family and their continuing participation in the parade. Family writ large is evident in the efforts that Mummers, through their clubs and divisions, make to reach out to others. Without exception and usually without fanfare, the clubs are good neighbors to each other and to other Philadelphians.

In examining the meaning of family in this chapter, I rely on the Mummers' words and their club histories. Contained in these oral and written accounts of family are stories of Mummers, past and present, whose lives embody the norms and values this play community cherishes and attempts to emulate. In celebrating these heroes, the Mummers promote normative expectations for members; these individuals are role models.

Family is important in another sense, because personal loyalties more often than formal structures influence the decisions made about the parade and the direction it takes. The Mummers' strength, and in some cases their weakness, lies in family.

Defining "Family"

"Family" is at once a familiar and an ambiguous term. It evokes warm and trusting feelings and reflects deep yearnings for connection with others. Family is *the* primary group to which individuals belong. In sociology, the primary group is characterized by face-to-face relations and cooperation. During this interaction, individuals learn values and norms, share in the common life of their group, and identify with the group's purposes and goals.

Individuals participate in many groups and are influenced by multiple institutions, family and church among them. For the Mummers, there is continuity between their family and religious lives. This is also the case for many of the children of these families. With the accelerating pace of contemporary life, children often spend less time with their families and more time in other settings. Yet, in the Mummer clubhouses, children find a second home and caring adults who hug, scold, and teach them the traditions of their play community. In this sense the Mummers are old-fashioned. Consider this contrast: in the suburban shopping mall, or even in visits to a middle-class friend's home, misbehaving children are rarely corrected by anyone except their parents; within the Mummers' clubs, a child's conduct and well-being are everyone's business. This feeling of being cared for and supported leads to a strong emotional link with Mummery as an extension of family life. As one longtime fancy brigade member pointed out in discussing young people and the clubs:

> As it [the club] relates to young men, and now it's more and more young women, it gives young people something in common with their parents and their grandparents and gives a forum for them to have something in common without fighting each other. And you have a sixteen-year-old boy who is at odds with his father. You have a common interest, right? Maybe you don't agree with how he's doing in school, you don't like your son's girlfriend, or his friends . . . you don't

like the way he talks to his mother, but there's always the club. . . . There's always that common bond, and what's nice about it is that if your grandparents are still alive and your grandparent is a member, you still have that, too. You still have that common thread. (Creedon, interview, 1996)

Children parade up Broad Street from the time they are able to toddle alongside their parents. One young father was at the Mummers Museum in late December 1997 asking whether his two-week-old baby would be the youngest to participate in the parade, assuming his wife would allow him to dress the infant in costume and wheel him up the parade route. (She did, and the infant became "the youngest"; years from now the videotaped interview with the proud dad and the appropriately costumed baby Mummer—with golden baby shoes—will connect another generation to the parade.)

In South Philadelphia and other parts of the city where the clubs are anchored, family ties and traditions are important. However, moving away does not always result in cutting the ties with clubs. Some individuals who have left the neighborhoods where they grew up can and do go home again; they maintain their links to the neighborhood by continuing participation in their neighborhood clubs. Of course, not everyone who grows up surrounded by Mummery chooses to become part of this life-world, but the individuals whose lives are the focus of this book are those whose connections to Philadelphia Mummery and their clubs are both intense and long-lived.

The Club *Is* Family

Paths to membership in the clubs show the links between family and the Mummer tradition. Those Mummers I came to know through observations over an extended time and through lengthy interviews, and others whom I spoke to casually, told me that the most prevalent gateway to involvement in one of the clubs was family or neighborhood contacts.

The concentration of clubs in South Philadelphia means that even if a resident wanted to avoid the Mummers' play, it would be nearly impossible. At present, all fifteen of the Mummers' fancy brigades are located either on or within two blocks of South Second

Street. Most of the string band clubhouses are on Second or Third Street. Interspersed among the fancy brigade and string band clubhouses are the comic New Year's Associations, and fancy clubs inhabit larger spaces in South Philadelphia.

As one walks up Second Street, beginning at Washington Avenue, where the Mummers Museum is located, and continues to Snyder Avenue, the signs or banners on the row houses proclaim the presence of the clubs. Nailed to the utility poles are announcements of party nights and bingo games, as well as benefits for Mummers who need help. Other neighborhoods with fewer clubs in their midst are similarly affected by the presence of the Mummers. Six string bands based in Northeast Philadelphia perform for their neighbors and raise funds through various events that draw residents. Thus family involvement and neighborhood residence are good predictors of whether an individual joins a club. Questioned about their introduction to Mummery, individuals identified the twin influences of family and neighborhood.

Jack, a lifelong Mummer, explained why he is Mummer:

> I think it's a tradition that's embedded in families. I can say that I had four uncles and a father who organized the Gallagher Club in 1931, and . . . they entered the fancy division. And having all those uncles when I was born, I was carried up the street the first year; and the second year I walked a little bit further [along the parade route] and I guess I *had* to do it more than anything as a child. I mean, my grandfather was with [one of the first clubs to march up Broad Street], and he was a great Mummer. I started into it, and [after leaving Philadelphia for a few years to play professional sports] I came back home and the tradition kept going. I got married and raised a family of seven children, and every one of my seven children have been in the parade—and six of them were *girls*! (Walsh, interview, 1996)

Jack's family has maintained their Mummer and family traditions through several generations, and it was with considerable pride that he described his family. "My grandsons and my granddaughters [are all active]. You know, I have ten grandsons and two granddaughters, and all but one of the grandchildren, only one—that's little Laurie Anne—have been in the parade. She hasn't because she's too little. ... My Dad was a Mummer, and there's me, and there's my sons [and daughters] and [their children], so that's four generations." The involvement of Jack's family—a pattern common in the Mummer community—goes beyond simply allowing the grandchildren to accompany their grandfather as he parades on Broad Street. Families also support the various Mummer clubs by buying tickets to and attending the many social events that occur as fund-raisers and present opportunities to have a good time.

In the past, and among some clubs even today, children of club members were given preference in joining the club; such ties formed a boundary that prevented nonrelatives from joining. In these cases, the young boy whose father did not belong to one of the groups was on the outside looking in at all the fun. As Bill, an active Mummer and leader of a brigade related:

> I lived across the street from [the captain of one of the oldest fancy brigades], and they used to have block parties. My father knew [the captain], but this club did not take children unless your father belonged. They only took so many children, and there was a long waiting list. My father drove a truck and worked crazy hours, so he [did not belong to a club]. But as a birthday present, for my eighth birthday, they [made it possible] for me to join a brigade. (Burke, interview, 1995)

Bill's desire to be part of the Mummer community was as intense as it was inevitable, given where he grew up.

> I used to follow [the club]. My grandmother lived at Second and Mifflin, and we used to go and watch the parade. Me and my friend would go, and we'd get Christmas trees and stick them down the back of our coats and hold on to them like they were [Mummer] backpieces, and we would dance down the street behind the [viewing] stands. ... Before we got home, or too close to my Mom's, we'd take the trees out. ... I'll never forget the one time I scratched my whole back

because the tree got stuck between my shirt and my back [instead of coat and shirt] and I smelled like sap. Of course, my mom asked, "What happened, how did you get this?" I smelled like sap.

Such accounts reveal the high profile of the clubs in the neighborhoods. Because the clubs are ubiquitous and because so much of the social life of the small communities is organized around them, children and adolescents grow up surrounded by the color and gaiety of Mummery. In cases like Bill's, the influences of family and neighborhood converge. Though Bill's father was not a Mummer, I discovered in my research that other family members were club members; thus Bill was admitted to a club.

The voices of the Mummers interviewed for this research are not the only evidence for the strength of family ties. In 1996 the Murray Comic Club celebrated its sixtieth anniversary and published a commemorative book that reveals through brief sketches on the New Year brigades the family connections forged in play. In this history we are introduced to the J. A. Murray Comic Clubs roots.

> The J. A. Murray Comic Club was created in 1935 by Harry W. Tyler. Like many other comic clubs, the Murray Comic Club consisted of Murray families. In 1936, the Murray Club, which was made up of Dudes and Wenches, took their first walk up Broad Street. . . . [The members] were mostly multiple generations of several families. The Tyler family, Harry Tyler, Sr.; Harry Tyler II; Joseph Tyler III; Bobby Tyler; and Jack Tyler all marched as a clan. The Herman family, Dan Herman, Sr.; Dan Herman, Jr.; Dan Herman II; Peter Herman; and Ed Herman were Mummers.

The Murray Club tended to feature children, perhaps because of its strong family ties; it is the only club to list children in the *Mummers Magazine*.

In an article on the Tyler family, Richman (1974) wrote about the five generations of Tylers marching in the parade, "Twenty-four years ago, four generations of Joseph F. Tylers marched in the parade. Last year, another four generations—great-grandfather (76), grandfather (50), father (26), and a son (2)—went down Broad Street with the

Murray Comic Club. Great-grandfather Tyler served as a marshal, and the three youngsters dressed up as 'The Martians.'"

Similarly, the Flying Dutchman Comic Club, a forty-year-old club from the Grays Ferry section of South Philadelphia, emphasizes changes in its ranks, informing readers that, "originally organized as a group of boisterous males, our club evolved into what is now a family-oriented organization. It has both male and female members, ranging in age from 3 to 70, and includes fathers, sons, daughters, brothers, sisters, cousins, and friends."

The Murray Club is primarily a South Philadelphia group, but some of the New Year brigades boast membership from Bucks County (north of Philadelphia), as well as from other sections of the city. One group, the Fearsome Foursome Minus Two, was founded by a dentist and an accountant.

Other sources confirm the pervasiveness of this emphasis on family. With few exceptions, the brief biographies provided for the 1996 parade specifically mention family connections, usually multiple generations for each of the small units marching with the Liberty Clowns, the Goodtimers, the Joseph A. Purul Comic Club, and the Landi Comic Club.

Three fancy clubs marched in the 1996 parade. Typical descriptions of their entries include this one: "'Watuzee [sic] Warrior,' an entry in the Fancy Trio category, has as carriers: Ed Cox, Sr.; and Ed Cox, Jr.; and John Cox. . . . The Cox family is well represented. Father, sons, daughters, and other family members are marching today. Ed Cox, Sr., and Ed Cox, Jr., are both teachers."

Although Mummers from other divisions commented that multigenerational participation is less prevalent in the string bands because of the requirement that prospective members perform well on a music test, this was not necessarily the case. (It is, of course, possible that musical talent is a family trait!) For example, family ties are highly visible in the Duffy String Band; under "miscellaneous facts" on their background information for 1996, we read, "Henry Kunzig, Sr., bought the band in 1956, and was its marching captain until 1986. He remains the honorary captain. This [band] is a real family affair. Captain Teddy Kudrick is the stepson of the club's owner. Teddy's brother, Michael [plays] bass sax. In addition, Teddy's sisters march with the band. There's Peggy on accordion, there's Cheryl on banjo . . . and Cheryl's daughters, Sharon on sax and Tricia on sax."

The Quaker City String Band's "club history" documents similar family connections: "Quaker City was founded as a social club with the emphasis on the family. At one time, there were 35 father/son combinations marching with the band; this year, there are 23." This band's clubhouse on Third Street (where it divides from Second Street) is always alive with the sounds of members and neighborhood residents participating in activities related to either preparing for the parade or raising money to finance the annual performances. Summarizing the pervasiveness of the tradition, a longtime member (now inactive) stated:

> The Mummers, like I said, there's a thread of family involvement, and so it spreads into every other social activity. [Participating in] the Mummers [Parade] is just one [part] of this thread, and maybe a large part of a person's leisure time [is taken up with it]. If you're a [member of] a family, you drag in your other family members or you try to get your other family members involved. . . . It's an activity that's creative, and something you can have experiences with your family. So there's no separation between family and social life. You take it home with you . . . you make friends within [the clubs]. . . . They might [also] be your neighbors and you incorporate your neighbors into your family and social life. It's a subculture, but really has long tentacles into every facet of someone's life. (Creedon, interview, 1997)

This pattern recurs throughout the divisions, and links across divisions are formed within the environment of the larger play community. This Mummer, whose familiarity with the clubs goes beyond his involvement in a brigade, asserted that the noncity clubs are an extension of the South Philadelphia neighborhoods; when asked if there was "something different" about the suburban clubs, he responded, "I don't know if there is truly one [a difference], because in [those clubs] there's always transplanted Philadelphians. . . . Even though they are [geographically] separate, there is that South Philly traditional influence, and they try to do things [in] the South Philly style. . . . I think their roots are here" (Giancaterino, interview, 1997). Family and neighborhood links, however, are not the only gateway to club involvement and membership, as the next section reveals.

The Club *as* Family

Other, less direct paths lead to becoming a Mummer: marriage, friendship, and a desire to join others in playing. For some individuals seeking connection, the Mummer clubs become a support network. One fancy brigade marcher declares herself "a Jersey girl, born and raised," but she is married to a South Philadelphia man; her fascination with the Mummers began early.

> I was raised in Jersey. I lived in Delaware for two years, but I've always loved the Mummers. I always wanted to be a part of it; but when I was a child, women weren't allowed. Women did everything behind the scenes. I [first] got involved . . . in high school; my boyfriend at the time, his younger brother was with Palmyra [now Palmyra–South Jersey String Band], and his parents took me to [see] the band. . . . The year Palmyra took first place, I was at the clubhouse with them, and I helped the captain with his costume. After the parade, they got me in it. (Mastroianni, interview, 1996)

From the string bands, this Mummer moved to a fancy brigade. For her, the clubhouse is home, not surprisingly, given the number of hours she devotes to club activities. Particularly intense are the two months before the parade. "Last November and December," she recalled, "getting ready for the parade, [I spent] four nights a week, about four or five hours, so that's twenty to twenty-five hours, three hours every Sunday. . . . I'd say a hundred hours or more [in those two months]."

Speaking about friendship within the club, she shared personal experiences that illustrate how connections to others are intensified by helping one another through the bad times as well as sharing the fun of play:

> This club is like my family. . . . I lost my father one New Year's Eve. . . . It was unexpected that it was gonna happen as quickly as it did, but I was here [at the clubhouse] when it happened. I had picked up Sue [a close friend in the brigade] to take her to board her dog at the vet's, and we had stopped to see my father. He was not well when we saw him, and then

my brother got a call on his car phone that my father had passed away not five minutes after we left [the vet's]. . . . Sue jumped out of the car and told everyone, and before my brother could move the chairs [to keep the parking space in front of the clubhouse open] . . . before I could put the car in reverse, I had somebody opening the door, helping me out of the van, and they kept me [in the clubhouse] until I calmed down and got myself together. [The club] dedicated their parade performance to my father. That was the nicest thing they could have done. . . . Guys from the club came to my father's memorial service, all the way in Jersey.

Though it is not unusual for friends and even work acquaintances to offer help and support in the face of loss, club members were in it for the long haul. "In [only] three years [as a member of the club]," this woman continued, "they were there for me. Asking 'Do you need anything? Call us, if there is something you need. . . . We'll take care of it.'"

When asked if she saw this offer as more than a polite gesture, she responded that she would have asked for help: "The closeness is there." Her experience reflects what members of club families expect from each other. Establishing intimacy is made easier by the many occasions when Mummers work together. One string band member told me:

I think just being around one another socially, what happens is you're with the same people so much that they begin to learn about your life and your problems and then you find out that there's a place every Wednesday night that if you have problems, there's [support] there. There's a little support network for all of us that maybe we don't experience in our own families. I don't . . . I'm one of five, but I can't say that if I had a problem, I'd run to one of my brothers. I'd run to one of my string band brothers before I would [go to my family]. (Lowery, interview, 1997)

Like the brigade member quoted earlier, this string band performer had no direct family connection to the Mummers or South Philadelphia and was drawn to playing in a string band by an interest in music. She works with a large law firm in the city, where Mummery is regarded as a somewhat odd way to spend time. "And my answer to [that] is, 'While you guys around here are popping your Prozacs and trying to cope with life and going to therapy once a week, I'm sitting in that clubhouse on Wednesday night, banging away on my banjo, having a ball. And I have never had to see a therapist or take Prozac.'" As much as competition creates bonds, she maintains that in her experience, "New Year's Day is not the end-all for me to be in the club. [Mummers] enjoy the camaraderie and having the club to meet every week, and going out on bus trips on weekends [to play paid engagements] and traveling and the whole thing. [They enjoy this] more than the competition."

The opportunities for socializing are seemingly endless; the string bands and fancy brigades compete with one another in baseball leagues and attend one another's family events—baptisms, birthdays, weddings, graduations, and funerals. As this Mummer commented, "There's a lot of time taken up with that." And on those occasions, as well as during rehearsal nights and traveling to engagements, friendships are formed and support given and received.

In a 1982 article titled "Oh, Dem Golden Wing Tips," attorney Jake Hart described his first memories of the Mummers:

> From my office window, I can see both the square [in front of City Hall, where the Mummers perform] and the line [crossed to begin the performance]. I look at them often; for I know that I will be there again in 1983, with the swelling crowds, braced by a small army of Philly's finest. It will be cold, maybe a light snow falling. Many spectators will be too drunk to see, certainly to remember. But the children will remember just as I did long ago. Peering from beneath an ear-flap hat with a gold painted acorn above the brim, each year I would be held by father above the crowd to hear the music and see the colors and the glitter and the feathers. (16)

His childhood memories of the Mummers led Hart to apply for membership in a string band, even though he does not mention family links to the parade. His involvement with the club changed many of his ideas about the Mummers:

Like many of you, I always believed that this fraternity was closed to all those who could trace their lineage to somewhere south of Broad [Street] and Snyder [Avenue]. Since I grew up in Germantown [north of the city] and now live in Wynnewood, I simply assumed that any true Mummer would regard me as a curious oddball at best, and, at worst, as an unwelcome alien. I was wrong. The fact is that being able to play an appropriate musical instrument with some facility, while at the same time being willing to appear in public dressed like a lunatic, are the only two requirements. (17)

Hart's entry into a string band, though not one of the "heavyweight" bands that most frequently win top prizes, followed soon after he demonstrated his talent on the tenor sax. Welcomed into the club, he found friendships with an extremely talented cadre of musicians and discovered the joy and challenges of performing on Broad Street.

Many string band members, Jake Hart among them, represent a subset of individuals who are not Mummers "by tradition." More often, though, the Mummers are homogeneous in other respects, including socioeconomic status and religion.

Homogeneity in the Play Community

A study of any community explores the characteristics, social and economic, of its members. But the Mummers, however cooperative in sharing other information about their lives, are remarkably closemouthed about socioeconomic status. Their reaction suggests that the "credentials" respected in the play world are those that most frequently appear in their public biographies and are mentioned in interviews: family roots in the parade; the length of time the individual has been a Mummer—particularly if he or she first paraded in a baby carriage or on a father's shoulders; special skills that the individual demonstrates in competition—dancing, musical ability, artistry in design or production, leadership; the number of prizes won in competition; recognition within the community as a member of the Mummers Museum Hall of Fame. Within their world, an individual's socioeconomic status is largely irrelevant.

Yet socioeconomic characteristics are important in explaining the convergence of values and ideals within the Mummer community, as they are in any community. The parade emerged out of the working-class communities of Philadelphia, and even as some Mummers have moved into the middle class, their connections to their old neighborhoods and family traditions remain strong. Thus the community as a whole is slow to adapt to changes in the wider culture. Who, then, are the Mummers?

In 1965 James Smart, in an article titled "Want to Know About the Mummers? Don't Ask a Mummer," noted that most Mummers refused to cooperate in a survey that attempted to gather the type of data that would reveal the socioeconomic status of club members. Smart did not specify how many responses he was able to collect, but he offered this summary:

> Of the employed Mummers, 15 percent work in offices and 12 percent in factories. Truck drivers make up 5.5 percent. Nearly 9 percent are government employees: 4 percent federal, 4 percent city, the rest state; 3.5 percent are policemen, 2 percent firemen. Self-employed Mummers make up 5 percent of the String Band sample. But only one-half of one percent of those are salesmen, storekeepers, etc. Most are tradesmen: plumbers, roofers, and electricians. As regards education, 31 percent are college graduates and 5 percent high school graduates. Half of the college graduates have music degrees, but only 30 percent of the total sample ever took formal music lessons. (Yet 26 percent play more than one instrument.) About 1 percent have master's degrees, and 1.5 percent have doctorates. Engineers account for 1.5 percent of the total; doctors, lawyers, and teachers together for only 2 percent. There are pharmacists, artists, mailmen, and others represented. Completely absent from the sample: dentists and clergymen. (Smart 1965, 5)

Anthropologist Andrea Rothberg (1980, 139–40) distributed a questionnaire to fifteen thousand Mummers. Less than 1 percent of those surveyed responded, and these responses were not, Rothberg acknowledged, "evenly distributed across divisions." Taken together, the results of these surveys are more confusing than revealing, partly because Smart and Rothberg's categories were not uniform. Yet there is some concurrence: Smart's assertion that 31 percent of the

Mummers were college graduates is close to Rothberg's finding that 27 percent were junior college or college graduates. Other findings in the surveys are quite different, though.

Given the reluctance of the Mummers as a group to participate in surveys, the only strategy for gathering socioeconomic data was to obtain it indirectly. The biographical information that the clubs prepared for broadcasters for the 1996 Mummers Parade provided some insights into the socioeconomic characteristics of club leaders, though it sheds little light on the membership generally. What is revealed in the "Parade Book" is consistent with observations of the community.

In 1996, many Mummers worked in the building trades as plumbers, carpenters, builders, and installers of heating and air-conditioning equipment. Another group were administrators or managers; for example, one club captain managed a dairy, another, a sporting goods store, and a third, a grocery store. City, state, and federal government workers were represented, including policemen. Auto mechanics and utility workers also marched in the Mummers' ranks. Relatively few computer and data-processing professionals or accountants appeared in the descriptions, but many worked in government and other areas where computerized systems are used. Beyond these general categories, there was a mix of other occupations, including one marble cutter, a court reporter, and an owner of a dental laboratory. And, of course, there was Jake Hart. Two Mummers also served on the Philadelphia City Council.

At the leadership level, these data suggest that the Mummers are likely to hold skilled or semiskilled jobs and administrative/managerial positions rather than high-level technical posts in data-processing or professional positions; so attorney Jake Hart is indeed an exception, or at least he was when these figures were collected several years ago. Because of the heavy time commitment required to be a club or brigade leader, the dearth of professionals is not surprising. However, based on limited information, generalizations about the Mummers are speculative.

Two Mummers (one of whom is a highly placed city official) provided some anecdotal information on changes in class position in an interview that sheds some light on upward mobility within the community. Describing the fancy brigade to which he belonged, one informant told me membership was no longer dominated by working-class people. "I mean, in my club, of the . . . hundred members, not counting the twenty to twenty-five older gentlemen, I'll bet you twenty of them are college-educated. It's still neighborhood people or recently transplanted suburbanites, but [now] they are accountants, people with criminal justice degrees; we don't have any doctors . . . and no lawyers" (Kenney, interview, 1996). His response suggests higher educational attainment reflecting generational changes, but once again it is difficult to generalize from one club.

The second informant shared these observations on class structure gained from his long association with the String Band Association and liaison activities with the other divisions:

> This entire tradition has its roots in very much blue-collar, working-class people, though I think that is changing somewhat. As with the rest of our society, you're seeing more educated Mummers, especially in the better bands—though I hate to say better because it sounds qualitative. I mean, in the more successful, talented organizations. You tend to see the expectations [people have] of kids in the band. He may not be my son, but the kid's a junior in high school and you're saying to him, "What college are you going to?" Nobody else in the family ever went to college, but you say to the kid, "You're going to college, right?" And [for the young string band player], he suddenly has fifty fathers, and they're all telling you to go to college instead of one father [guiding you]. And [as a result] you can see a slow rise in the class structure, and the [younger members] are leaving the blue-collar ranks and becoming white collar or becoming technical—you know, [computer] information systems kinds of folks . . . and they're separating themselves from that traditional blue-collar background. . . . There's still a lot of blue-collar folks in this, but I think as generations move on, the good social aspects of Mummery are providing a stimulus for people to change their lives. (Creedon, interview, 1997)

Though older Mummers may lack higher education, these comments on their strong encouragement to young men and women to go to college are consistent with the observations I made during the four years I spent in and around the clubhouses.

However, within the clubhouse setting, the Mummers discussed neither their work nor their own education—unless it was to establish that someone they encountered had attended the same high school. (Most Mummers are alumni of Philadelphia's parochial schools.) Huizinga (1955, 7) maintains that play is "set apart from the ordinary or mundane." Immersed in the process of playing or preparing to play, individuals are not judged by the standards that prevail in the work world. Thus, they find a place as Mummers where they can be special as artists and performers.

The Play Community as Family: Moving Beyond the Clubhouse

It is 10:30 on a Wednesday evening at the string band clubhouse. The band has just moved into this former row house on Two Street, in the heart of "Mummers Row." Construction material is pushed toward the walls, and the smell of fresh paint almost masks the smell of beer as band members refresh themselves after an hour-long practice session of music for the 1998 parade. A man in his seventies, known to the club and other Mummers as "Pop," is seated on a stool at the bar, a fixture in the clubhouses, strumming his banjo. With him is his sister, keeping a watchful eye, and his son, who has led this band up Broad Street for a decade. As the son talks to me about his Mummer career, he too glances frequently at his father. Pop is a lifelong Mummer. After my interview with Pop's son, one of the club members tells me sorrowfully that Pop is terminally ill. The doctors have stopped treatment and sent him home. Band members have all made it a point to go up and speak to Pop, the men patting his shoulder and the women giving him a hug and a kiss on the cheek. He looks around contentedly and begins to play a few banjo "numbers"; there's no need for the sheet music as his fingers find the familiar chords. One by one, others go back for their instruments and add their music to his; within just a few minutes, with no words being spoken, he is the featured player in the midst of violins, a bass, and a saxophone or two. It is a startlingly intimate occasion; the feelings of affection and respect of all the club members are palpable. It is also a moment when I feel very much like an outsider. Pop is part of the band "family." He is still playing when I leave the club-house at 11:30 that evening. (Field notes, 7 May 1997)

This vignette illustrates the closeness of family ties in one string band. During the months that followed my visit to this club, Mummers from other clubs and other divisions spoke of Pop's illness and their concern for his family. Among the announcements on the utility poles along Second Street the evening of my club visit were posters advertising a party for Pop to which everyone in the neighborhood was invited. It was held at one of the fancy brigade club-houses—the largest one offered to host the event—and the proceeds from the food and drinks served were given to Pop and his family "to help with expenses." Pop's string band performed, as did many others, and the comics and others added their entertaining skills to the event. "You see," one Mummer told me, "we wanted Pop to know that we care about him and his family. He's one of us."

In March of the following year, Pop died. The evening before the funeral Mass at Our Lady of Mt. Carmel Church, where the string bands host a family Mass just before the parade, several hundred people had extended their condolences to his family at the wake. On this occasion, too, his club members played Pop's favorite music, as did one of the other string bands. The next morning at the funeral Mass, Pop was eulogized as the club's "father," teacher of music to many of its members, and a role model for a life passed productively and happily. A small Mummer doll, dressed in spangles, feathers, and glitter was placed inside the altar rail, as were a pair of golden slippers and a miniature plumed backpiece.

An older Mummer whom I had grown to know well during my frequent trips to Philadelphia and the Mummers Museum told me after the Mass that Pop had continued to play his banjo until his last days. "He was always willing to show someone a tricky passage, and he played for hours," she said, "even though he held the banjo right up against his body where the tumor was growing. And you know, banjos are heavy, so it must have been painful. I guess he didn't want to stop playing his music."

The support given to Pop and to his family was not unusual. In 1996, seventeen-year-old Chris Brinkley, who had just graduated from high school and would be entering college in the fall, was killed in a convenience store robbery in the Grays Ferry neighborhood of South Philadelphia. He had been excitedly telling his friends about being accepted into one of the top five string bands shortly before his death. The young man's string band suit was on display at the Mummers Museum the week before the parade. In his case as well, posters on the neighborhood utility poles announced a benefit, with many clubs helping to raise money for the Chris Brinkley Scholarship Fund. These efforts were another example of the four divisions joining together to commemorate the life of one of their family members.

The Mummers as clubs are fierce competitors; as divisions, they are fractious; but in helping one another, they exemplify community as a potent force in knitting people together. If the club is family on the smallest scale, with intimate knowledge of one another and of one another's problems, the four divisions together represent family in the most expansive sense.

An interview with a longtime Mummer and leader in the comic division provided a glimpse into the network of support that the Mummers offer one another. Our meeting had been scheduled for two weeks, when he learned from his physician that a physical exam had turned up the possibility of a tumor. I offered to postpone our meeting, but his wife assured me that he would welcome the distraction of company. So we met at his home on a Saturday morning to discuss his experiences as a comic. I asked him the standard question that I asked everyone I interviewed for this research: "If you were in some kind of personal trouble, or needed help, who would you turn to for help?" His responses and his wife's interpolations were revealing:

> I'd say Mike, and Jenks, and Henny, and our club captain, Denny. But my top three would include Mike, who I just talked to on the phone. I'll tell you the truth, he's like a brother to me, I guess. When this happened, he called me and said, "If your family needs anything and stuff like that," so I guess I'm gonna get a little choked up here. And there's one kid, Denny, in the club who just got engaged, and he called to tell us. They call her [his wife] "Mom," and me, "Dad," and he brings his girl by to show us the ring. (Porco, interview, 1997)

His wife added, "Another friend, Bobby, called the house last week, and he came by and said to me, 'Maggie, don't worry, you'll want for nothing.' I can't tell you how much this means when you've gone through this kind of scare."

Moving beyond his club, this man described help from one of the string bands after his club had helped them:

> Anthony from Ferko, he's a friend. I could say that I have no problem with anyone. [Agreeing that it's a big community, he added] . . . We did a big benefit for a kid who was born. Remember that little baby, Maggie? One of their [Ferko's] members had this kid with a problem, and they were having a benefit for him. And we couldn't be there that night . . . but at a meeting in our own club, we said, "Whatever you guys collect here, we'll double it." So we collected $150, whatever it was. We went up to their clubhouse that night, the benefit hadn't even started. Ferko's members weren't there because they were having it at [another] string band's clubhouse. So we went up there, and I gave it to a guy and said, "Look, here's an envelope here with a check; it's from our club." He said, "Stick around, we'll announce you." But I said, "We can't. You don't have to announce our name."

Months later, the kindness was remembered when the club of which my informant was president hired the Ferko String Band to perform for their annual banquet.

> The best part about it is, we hired Ferko String Band to do our annual banquet. I always do something as a surprise at our . . . club banquet. Well, I called Anthony [the band's president] up, and said, "Anthony, why don't you come in late, at least twelve pieces you know, ten or twelve pieces. And Anthony says, "All right, Rich don't worry about it." So I invited him and his wife and Ferko's captain . . . and his wife. When it came time, well, I can't tell you about it—

At this point, he was so touched by the memory of an unexpected kindness, he couldn't continue. His wife picked up the story. "The whole band [all sixty-four musicians] in costume parades right in, because they didn't forget what our club did for that little kid. And they wanted nothing [for the performance]. They wouldn't take our check." Efforts to reach out on an individual level in dozens of small ways strengthen the Mummer play community, but the Mummers' reach includes the larger community of Philadelphia as well.

The Play Community as Neighbor: The Community and City

The Mummer clubs individually and the divisions, together and separately, are active contributors to the neighborhoods and the city throughout the year. Within the neighborhood, the relationship between the clubs and residents involves mutual support. The residents of South Philadelphia and the neighborhoods surrounding the other clubs in the Northeast contribute generously to the fundraising events that are the financial base on which all the clubs rely. Their support is substantial. Prize money from the city peaked at $315,000 in 1984 and has decreased every year since, and expenses have increased as the club productions have become more lavish. Other revenue comes from broadcasts of the parade. Some clubs generate support from local businesses. One comic club president explained that only the club banner car may carry an advertisement for a company sponsor. Regulations are so strictly enforced that the names on rental trucks used to carry scenery must be covered.

Three divisions—the string bands, the fancy clubs, and the comics—make appearances throughout the year for which they are paid. The bulk of money raised by the bands comes from these engagements. Members accumulate points by going on paid engagements, and these points "qualify" them to march on New Year's Day.

The other divisions turn to families and neighbors for financial support, and fund-raising is an ongoing project carried on through entertainment in the clubhouses, raffles, bake sales, and selling Philadelphia's signature hoagies. This dependence on the goodwill of neighbors, coupled with a desire to be part of the Philadelphia community, leads the clubs to reach beyond immediate family in a variety of ways. Press coverage of these efforts is rare, with only brief mention of the Mummers' good works in local papers.

Each time I spoke with a Mummer, I asked about involvement in charities, because this kind of participation is an indicator of attachment to "the community" outside the clubhouse. Each club, without exception, could identify some activities that reflected good citizenship. In some cases, the groups banded together in intradivisional outreach. For example, for many years the Mummers paraded on Second Street to raise money for the Edward O'Malley (EOM) Athletic Association, a South Philadelphia Boys Club. Marching twenty blocks in the freezing January weather, all of the Mummer units collected money along the route to help the boys club construct a sports facility.

The EOM parade was not simply fund-raising; like any activity connected with Mummery, it incorporated play and pageantry with "good works," as this account by Art Carey (1978) related:

> As any Philadelphian knows, though, cold weather . . . has never stopped the Mummers. Give them a stretch of pavement, block off some streets, throw in a couple of thousand spectators, and the "Two Streeters" will strut their stuff. That's exactly what they did yesterday. Many of the string bands—along with the comic and fancy brigades that turn Broad Street into a riotous carnival of sequins and plumes every New Year's Day—brought their foot-stomping rhythm, kaleidoscopic color, and clownish antics to Second Street. . . . As their procession moved deeper into South Philadelphia, more people lined the streets. Toddlers bundled under layers of clothes and blankets clapped and giggled. Some tots watched from their homes, pressing their noses to the glass of bay windows and jiggling their bodies to the beat of favorites like "Dem Golden Slippers," and the theme from "Rocky." Perhaps no one was enjoying the spectacle more, though, than Catherine Blance, 76, a great-grandmother who kept herself warm by strutting in place on the sidewalk at Second and Federal Streets.

This event continued through the 1960s and 1970s. It was discontinued because the neighborhood composition changed, and as one Mummer said, "people stopped moving their cars off the street, so we couldn't parade." Yet the Mummer tradition of community service continues into the present on a smaller scale.

Sometimes the outreach takes the form of entertaining; the Mummers have close ties to the Catholic schools and convents that are scattered throughout the neighborhoods, so their first stop on parade day will frequently be a visit to neighborhood convents where they entertain "the Sisters" (Dougherty 1992). Clubs visit individuals who are confined to their homes; for example, one of the large comic brigades always remembers a member who is unable to come to the parade, so they bring their performance to him. One club leader recalled, "I found out after the second year [that they marched with his club] that they have a fellow . . . who [formerly marched with their club] who broke his neck. I don't know how many years ago this happened. And [every year] they serenade him for a few minutes before they go to Broad Street. Not many people knew that. I asked around, and no one knew—not TV, not the papers" (Cloney, interview, 1997).

As president of one of the clubs, this man mentioned that his groups are involved in many different types of "community things, though we used to do a lot more. People have such hectic schedules." Among the groups they entertained or raised money for were Hands Across America, the Special Olympics, and the Easter Seals Telethon.

The fancy brigades are equally active, though once again their efforts receive little publicity. Commenting on the press's tendency to overlook this activity, a fancy brigade captain told me, "I asked [a reporter], 'How come you don't show up when we're out there and we go to the orphanage every year to see the kids that nobody wants to see . . . the handicapped kids. Or, if somebody needs help somewhere, or [the brigade association] does a food drive, or whatever. Why don't you show up when we're giving blood on the table—there's nobody [from the media] there'" (Burke, interview, 1995).

It isn't just public relations that motivates these efforts. As a longtime fancy brigade performer told me:

> We have done appearances at the hospitals for the children a couple of times. . . . It's a rough experience, but a very enlightening experience. It's hard to go in a costume designed for merriment and good times and go into a wing where the children are facing basically life-threatening diseases and try to be happy for them. . . . They don't want you to dance, they just want you to come in a costume, just to say "Hi," and shake their hand and talk to them for a minute, just to show them that you're there and care about them. (Sexton, interview, 1996)

The good news for the clubs is that recognition of their efforts to give back to the community has increased. An article titled "A Soft Spot in Mummers Hearts" (Giancaterino 1996) reported:

> One creative good-will campaign is a 900 telephone number established by the Philadelphia New Years Shooters and Mummers Association . . . that will give [fans] a chance to vote unofficially for the first-prize selections during the parade . . . 25 percent of the profits will support the Philadelphia Police Department program to provide funding for the force's bulletproof vests. . . . Tomorrow, members of the fancy brigades and the Quaker City String Band will visit the Greenwich Home for Children in the city's Olney section. The groups donate their time and money to these needy youths. . . . [On] Sunday, Quaker City String Band, led by Santa (will he be wearing a backpiece?) will march along Two Street. A 50-year-old tradition, members will hand out candy and perform for shut-ins and other residents who will not be able to make the New Year's Day Parade.

These connections are important; they affirm the Mummers' role as contributors to the neighborhood, community, and city. And for groups whose purpose is to bring laughter and fun, outreach to those in the community who are in trouble is yet another avenue for reducing the distance between individuals.

Clearly, strong bonds exist within the clubs and the play community. Robert Putnam's (1993) research affirms the importance of trust and reciprocity in strengthening civic life; in the Italian regions that he studied, groups have ties that extend back several generations. His emphasis is on the extent to which these networks are related to democratic civic communities. Play creates cultural capital through the shared experience of fun and the cooperative efforts to create it. The contributions of the clubs to neighborhood well-being was acknowledged in the comments of one Mummer who holds office in the city government: "I view the continuation of these [clubs] as providing stability in the neighborhoods. They are better for the neighborhood in general than the parade is good for the city as a whole" (Kenney, interview, 1996). But there is a limit to the help the Mummers can give neighborhoods, and the option of moving to the suburbs is an attractive one. Another Mummer interviewed during this research talked about the quality of life in Philadelphia:

> [When you talk about deterioration in the city quality of life], what is meant is you can't leave the door open. You aren't gonna pull into a nice, tree-lined driveway. You don't have grass and trees around you. There is a lure to getting out of the row house. I have resisted it thus far. But it is getting stronger and the problem is that things like Mummers will keep people in the city of Philadelphia. Being affiliated with a club and having friends in the city will keep people, if not in the city boundaries, at least close enough to commute in. (Creedon, interview, 1997)

Yet the problems of the city are not avoidable. In speaking about the experience of one string band that had recently relocated, he said:

> That band was in the Overbrook section of the city until two years ago. They were housed in [a club run by one of the ethnic associations], which was really a neat place. The residents tried to rally around in that neighborhood because it was deteriorating. But the [string band] finally moved out of there because they couldn't attract members because cars were getting broken into, people were being accosted during rehearsal, and it became a safety issue. They've moved to the suburbs, but I think that bands in a lot of these neighborhoods that are now deteriorating tried to hold out as long as they safely, or financially, could before they had to get out.

The Second Street area, with its very long traditional ties to Mummery and dense population of clubs, is a stable area, one where the streets are "safe" after ten o'clock at night, and one where the triple links of family, club, and community have a beneficial impact. But in neighborhoods like Overbrook, even the desire of residents to retain the Mummer club as an anchor were not sufficient to overcome the deterioration. It is understandable that neighborhoods would want to have the Mummers' clubs as neighbors because the groups have a long tradition of reaching out to help those in need. They find models for this outreach in the individuals they recognize as exceptional within their divisions and across divisions, as well as in their veneration of past Mummers, such as the two men described in the next section.

Ideals and Values: Teaching by Example

Individuals are brought together through shared interests, goals, and backgrounds. As they interact, members of a community create consensus regarding their values and the norms that govern their treatment of one another. Norms are codified: professional communities write ethical guidelines, and religious communities find moral role models in the lives of their founders and prophets. Most children in the United States know the story of George Washington's admission that he did indeed chop down the cherry tree and risk punishment rather than lie to his father. Narratives focused on the lives and deeds of leaders of communities reveal the characteristics that its members value.

The Mummers have heroes and role models, and they honor them through the formal mechanism of the Hall of Fame at the Mummers Museum, as well as in the stories that are shared within the play community. On the museum walls are photographs of the men (and thus far they are all men) who represent the community's ideals: hard work, artistry, generosity, fair play, and competitiveness.

In 1997 the Philadelphia New Year Shooters and Mummers Association's *Mummers Souvenir Book* was dedicated to Thomas Howley. After presenting Howley's biography, the dedication focused on his contributions to the play community; first, he was a man who loved and succeeded at competing:

> Upon completing his [military] duty, Tom came home and resumed his love of the Mummers. He paraded with the Hog Island Fancy Club and eventually became their captain. [After he had won] many top prizes in the fancies and [put in hours of] . . . hard work, Mr. Joseph Ferko asked Tom to join in the Ferko String Band, which he did. For the next few years, Tom was a vital part of the drill presentation, and in 1963, Tom won the role of dancing with Mr. Joseph Ferko himself in the drill that established Tom Howley as a top performer on Broad Street.

Howley moved from Ferko to the Hegeman String Band, where he had a winning record as captain. The dedication tells readers,

> But we must look further at this man. He did not only serve the clubs he was with, he served all the Mummers in many ways. He assisted all three divisions for many years, made backpieces, frame suits, and did the many things necessary to get a club on Broad Street. He worked endlessly on matters for the String Band Association, doing everything possible so that the Show of Shows[1] would be a success; or a Mummers Parade would come off good by working with the TV people, fixing suits on Broad Street so that the men in the suits could continue to march. He brought help wherever help was necessary. He served the Philadelphia New Year Shooters and Mummers Association for over thirty years . . . and held the office of Recording Secretary for the same amount of time.

In this brief dedication, some of the ideals guiding the Mummers are exemplified in the life of Howley, a life of service to others, of creativity, and of hard work. He is one of many men (and a few women) whose names recur in the stories Mummers tell about their tradition.

 In the panoply of Mummer heroes, no one is more prominent than Joseph Ferko, founder and captain of the Ferko String Band. Joseph Ferko was born in 1895 in South Philadelphia, where Mummery itself was born. On the hundredth anniversary of his birth, Ferko String Band members Dave Bradshaw and Tom Frangicetto published *Joe's Boys: The Story of Joseph A. Ferko and the Ferko String Band*. The story follows the model of a Horatio Alger myth.

> Joe was a junior at the Philadelphia College of Pharmacy & Science, and a bright and serious student. Every day after his last class, he would hustle back to his South Philadelphia neighborhood and his job at Fralinger's Drugs on Second and Siegel Streets. . . . Joe knew he wanted to become a pharmacist someday. In 1912, at 17, Joe graduated from Southern High School, but his career ambition, his "dream" was clearly not within his grasp—he didn't have the money to pay for college.

Dr. Fralinger not only liked Joe, but he saw in him the unique potential that would later be realized in so many different ways. He gave Joe the opportunity he needed to pursue his dream. (5)

In 1914 young Joe was busily pursuing his dream of becoming a pharmacist, with Dr. Fralinger's help, but he, like the other young men in the neighborhood, was drawn to the Mummers. "New Year's Day was then, as it is now, a thrilling day for Philly kids of all ages who loved the pageantry and fun of the great parade. Once they'd witnessed the unbridled joy and superb talent of skilled mummery, many of those kids were hooked. Kids . . . like Joe Ferko and his pal" (5).

It was in 1914 late in the year that Joe Ferko and his friends approached Dr. Fralinger and asked him to sponsor a string band. He agreed enthusiastically, and the Fralinger String Band made its Broad Street debut in 1915.

A successful performer and an excellent leader, Ferko marched for several years with the Fralinger group, winning a first prize in 1920, just about the time that the string bands were coming into their own as a division of the Mummer community. Early on, he established his credentials as a winner. But Ferko moved out of South Philadelphia when he bought a pharmacy, Ferko & Jones, in North Philadelphia. His pharmacy became "a mainstay of the community."

It was a wonderful place. There was a soda fountain and shelves full of everything—candy, toilet articles, perfumes, cigars, school supplies, and hundreds of other "things you need every day," including, of course, Ferko's Foot Powder. Now and then a portly and popular visitor at Ferko & Jones—Santa Claus—brought gifts to the children during the Christmas holidays. And a gigantic bunny brought Easter candy for the little ones in the springtime. . . . The people in the neighborhood could count on Joe Ferko. There was a "night bell" on the side of the door, assuring all customers of "service at any hour during the night." Mike Caputo, a [Ferko] band member who worked in the store as an errand boy in the early thirties, remembered the small boy who long ago came into the store with a note from his mother pleading for medicine—*and*—two dollars. Without hesitation, Joe "filled" his mother's prescription. Sister Rosemary Hendry was just a little girl when she lived in the North Philadelphia neighborhood close to Joe's drug store. She recalled fondly: *"I can remember the times when our family needed a prescription filled, but didn't have the money then and there. Mr. Ferko graciously filled the prescription, and even had a way of making you feel comfortable in such a situation, and even gave us kids a piece of candy as we left!"* (9)

Though surely a shrewd businessman and a successful one, what the Mummers emphasize about "Mr. Ferko" is his generosity. He is a legend in their community, and many of the older Mummers' lives were directly affected by his actions. For example, one lifelong comic said of this unique man:

> I don't know how "saintly" [others you have interviewed] make Joe Ferko sound, but I will say this once again about that particular individual—wrapping up all the things we said, all the positive angles of Mummery into one [ideal] and [applying] that [ideal] to one man, it would be Joe Ferko. . . . He gave of himself in a gracious manner, never making the receiving person feel that [he or she] was humbled in any way [in receiving] what he gave them. . . . In my life I have yet to meet up with another individual of his caliber. It's so unusual that anybody who touches on this particular person, whether they be male or female, knows that they've been touched by somebody special. Somebody that you just don't run into, and I'd have to say that all these [good qualities] described Joe Ferko. (Heller, interview, 1996)

Beyond the ways in which Ferko affected those who came into contact with him, he was also, as one older Mummer who knew him personally tells it, active in the larger community: "He served his community. He was the state representative for a number of terms [in Harrisburg]. He was involved with everything; I think in the formation of a couple of hospitals. . . . When you, me, or the next person said, 'Let's get this hospital off the ground,' he was right there. He raised money for community projects and made life better in this city for the people" (Conners, interview, 1998).

Clearly, Howley and Ferko modeled behavior for the Mummer community. Though he is a figure from the distant past to most of the members of Ferko's Band today, the values Joe Ferko represented still govern their behavior and interaction with others. As a longtime brigade member commented:

> Competitiveness . . . sometimes very acrimonious, [occurs among the clubs,] but [Ferko] is not on Mummers Row [Second Street] . . . and they're removed from the competition because Mr. Ferko's influence on that band still exists today, despite the fact that he's been gone for years. They have a different mentality when it comes to the way they present themselves, not that other bands present themselves in a bad way. But [with Ferko] there is an overriding sense of dignity and decorum when it comes to Ferko. From the red jackets [they wear] in public and the way they present [themselves]. They're just very much a continuation of the tradition that the old man started. (Kenney, interview, 1996)

Ferko has his successors also in present-day leaders of the clubs, many of whom are highly respected in the larger Philadelphia community.

Socialization Through Playing Together

In earlier chapters and in this one I have discussed the influence that the Mummer clubs exert in the lives of their members and on the wider community as well. Role models like Howley, Ferko, and Pop are highly visible and respected. The Mummer tradition would not have continued without the intense attachments to family that motivated individuals to continue their parading. For many individuals Mummery begins in childhood, and the interaction with parents, extended family, and club family becomes part of growing up. Within the clubhouses and through everyday contact, the individual Mummer is socialized to share in the common life of the group and to identify with its purposes. This "common life" includes the norms that govern interaction between individuals and among groups and the values that the community cherishes. The Mummer play community is a human community, not a heavenly one, so individuals fall short of the ideals that are exemplified in the lives of heroes like

Ferko and Howley, but this does not invalidate the ideals or make them less "present" in the clubhouses. These ideals are taught, though not through preaching; instead they are demonstrated.

The clubs themselves have from the earliest days of the parade adopted the role of teaching and training the young men in the neighborhood. Now, of course, the clubs also welcome young women. Musical talent is developed, for example, within the string bands, and not only music is learned. As a string band member who had been in the Mummers since his own adolescence commented:

> The strength of [our] band is that there's this real under-standing that you're not going to find great musicians, you have to develop them.... For the most part, you grab your son. I mean, I have a fifteen-year-old son who has been tak-ing lessons since he was eight or nine with [one of the music teachers]. As a freshmen, he was second chair, all-Catholic in Philadelphia. And it has made a wonderful difference in his life because he grew up in a [demanding] environment. You know, he's eleven, twelve years old, putting on a costume, and he has to play as good as that guy next to him or he's let-ting the rest of the organization down. So it creates a very high standard in that these kids have to become men, maybe not physically mature men, but adults in another way. (Cree-don, interview, 1997)

I told this man that other Mummers had told me that from the earliest times, the clubs were a place for young boys to be with their fathers, both to learn music and to stay out of trouble, and I asked if this was his impression as well. He replied:

> It's a pretty successful social experiment, [though not hav-ing demographics] ... I would [estimate] that the number of string band kids who get in trouble with drugs, drop out of school, get arrested, is significantly less than the general population because these kids spend a lot of time [at the club]. I mean, they have someplace to go ... something to focus their lives on. If a kid gets in trouble in school, he's not [allowed to participate] in the band. You know, if a kid flunks [in school], his father yanks him from the club—"You aren't coming to string band until you get that grade up!" It was a

punishment. For that reason, I've seen some wonderful young men, some who were wise-ass young kids, grow into wonderful young men because they went through that almost "boot-camp" experience, the teaching of responsibility.... Some of the fresh young kids I knew are now people I'm proud to know—they're Philadelphia policemen and doctors and lawyers. When I see them today, there's a special bond because they were in the band.

In the clubhouse where I was a participant observer, the enthusiasm of the young members was impressive. They were learning to finish suits, developing different props, practicing their rollerblading (part of the show planned for that year), and bonding with one another. All this occurred with parents close at hand. Their parents work hard at getting ready for the parade and model devotion to Mummery—to winning, to working hard, to supporting each other. It is in this nurturing environment that multigenerational links are formed.

Familial Ties and "Formal" Structures Organizing the Play Community

Claude Fischer (1976, 106) developed a model of how groups might come to create a formal organization. His model accurately describes both the emergence and familial nature of structures within the Mummer play community as well as the ethnic organizations that were so influential in the early years of the parade.

Rural migrants to cities commonly establish formal organizations soon after their arrival.... These associations seem to substitute for rural kinship groups ... [but studies suggest that] their formal authority quality is usually only a veneer, applied (often for political purposes) to a set of essentially informal relationships based on ethnicity.... For instance, a group of migrants to the city who have come from the same village may wish to participate in the annual carnival parade. ... To do so, they need official recognition from municipal authorities; so they constitute themselves as a formal club, complete with officers. This kind of group is not very "formal" in the sociological sense.

In the earliest days of the parade, the clubs were simply a veneer for family groups, so Fischer's findings are particularly relevant to the Mummers. Family links and personal loyalties have always shaped interaction within and between the divisions of the Mummers, and these same family ties can make disagreements within the clubs intense and extended. The expansion of the parade and elaboration of the Mummers' art during the twentieth century led to what appeared to be formal organizations charged with negotiating logistics with the city and devising and enforcing competitive rules within and among the divisions, as discussed in Chapter 2. The clubs in all four divisions—comics, fancy clubs, string bands, and fancy brigades—have umbrella associations that represent their interests to the city's Department of Recreation. Within the divisions, clubs elect officers and appoint committees that have specific responsibilities, from choosing a parade theme to raising and managing funds. Officers are elected "democratically." Or so it appears.

A disagreement that occurred in the mid-1960s between the fancy brigades and the other divisions reveals how important it is to understand personal loyalties in any analysis of a community that is also a "family." The conflict began with the resignation of the executive director of the Mummers Museum owing to what was described in news accounts as "differences about the scope and nature of his duties." The executive director was a longtime member and former captain of a fancy brigade; he had, in addition, extensive professional experience that made him appear highly qualified to direct the museum. Yet more than his performance was at issue in this dispute. When he resigned, the Fancy Brigade Association withdrew its support of the museum as a way of protesting the treatment of the executive director by the museum's board. Their support of museum activities included participation in fund-raising activities such as an annual banquet, to which tickets are sold, and a yearly telethon. Because of the chronic underfunding of the museum, their withdrawal had negative consequences.

Many brigade members believed that the resignation occurred because the string bands sought control of the board's decisions, an assertion that it was not possible to prove or disprove. What was most important to the brigades was that the director was one of their "family." Taking the side of the director became a matter of loyalty and friendship—making it impossible to discuss the museum's priorities. Brigade members would not budge from their stance, despite the museum's new executive director's effort to bring them back to the museum's board, and despite, in many cases, their recognition that the museum deserved and needed support. In this case, personal links were more important than being part of the museum's board, even though the board was effective in representing the interests of the Mummer community to the city. (Revisiting this issue in 2004 as I was preparing this book, I learned that relations with the museum had been repaired.) This self-imposed isolation from the other divisions, though temporary, may have led to a decision by the Fancy Brigade Association (FBA) to break with tradition in 1997 in an attempt to solve some of what their leaders saw as problems with the parade.

The FBA in 1997 had six elected officers: president, first vice president, second vice president, secretary, treasurer, and sergeant at arms. In addition, the FBA appoints a parade coordinator. Duties and responsibilities are specified in the association by-laws: who attends meetings, who writes checks, the length and terms and processes of nominating and electing officers, and other operating procedures. Thus the association appears to be a "formal organization." Yet what makes it operate efficiently are the close ties within the leadership.

Interviews with brigade members and comments of others in the play community praised the efficiency of the association in raising funds though annual assessments and joint events. In 1998 the FBA broke with the other divisions by deciding to perform inside the Pennsylvania Convention Center and charge admission after the Broad Street Parade; it negotiated this break with tradition with the city's Recreation Department, the Convention Center, television stations, and hotels, all of which were interested in devising a way for the Mummers to entertain tourists regardless of the weather. (Promoting an event that may or may not occur, depending on weather conditions, has always posed a problem for the groups promoting tourism in Philadelphia.) They decided to take this step without consulting the other three divisions, though they did, after striking a deal with the city, invite the others to join them in the Convention Center. The invitation was declined.

The Convention Center deal certainly caused dissension within the larger Mummer community. But what is interesting sociologically is that orchestrating the event was only possible because of the long-standing relations among the eight men who made up the brigade's leadership. The president of the association told me:

> Now [after the 1996 parade], the next problem we came up with was: How can we better our show? How can we make us more marketable? A guaranteed January 1 performance [so that the brigades could be part of a hotel holiday "package"]? How can we do that? So, going into the Convention Center was suggested. We went up, we talked with a few of our friends [associated with the city]. Then we did our research. Four of us did it in a matter of forty-five days. Come up with this game plan [which was] then presented to the city. (Cloney, interview, 1997)

Working through personal friendships, the brigade association obtained approval of their plan from the city government and circumvented normal channels of control exercised by the Department of Recreation. As this officer told me, "first of all, we have to use some of our friends to make all the appointments [with city leaders]. I guess you know who those friends are [and he identified some individuals well placed in the city power structure whom I knew to be members of Mummer groups]."

The idea grew into a fully developed plan that successfully solved some of the problems the brigades had identified; the props for the their presentations had gotten so large that it was easier to mount the productions in the Convention Center and to use only hand props on the parade route. This approach had the added advantage of shortening the fancy brigade division's march up Broad Street, and the members felt they had more time to emphasize their performing skills. Attendance at the Convention Center performance has steadily increased over the years, and the television coverage includes the brigades' performance.

Stressing the personal relationships within the group, this officer told me, "[as a group], we've worked together great for the last thirty years, and it's a proven fact, what we've accomplished [as fancy brigades]. . . . I mean, we started out with an idea, four of us [with the idea coming from another close friend who is captain of one of the clubs] . . . and we attended all the meetings, worked together . . . and the four of us know what all the others are doing."

Implicit understanding and respect for each other's ability, only possible within intimate groups, coupled with the respect for their leaders within the brigades, made this coordination possible. And this closeness was built on the personal ties that I learned about when I interviewed another brigade officer. I found that the vice president is the second cousin of the president; their families live within a few blocks of each other in South Philadelphia near Second Street. All eight of the men grew up near each other in South Philadelphia, and they all (or their families) still own homes there. Seven of the eight men graduated, though in different years, from the same Catholic high school. As a child, the first vice president lived across the street from the family of the FBA's representative to the Mummers Museum, and was in fact introduced to Mummery by the representative's father, who is legendary in the Mummer community for his leadership during the earliest parades.

Emerging from this research was a consistent pattern of personal relations that governed decisions and alliances. This is both a strength and weakness within the community. It is a strength because these personal links to the tradition ensure its transmission across generations. It is a weakness because the dependence and emphasis on personal ties makes it difficult to formulate decisions that could benefit the parade as a whole.

The Mummer Family

This book demonstrates how the process of playing together generates normative culture. This chapter affirms the importance of the clubs for families, strengthening ties through the continuation of a family tradition that links the generations. In the clubs, the burden of parenting is shared, with surrogate mothers and fathers providing guidance to the children. For those whose family connections are not strong, the clubs can provide a social support network. In effect, the club can function as a primary group in the absence of kinship ties.

The small communities (and the larger community of Philadelphia) also benefit from the civic involvement of the Mummer clubs, many of which repay the support of their communities and extend helping hands to those who face problems throughout the year. Their contributions include not only the gift of fun and entertainment but also the practical assistance of money for medical procedures and other needs that are beyond the means of families. Most often, the Mummers use the occasions of charitable and community activities as opportunities to bond with one another and even to play together.

Personal conflicts do arise among the fiercely competitive clubs and divisions. But, although these conflicts can lead to fissures in the play community, the Mummers join one another in supporting those outside their play community who need help and those within their community who confront serious difficulties.

The Mummer play community is an important component in the culture of Philadelphia's neighborhoods and in the lives of individuals, as this discussion of family and neighborhood links shows. Equally important is that the Mummers contribute to the civic life of Philadelphia through their voluntary activities and their play. They do so because, like marching in the parade and wearing sequins and plumes, helping others is a tradition that enriches the giver as well as the benefactor. In the lives of early Mummers these values are demonstrated, and through passing on stories of exceptional men, their heroes, the heritage of Mummery is strengthened.

Ferko's club chaplain, William Conners, reflected on his fifty years as a Mummer (Bradshaw and Frangicetto 1995, 107):

> After 50 years with the Ferko String Band, I can look back and thank Providence for the lessons learned in this association. After Joe's death, I made it my business to read to the men a few times a year a set of rules, he thought we all should follow:
>
> > Do unto others as you want others to do unto you.
> > Bear in mind that life is too short to be wasted in fault-finding, hatred, revenge and destruction.
> > The road to a friend's house is never long.
> > A good reputation is worth more than gold.

7 The Experience of Play

And you know, even going back to the days [when I was in the
comics], when I was on the street, I didn't think that anyone else was
around me. . . . And it was the same way in presenting your suit at
the judges. . . . I was performing. And that was it. You were a ham,
you were—it was your day—when they announced you and you
were at the line [designating the performance area], that's it. There
was nobody [else]; that was your stage. That was your five minutes
in the limelight, and as far as the performing, I enjoyed that four
and a half minutes.

—Conner, interview, 1997

From comic to fancy club member, from string band musician
to brigade dancer, whatever the individual experience, "having fun" is at the core of Mummery.[1] Play for the Mummers
encompasses the creative work that goes into competing and the
experience of performing.

"Fun" and "play" are relatively neglected in the social sciences
because sociologists tend to concentrate more on the outcomes of
interaction than on the fleeting quality of human experiences as
important in themselves. Yet, in answering the question of why they
parade, the Mummers consistently identified "having fun" as the primary reason for being part of the play community. That the Mummers are bonded so intensely through their play affirms the importance of this experience in generating community cohesion. The
ostensibly frivolous activity of play in its ritualized forms creates
community.

Play is expressive, challenging, liberating, and *fun*. Beginning
with the earliest Shooters' processions, play assumed myriad forms.
For some immigrant groups, such as the Swedes, the solemnity of a
religious celebration was coupled with opportunities to socialize, as

their community affirmed their shared religious faith and strengthened familial and friendship ties. For the Irish, play was irreverent, following the village traditions of house-to-house entertaining. The droll verse that today is emblazoned over the entrance to the Mummers Museum aptly describes their hijinks:

> Here we stand before your door
> Just as we did the year before.
> Give us whiskey, give us gin
> Open the door and let us in.[2]

Despite the differences in their celebrations, all of the immigrant groups played.

Overview of Play

In 1938 Johan Huizinga examined the history of ancient and modern civilizations, from Greece and Rome to China and Japan. He acknowledged that play serves biological and psychological functions but maintained that the experience of play is irreducible to these functions.[3] It is apparent from his tracing of the evolution and varieties of play that as cultures become increasingly complex, the forms that play assumes grow more elaborate. The oral history of a tribe becomes the folklore and literature of a literate society; spontaneous and rhythmic movement becomes stylized ballet. Yet the spirit underlying both simple and complex play and performance is unchanged. As Huizinga (1955, 47) put it, "At any moment, even in a highly developed civilization, the play 'instinct' may reassert itself in full force, drowning the individual [performer] and the mass in the intoxication of an immense game."

This return to play, to the "intoxication of an immense game," renews and reinvigorates the Mummer community and ensures the continuance of traditions. In organizing to parade, club members strengthen old ties and form new bonds with one another.

Providing a slightly different perspective that is relevant to the Mummers, Roger Caillois (1961) concentrates on games as a highly social form of play. Four categories of games allow individuals to satisfy different impulses.

The first category of games is *agon*. Competitive play engages individuals and groups in tests of skill and ingenuity. The rules bounding such play are designed to create a level playing field among competitors. Ideally, the winner is recognized as the best, based purely on merit. What individuals learn through play is how to both cooperate and compete within a normative structure. *Agon* "presupposes sustained attention, appropriate training, assiduous application, and the desire to win" (Caillois 1961, 15). Athletic games[4] are an excellent example of *agon,* though competitive artistic performances fit into this category as well.

Alea, or chance, is the second category of games. Within this classification, Caillois places lotteries; no skill is tested in this form of game, which relies on chance or luck. Drawing for position in the parade introduces the element of chance into the Mummers' play. Because parade position is associated with more or less success in winning, the Mummers see the drawings as fateful. Risk is present in the decisions that clubs make to experiment with new themes or novel presentations. For example, a string band once presented a show inspired by the film comedy *Sister Act,* with dancing and cavorting "nuns." The club, as interviews after their City Hall performance indicated, saw this theme as "risky" because it might have been perceived as "disrespectful." The majority of Mummers attended Philadelphia's parochial schools and have a healthy respect and affection for "the Sisters." Similarly, the Vietnam War Memorial and songs from that era served as the theme for another band, whose members were most anxious about treating a serious topic in the playful parade context. The tone of the presentation was commemorative, but the sequined military "fatigues" and up-tempo music (the only type of music that the string bands play) were discordant. In an interview after the performance, the band's captain stressed concern about bringing the theme into a parade where fun and celebration dominate. In both cases, the clubs felt they were taking a chance, but this risk was weighed against the possibility that something "different" would make their performances competitive and memorable. And in both cases, though approached as entertainment, the themes honored individuals whom the Mummers revered—nuns and veterans.

Pretense and illusion are the hallmarks of Caillois's third category, *mimicry.* The impulse to mimic others begins in infancy and continues through the life cycle, though full awareness of the boundaries of self and of the role being played distinguishes the adult at play from the child, who enters fully into a role. The fun of passing for another, experimenting with alternative identities, or revealing a hidden "self" draws individuals to this game form. Although the clown or comic is the prototypical mimic, any costumed performer assuming another persona engages in mimicry. Within the Mummers' play, pretense and illusion are the basis for all performances, with mimicry ranging from totally improvised to tightly choreographed performance.

Caillois's final category is *ilinx,* the type of game in which individuals pursue vertigo, "momentarily destroy[ing] the stability of perception and inflict[ing] a kind of voluptuous panic upon an otherwise lucid mind." *Ilinx* is experienced vicariously, in watching the tightrope walker in the circus, or directly, in riding a roller coaster. Stilt walkers or in-line skaters (a regular feature of the fancy brigades' performances) offer the vicarious experience of *ilinx* to Broad Street spectators.

The Mummers combine these four categories as they play, when, for example, they blend mimicry and competition in the performances of comics and brigade members who assume the roles of jesters and kings and draw the audience into a make-believe world. The most effective performances are seamless, with no break in the theme and no distracting "mistakes" that interrupt the fantasy. Competition emerges as the clubs attempt to present a "flawless" fantasy. The parade is street theater, but the rules of competition impose structure on play, and the conventions of folk art are used in judging the merit of a performance or entry.

Play and "Flow"

Another way of understanding the seductiveness of play is through Mihaly Csikszentmihalyi's (1975, 1981, 1990) work to discover what makes an activity enjoyable or "fun." He identified multiple components of enjoyment that create "flow." The parallels between Csikszentmihalyi's, Huizinga's, and Caillois's work are striking, and the ideas of the these scholars are linked in the following summary of "flow":

1. Positive experiences are those in which the individual's attention is concentrated; absorption in the task at hand

adds pleasure. "People become so involved in what they are doing that the activity becomes spontaneous . . . they stop being aware of themselves as separate from the actions they are performing" (Csikszentmihalyi 1990, 53). In Huizinga's framework, this component is equivalent to the sense of immersion in play to the point where the ordinary world recedes (1955, 8).

2. Total concentration on the task of playing or performing is possible because clear goals are set out and immediate feedback comes from audiences or judges. At City Hall's ultimate performance, the crowd's reaction energizes the club members, who see this as a "true test" of their ability. Although certain activities that provide the flow experience may take a long time to complete (as, for example, in the hours of effort that creating a fancy club entry requires), even in that case goals are clear and feedback is anticipated as the fancy artist works. Specifically, "in creative activities, a person must develop a strong sense of what she intends to do" (Csikszentmihalyi 1990, 56). Huizinga (1955, 10) has identified the goal of perfection as achieving an aesthetic aim with play; in performance, the player is assured of feedback from judges and spectators who appreciate harmony and balance. Goals may be specified at the outset, but often the individuals involved in the flow experience may have an internal standard that they are reaching to attain. In the case of a group experience, a standard develops through comparison with other groups or through an explicit standard for competition.

3. During flow, individuals control their actions rather than feeling controlled. This is an important distinction between flow and ordinary activities, where individuals are vulnerable to negative consequences of failing to meet the requirements of a task. Caillois noted that "enjoyment often occurs in games, sports, and other leisure activities that are different from ordinary life, where any number of bad things can happen. If a person loses a chess game, . . . he need not worry. . . . Thus, the flow experience is typically described as involving a sense of control—or more

precisely, as lacking the sense of worry about losing control . . . typical of . . . situations . . . in normal life" (1990,
69).

4. Csikszentmihalyi found that when immersed in activities
associated with "flow," the sense of time is suspended—
"hours pass by in minutes, and minutes can stretch out to
seem like hours" (1990, 49)—a point that Huizinga made
as well.

Experiencing flow is, Csikszentmihalyi (1990, 49) asserts, so
psychologically compelling that individuals will invest tremendous
energy "simply to be able to feel it again." Paradoxically, then, individuals will "work" to play. The flow experience is "autotelic": one
plays merely for the pleasure of playing, performs for the sheer joy
of pleasing oneself and entertaining others. The joyfulness of play is
apparent in the accounts the Mummers presented in explaining their
longtime involvement in the parade.

The Comics at Play

The comics are the "first act" in the Mummers Parade. In 1992 almost
eight thousand men, women, and children "clowns" filled Broad Street
with their antics. They were organized into one hundred entries, competing in several categories: "best captain," "best brigade," "best float,"
"juvenile," and "original costume." Many marched in multigenerational family clubs. All Mummers acknowledge the importance of the
comics' contribution to the parade, though sometimes with ambivalence. As one veteran Mummer pointed out, "there wouldn't be a
parade today if it wasn't for that guy with the wig. Maybe he's got
a can of beer and his umbrella, and he's out there dancing 'cause that's
where it started and that's where the tradition was born" (Stermel,
interview, 1996).

In a procession of "kings for a day," the comic is the court jester,
testing and sometimes defying boundaries—of taste, political correct-
ness, and law. Nineteenth-century Shooters were clowns long before
they became self-conscious entertainers. Before Broad Street, parading through the neighborhood streets, they used their flour-filled
stockings to "sock" bystanders and took advantage of every opportunity to kiss the girls. In the process of "having fun," they chal-

lenged the standards of behavior that more sober, respectable city residents embraced. Their unstructured play continued well into the twentieth century. Today, while individual comics compete in traditional categories within the parade, groups of comics make up the wench brigades discussed earlier. For the comics, the parade experience has changed, but the spirit has not.

One longtime Mummer, still active as a club officer though he no longer performs, recalls how it was in the 1940s, when the comics marched in the Broad Street Parade:

> In my day, we used horses still, because they were much better to take in a parade than in a vehicle. The late '40s, we didn't have automobiles [because of the war effort], so for the Mummers to use a car in the parade, they generally had . . . Model-T-type cars. We used to buy a car for $10 or $5 and the cars would explode on Broad Street. You would get them overheated and they would explode, a geyser coming out of the radiator. . . . But for $1.50, you could get a horse and wagon, for another twenty-five cents, a pouch of food for the horse. Take the horse and put on her head, through her ears, a little Mummer hat, so the horse was part of the parade. Then, they [comics] used to be sociable, so as the men were taking a drink, they would give the horse a drink. After a while, as we paraded—and we used to parade all the way to Girard Avenue and then down to Girard and Second Street, then south on Second [a route that stretched six miles]—the horse would dance. So, when we would play, she would dance right along with us, her whole rear end moving. She would dance right along with the Mummers and you had a great time with the horse, and when we would stop, she would stop; we would move, she would move. At the end of the day, you didn't even have to take them back to the stable, you'd hit the horse on the rump and she'd walk back herself. We had carts where we used to put the kids and what have you. (Heller, interview, 1996)

The carefree informality of the early processions is obvious in this description of earlier parade. In those days, consuming alcohol, usually beer, was part of the fun of parading. Today's comics are less likely to associate drinking with "fun"—and rules against this practice are accepted and followed, at least on the official parade route, if not in the neighborhoods.[5] For the most part, as their tradition has matured into public performances, the Mummers have redefined "playing," and drinking on Broad Street is not encompassed in the redefinition.

Mike, a retired Philadelphian policeman and lifetime Mummer, eagerly shared his stories of parading. He is a large, soft-spoken, almost shy man. This is how he describes his fifty years of parading:

> I love it. I love being in the parade. I love entertaining people. I love getting dressed up in different costumes. People say, "How do you do that?" Well, you gotta think realistically, people can't see you under that costume, so you don't have to worry about being embarrassed about what you look like 'cause it's not even in your thoughts. You just go out there and do your thing. You could be the silliest person in the world. And people don't know what you look like, and it makes them happy. . . . And this is the big thing, if you give people pleasure and happiness by entertaining them, that's the whole thing. That's what we do. . . . I'm sure that all of us have different personalities. [Being a comic] is taking on another personality. (Stermel, interview, 1996)

As he reminisced, Mike often smiled, especially when he described his father's career in the comics, which led to his own immersion in the Mummers' world. His father, known as "Mr. Clown," teaches visitors how to do "the Mummers Strut" in a museum freeze-frame display; he has been dead many years, but for Mike he lives on in this "special" performance. "I'm lucky," Mike said, "to be able to visit my father here [in the museum] any time I want." Mike's roots go back to the earliest South Philadelphia processions; and in reading an interview of his father in the *Mummers Magazine* (undated), it is obvious that Mr. Clown's authentic self was projected in performing as a comic. For Mike, the pleasure of performing is intensified by the sense that he is following in his father's footsteps—that he and his father are linked by a common experience.

Mike's emphasis on the joy of parading is echoed by another longtime Mummer, currently president of one of the clubs: "It's fun.

The biggest [part of it] is the performance. I guess it's like being an actor. Playing the role, practicing the role, and then making it come to life. You think about how you're doing it. And when you get to the judge's stand, it's like—it goes so quick—but while you're standing there, the thrill of it hits like a big rush" (Porco, interview, 1997). The comics of Philadelphia's parade are connected to the comic—clown, "fool," or jester—a staple in the broad carnival tradition. He or she is masked or made up, hiding behind the exaggerated smile or frown, wearing a wig, in full costume, or more simply clad in an inside-out coat or tattered dress, the only "costume" the early Shooters could afford. The mask, William Gradante argues, is both a disguise and an affirmation of the clown's liminal status; the protective coloration masking affords is used to step away from the world of responsibility, to be released from the obligation to respect authority, and to mock the pretensions of rulers and elites. Providing comic relief and questioning the taken-for-granted arrangement of the social world are the clown's tasks. Gradante (1986, 173) in describing the role of the royal jester, reveals the essential nature of the clown: "Because of the fool's feeble-mindedness, whether it be real or feigned, his famous privilege and power of 'speaking the truth,' even when his master could not do it, was based on the convention that, for the jester, everything, including the most sacred matters, was mere play."

Mummer historian and former comic performer Al Heller, recalling the Shooters' history, maintains that the Mummer tradition of political satire is rooted in the revolutionary history of Philadelphia (interview, 1996). Once the Shooters made their debut at City Hall, they quickly used this stage to challenge local and national politicians, speaking for their South Philadelphia neighbors. The marching ballot boxes of the early parade have been replaced by contemporary political figures, among them Philadelphia's mayor and former Speaker of the House Newt Gingrich, who were portrayed on Broad Street in 1996. Philadelphia's former mayor and now Pennsylvania governor Edward Rendell was portrayed by one comic in a mask with "two faces," a typical political stereotype. "Newt Gingrich" was portrayed by a comic wearing a box painted to look like a large speaker, with a wing on the right side. His sign proclaimed him a "right-wing speaker." Though far from sophisticated comedy, these entries had a political point.

Generally speaking, competition plays a smaller role in the comic division than in the other three divisions, though many of the comics use the relatively small monetary prizes to create their entries for the following year. And, as with other Mummers, recognition is its own reward.

Changes have occurred within the comic tradition. One comic, whose involvement with the parade began when he was an infant wheeled up Broad Street in a baby carriage, marveled, "You know, the entries have grown, and it's just unbelievable what the comic division has done. They have spruced themselves up and it's a pleasure to sit and watch them. . . . They spend money and they have props and do little drills in two minutes . . . and they really are something to look at. . . . [The comic is a real New Year Shooter] who goes out there to bring joy for the people on Broad Street and [entertain] himself" (Walsh, interview, 1996).

These comments from a lifelong Mummer illustrate the shift in play from spontaneous mimicry to more polished performances. Yet the transition is incomplete, and pictures from the earliest parades bear a striking resemblance to photographs of the "wench" brigades that today fill Broad Street in the early morning hours.

The strength of tradition and the seductive quality of the Mummer experience was highlighted in the Murray Comic Club's sixtieth anniversary commemorative book (1996, 48) in a short article titled "What Is a Mummer?"

> Exactly what makes a Mummer? Some say it's in the blood. In fact this may be true, for some three or four generations march together on the first of the year [and] there are some captains who have been marching for half a century . . . [who] should be in rocking chairs. No one who sees a "two streeter" strutting to the mystical magic of "Dem Golden Slippers" will ever forget it. When you stand next to a group of Mummers, they are ordinary people just like you, but put them in costumes, hear the tinkling of their music, [see] the flash of banners and their charging strut of determination as they face the test: the judging. Yes, a Mummer is just a way of life. It belongs to people who seek a quest, something impossible. And yet they find it, in the applause and laughter swept up in the chilling January wind. It's something beyond us, the secret of the Mummer.

The String Bands and the Play of Music

South Philadelphia has always nurtured and respected people with musical gifts. Its neighborhoods count as native sons opera tenor Mario Lanza and 1950s rock-and-roll stars Fabian and Bobby Rydell. Thus it is no surprise that, from their first appearance in 1902 as a "novelty," the string bands emerged as stars in the Mummers Parade because they could draw on the love of music that was part of their neighborhoods. Twenty-one string bands competed in 1997; mergers (some due to the increasing cost of parade appearances) reduced that number to eighteen in 1999. In a community of truly ferocious competitors, the men and women in the bands are the first to insist that when they go up Broad Street, they have only one objective in mind: winning first prize.

String band performers take their music seriously. Professional judging began in the 1930s; the bar was raised in the 1990s. A member of one of the top-tier bands discussed the stringent standards in place today:

> The string bands totally revamped the [judging] process. We actually took ownership of the process. We [the bands] pay the judges. . . . Because of the need for anonymity and confidentiality, we do not select the judges. The city [Department of Recreation, which overseas the parade] selects two professional judging coordinators who are experts in their particular areas . . . and those judging coordinators each select five judges. The judges [have] credentials. The city reviews their credentials. None of us know their names in advance. . . . And they're paid $200 apiece for two hours, but I would tell you that none of them do it for the money. They think it is one of the neatest things they've ever judged. (Creedon, interview, 1997)

The judges' backgrounds are in music, arranging, costumes, theater, and choreography, and they come from different parts of the country. The string bands saw the need for professional judging because they had begun to play increasingly complex music and invest substantially in production. Today, the judges' comments are taped and later shared with the bands. This change is revealing because it indicates that the string band members feel the need to "prove" their superiority, and the judges—as outsiders who have no vested interest in any one club—ensure that the winner's prize is awarded on merit alone.

The judges' taped comments are used to improve musicianship and thus strengthen the competitiveness of the bands. Elaborating on how seriously the judges' assessments are taken, the band member commented:

> If [one judge] gives you a 34 in music instead of 40 [the maximum number of points that can be awarded], you go listen to the tapes. One of the things that was phenomenal to the judges is . . . that the bands actually listen to the tapes. And the judges said, "Oh, like the music arranger listens?" And I said, "No. The bands actually have a gathering the day after the parade or two days after the parade where every member is there, and they play these tapes." And you can hear a pin drop in the room. Because everyone, *everyone,* is hanging on every word of the judge. And you're listening to the judge's inflection. You know, is he laughing? Is he enjoying it? Did he like the move we just did? Because you visually imagine [what the judge sees] because you hear the music [and know the routine so well].

Competition is central to the string band experience. A musician with one of the string bands based on Second Street is one of a few dozen women performers in the division. Her brothers are professional musicians, but she received little encouragement to follow in their footsteps. Playing the banjo in a string band provided an opportunity to use and develop her skills. Other women in the band are equally dedicated musicians, including a "grandmummer" who is a classical violinist. Her account of performing shows both the pressure of competition (*agon*) and the thrill of performing (*mimicry*) before a live and enthusiastic audience:

> I . . . think it's just an unbelievable high. . . . If you're at the parade at the judging area [in front of City Hall], and those bands are coming up, they say you can feel the emotion com-

ing from the band. The anticipation, you can feel it just generating outward [to the viewing stands]. Like we're on such a high standing at that line and knowing you've worked all year for this. And I had a fellow, this was two years ago, and he's probably one of the best banjo players in the city—Joe [next to me]. He was always a quiet, reserved guy, softspoken. This was a guy that I admired for years—he's done so many parades. And he says to me, "I need a cigarette." Well, there was a little delay at the line. . . . And I'm like, "Joe, what's the matter?" He says, "Pat, I can't take this anymore." And he was a wreck. I thought [to myself] that I'm fairly new to the parade, yet I'm the one saying, "Joe, calm down, you'll be all right." And he said, "I'm all right, I'm all right." That's the high I'm talking about. When the hairs on the back of your neck are just standing up. My biggest thrill is when you're rounding the corner, and the [television] lights— they're as bright as day. And you know, this is show time. This is it, the cameras are on you and that crowd . . . that crowd is roaring. It's like the smell of the greasepaint, the roar of the crowd. That crowd is roaring. And they love [our band]. As soon as they know we're coming around the corner, and we start across the line, the roar is deafening. And that's what you get from it. You don't think about performing, because you're just thinking about what you're supposed to do and where you're supposed to be. (Lowery, interview, 1997)

The connection between play and music is, Huizinga (1955, 158–59) maintains, so strong that "we have to assume some deep-rooted psychological reason for so remarkable a symbol of the affinity between music and play. . . . The most we can do is to enumerate the elements which music and play have in common. Play . . . lies outside the reasonableness of practical life; has nothing to do with necessity or utility, duty or truth. All this is equally true of music."

Music is central to rituals and celebrations of all types because it has the power to elicit emotion—joyous, solemn, patriotic. Music pervades all of the Mummer rituals, drawing people together as it does in the New Year's Day Parade. "In feeling music," according to Huizinga, "we feel ritual. In the enjoyment of music, whether it is meant to express religious ideas or not, the perception of the beautiful and the sensation of holiness merge, and the distinction between play and seriousness is whelmed in that fusion" (1955, 159).

Competitive musical performances illustrate the fusion of *agon* and mimicry because the string band performances have moved beyond the simple, straight-line drills of the early years to productions that include dancing, clowning, and mime. However, the criterion for winning that remains most important is the virtuosity of the band's music. Musicianship matters.

Of all the accounts of performing that I gathered from the string band members, the most vivid and illustrative of the congruence between the Mummers' "definitions" of play and those of theorists who have written about play was written by Bill Conners, who was such a valuable resource on all aspects of Mummery. Mr. Conners joined one of the top three string bands in 1941.[6] He grew to love music as a young boy in a neighborhood band and honed his musicianship playing saxophone in a military band during World War II. Born in South Philadelphia, Mr. Conners, until his retirement, was senior teller for one of Philadelphia's large banks. For seven years he held the highly prestigious post of music director in his band, and served until his death in 1999 as club chaplain. He received what is Mummery's highest recognition: induction into the Hall of Fame. After his retirement in 1970, he turned his attention to maintaining and preserving the history of his own band, as well as the history of the Mummers Parade. Several years ago, he wrote an essay titled "Four Minutes," which begins:

> The band is at South Penn Square and your thoughts are, "This is it. This is what we practiced and rehearsed for. Remember the sessions in the schoolyard, the Armory when it rained, getting the bugs out of the music at the club? We smoothed over some rough spots on the way up the street, clicking at Spruce [Street] and the Academy [of Music]. Boy, there's a crowd that knows what's going on. I hope I don't make a mistake. I hope no one makes a mistake. Is the right number up? There's the whistle. Here we go. NUMBER 1."

This opening paragraph conveys the sensation of tension. As Huizinga (1955, 10–11) wrote, "The element of tension in play to which we have just referred plays an important part. Tension means uncertainty, chanciness; a striving to decide the issue and so end it. The player wants something to 'go,' to 'come off'; he wants to 'succeed' by his own exertions." The account continues in a similar vein, though Conners brings the element of chance or luck to it in his reference to the possibility of a string breaking. The limited time that the Mummers have for preparation and their tendency to improvise also adds uncertainty to their play:

> You're up to the LINE and you have finished your "coming up" [the street] number. In a few seconds, you'll be into your theme's opening selection. Our time begins when the first rank of musicians steps over the LINE. You look around. Are we lined up right? Do I remember everything? What about that tricky turn at the 16th bar? Don't wave to anyone. Don't stop to pick up music if you drop it. If a string breaks, forget it. . . . There's the whistle. We're on. I play, I turn, I step this way and that way. My heart is thumping. I guide right. I guide left. I do fifty things at once—or so it seems. How much time has gone by? Seems like half an hour. Here comes the going-away number.

Play, Huizinga (1955, 9–10) writes, is secluded and limited:

> While it is in progress all is movement, change, alternation, succession, association, separation. . . . All play moves and has its being within a playground, marked off beforehand either materially or ideally. . . . The arena, the card table, the magic circle . . . the stage, all are in form and function playgrounds . . . hallowed, within which special rules obtain. All are temporary worlds within the ordinary world, dedicated to the performance of an act apart.

In the City Hall performance, the Mummers inevitably mentioned the sense of timelessness they experienced. Paradoxically, they reported a heightened sensitivity to the passage of time because of the penalties for going beyond the allocated minutes. Thus the "line" has a double meaning, linked to its function as a boundary around the play area and as the point at which a performance "begins."

Conners's account also provides a glimpse into the "flow" experience of play. As the individual experiences play, he or she moves in and out of flow, with periods of intense concentration on the music, which is practiced until it becomes "second nature," and awareness of the mechanical actions required to perform. Conners's experience oscillates between the two poles of complete immersion in playing and preoccupation with steps and turns.

The account continues, this time with a focus on the camaraderie that all Mummers, regardless of division, feel:

> You turn up Broad [after finishing]. Halfway to Arch Street, the band stops. Everyone is talking. How'd we do? Any mistakes? Did you see the judges nod? I think we got it. . . . It was perfect. Whatta band. And so it goes—all the way back to the club. You undress and go down to the [clubhouse] bar where by now everyone is watching TV where the rerun of the parade is on. Then to dinner, then wait for the prize list.

The intoxication of performing together temporarily leads the club members to suspend criticism. All clubs—no matter the problems that they encountered in going up Broad Street—are "Number 1" as they step into and out of the bright lights of the square in front of City Hall. There is plenty of time in the months that follow to dissect the performance and identify the flaws, but at this moment, in this place, nothing overshadows the thrill of performing. As Conners wrote in summing up the experience of "playing" on Broad Street,

> There will come other times in a man's life when a minute or two here and there will be important, but at this particular time, on this particular day among your friends, all striving for perfection in this endeavor, there are no MORE important FOUR MINUTES than these.[7]

The Fancy Artist

The fancies, or fancy clubs, have a long and distinguished tradition; they marched in the neighborhood processions and in the 1901 Broad Street Parade. In their dazzling suits, the working-class men's desire to match the ostentatious displays that were so much a part of Philadelphia's respectable parade tradition was and is apparent. Early immigrants (and their children, following their models) showed off the crafts and craftsmanship that many had brought from other countries. The Mummers' extravagant displays are strikingly similar in many respects to the costumes and floats that appear in the Brooklyn Carnival, held annually by Caribbean immigrants in New York (Kasinitz 1992), the carnival celebrations held in Trinidad, and in Rio de Janeiro's world-famous carnival.

Interviews with the members of fancy clubs suggest that applying imagination and skill to executing an individual vision are play; in Caillois's game classification, their activities fit within *ludus*. In collaborating with others as they attempt to overcome specific design challenges, fancy club members confirm the personal ties that they form as artists, but of all the Mummers, the members of this division come closest to the image of solitary artist.

From the nineteenth century until the mid-1950s, the fancies created the block-long elaborately decorated capes carried by up to a hundred "page boys" that were the wonder of the early parades; Broad Street was the stage on which their art was presented. Today, the club entries fall into several categories and often have many components. For example, in the 1994 parade, one fancy club sent an entire "carnival," including an elaborately decorated mechanized merry-go-round and Ferris wheel up Broad Street, thrilling adults and children alike. Though their ranks have thinned in recent years, the three fancy clubs still manage to put on quite a show for Philadelphians and tourists.

Both of the fancy club members interviewed at length for this research were members of Golden Sunrise Fancy Club, established in 1959. The club's organizers came together from many older clubs that had disbanded owing to either financial pressure or internal disagreements. Several other members offered their impressions and experiences during a visit to the club's headquarters, located in a converted slaughterhouse in South Philadelphia. Golden Sunrise is a family club, with children and grandparents all involved in creating the show that goes up Broad Street.

Palma has never performed in the parade, but she is no less a Mummer than others who have. I present her account because she exemplifies the nonperforming Mummers who are so central to the art of the parade. Surrounded by racks of costumes from previous parades, she spoke of the creative challenge of making a fancy entry. Professional costumers make elaborate sketches of the suits they provide to the Mummer clubs, and Palma has watched them at work and adapted their techniques. She insists that she is not a "professional,"[8] but making costumes for the clubs that carry through a float theme has been a learning experience, making her more conscious of color and construction techniques. There is, she says, a satisfaction in getting it "right" and in watching the spectacle her club produces; she defines herself a folk artist. The creative process is play; it is an expression of Palma's inner aesthetic vision.

Palma grew up in South Philadelphia and raised her children in the neighborhood where she still lives; she became a Mummer, as many women did, through marriage. Understanding her husband's passion for Mummery, she started out by "helping" and today is responsible for many of the Golden Sunrise costumes that go up Broad Street. She is not involved in constructing the wooden and metal frame components of the entries, an area dominated by men, but her costumes are integral to the theme presented by the floats.

During an interview, she recalled the first time she designed a piece for the parade; she told her husband that she was looking at a piece of wire and "saw a butterfly." He smiled and said, "Go ahead and make it then." On her own, she worked with the wire, forming and reforming it, adding material, a little glue here, some sequins there, to create the butterfly. Her entry won first prize. Palma didn't say so directly, but from the way she described her ongoing activities, it was clear that the success of winning made her want to go further with learning to design.

Surrounded by sequins, plumes, glue guns, and glittering fabric, she talked about why the hours invested in making the suits are well spent. "You see, it's really the kids along the route. You should watch them when you're at the parade. They see the club coming and their eyes get wider and wider, and it's almost like magic to them. I like being part of that . . . it isn't like anything else that I have done" (Lucas, interview, 1994).

Ed, an accountant in his fifties, is a lifelong Mummer. Rather than make body suits, as Palma does, he is involved in constructing frame suits and larger floats.

I was raised at Front and Dailey [about ten blocks from Second Street and Washington Avenue, Mummers Row]. At that time when you grew up, just about everybody, maybe when they were ten years old, started going in the comics. My father, my family has been in it from—I wouldn't say day one, but my family were charter members of the old Gallagher Fancy Club [which marched in the earliest parades]. . . . I started in the comics in blackface, paraded with Bill McIntyre's Shooting Stars [one of the oldest fancy brigades]. You became of age, and you started parading. I started parading with the Murray Comic Club, just around the corner. There was no clubhouse. It was really the owner of the club who lived just around the corner and that was it. (Conner, interview, 1997)

Asked to elaborate on his earliest connections to the parade, he explained:

I started as a page [carrying part of a long cape], along with other relatives of mine. My father was not too much involved, he was into some other things, but an uncle and the family he married [into] were really [involved in the fancies]; they were costumers. They really worked; they spent all year on [building the suits]. The [fabric] flowers they used, we don't really use [those kinds of flowers]. If we didn't have our shoemakers' glue and our glue guns. . . . Back in those days, they [the women at home] made all the flowers, and did most of the sewing . . . they worked all year.

Ed's words show the respect that those who march as fancies have for the craftsmanship that has historically distinguished their art. He agreed with my characterization of the fancies as the solitary artists of the parade.

[Those who are artists] is probably most. That's probably why we're around; we're the ones [in the parade] who will probably build. The [fancy] brigades, they have costumers, although [their members] still build their floats [and scenery]. But I guess with a lot of us [the fancy club members], it's just instilled with the old Mummery tradition to build this [the suits and floats]. There's nobody around who builds frames, or frame suits anymore, or likes to work with that.

When I mentioned another fancy club captain I had interviewed, he agreed that John, a Mummer we both knew, worked from sketches that represented an idea he had in his head. However, Ed contends that he is "not much of a sketcher," but simply gets an idea in his head that he develops as he works with the materials. The challenge is in making the vision in his imagination a reality, a piece of folk art that has no utility but is intended to impress an audience because of its complexity and beauty.

Ed stressed the teaching of techniques that connect today's fancy artists to a long tradition, noting that he learned through the "handing down of skills." Yet he is concerned with what he described as a dying out of the fancy's art, commenting regretfully on the practice of some clubs that rely on designers, rather than developing ideas of their own, and then using the design as a basis for making entries. At the root of this change is a lack of willingness to commit the time that constructing traditional suits demands, although the fancy brigades produce large-scale props that use many of the skills required in making a fancy club entry. He chose his words carefully here.

> I think a lot of people, younger fellas today, they don't, they're not into the old thoughts about the parade, especially the fancy division, with frame suits and trios[9] [traditional categories] that require that you take the suit up the street; it's work involved. You're gonna come home with sore shoulders. It's a day's work. Nowadays people are changing, I think. . . . I think maybe it's a dying art, of building frame suits.

In addition to the artistic impulse that draws individuals to the fancies, Ed also described the satisfaction of performing. His description of performing opens this chapter. Consistent with Huizinga's (1955) and Csikszentmihalyi's (1990) description of play as set apart, his comments describe the momentary isolation of performing:

> Oh yeah, you become immune to all the surroundings. I think [there is something magical about that moment], I think you

get three individuals who don't have much money. They're building their own suits. They might have their wives helping them down in their basement. But here they are. They're being able to perform, and whether they win or not, I think they perform [because of] an inner ego or something in [themselves] that says, "Gee, look *me* over."

This artist finds an outlet for his artistic and competitive impulses in the fancy club, though he also builds props for one of the string bands. Like their string band and comic counterparts, fancy club members spoke about the key elements of the play experience: the creativity used to transform an aesthetic vision into concrete form, the thrilling experience of presenting this vision to an audience, and the transcendence of self and setting that is achieved within the magical circle of the play experience.

But there are also variations in play as it is experienced by individuals in different divisions. The theoretical descriptions of play from Huizinga (1955) and Caillois (1961) describe differences between the plastic arts.

In his chapter "Play Forms in Art," Huizinga (1955) proposes that the production of the plastic arts differs from the musical arts (which were the focus of string band accounts) in two important respects. First, the artist is never completely free of constraint when he or she produces architecture, sculpture, paintings, or decorative art objects, because of limitations in form and materials; the artist is less free when the product of his or her artistic expression also must serve a function, as it does in architecture. Second, music is performed, albeit within the limitations of the sounds produced by instruments and the protocols governing musical composition, while art lacks a "public action in which the work of plastic art comes to life" (166). Huizinga also argues that, "however much the plastic artist may be possessed by his creative impulse, he has to work like a craftsman, serious and intent, always testing and correcting himself. His inspiration may be free and vehement when he 'conceives,' but in its execution, it is always subjected to the skill and proficiency of the forming hand."

The limitations he identifies led Huizinga to write that the strenuous work involved in a work of plastic art obstructs the play factor; the practical purpose for which the art is made or the limitations imposed by the materials used determine its nature. In the case of the Mummers' play, Huizinga's distinctions are not entirely relevant. For the fancy club artist, the restrictions imposed by the materials used are part of the play. In an important sense, the materials are the challenge against which the artist struggles to realize a particular vision. The Mummer artists attempt to overcome obstacles and to invent new designs that conform to traditional categories of art. Thus the challenge that the fancy artists enjoy is taking the dimensional limitations that define a "frame suit" and creating an entry that looks strikingly different from others.

In presenting his or her creation, the fancy artist enters into competition. He or she invites spectators into a world where fire-breathing, green-sequined dragons become, if only momentarily, real and "scary"; the "performance" in this case is the creator's ability to manipulate an object so that it comes alive. Inside the sequined dragon is the individual performer, who assumes the identity of his or her creation.

Mimicry, the ability to bring others into a play world through performance, is coupled to *agon,* or the drive to win a contest that requires imagination as well as technical skill. Although the fancy club artist is invisible, his or her creation is an extension of the self. Like stilt puppets or costumed characters manipulated by performers who are to invisible to audiences, the fancy club suit is part performance and part plastic art. Placed along a continuum from totally improvised to highly structured, the fancy's play clearly falls into the structured, disciplined, and rule-bound ludic realm. The creation of art is, for the artist, play.

The Fancy Brigades: Production as Play

In 1995, in press releases the Mummers prepared for the parade, the fancy brigades were described as string bands without instruments, but this does not do justice to the truly innovative performances they create. Represented within the brigades are a wide range of talents and skills, from the backpiece specialists to the dancers who are at the center of the show. The brigade members are generally younger than their string band counterparts and reflect the interest in movement and special visual effects that are often used in the similarly brief music videos that appear on Music Television (MTV). They, like string band musicians, are driven to win, and their members are closely linked in a collaborative relationship where every individual knows that performance is judged by the overall effect. My interviews with fancy brigade performers revealed that the same experiences of performing occur within this newest division. What is different in this division is the experience of play as "production." Interviews with the leaders, who are sometimes, though not always, captains of the brigades, reveal that their desire to play is fueled by the satisfaction they derive from putting a production— from concept to final performance—on Broad Street. Bill Burke Jr., Golden Crown's captain, compared his role to that of a producer or director. (My first contacts with Bill Burke Jr. and my subsequent involvement with the Golden Crown Fancy Brigade are described in Chapter 4. The elaboration of the theme "Fire and Ice" is also discussed in that chapter.) After each presentation during the parade, the captain traditionally speaks with television reporters, and without exception these captains echoed the comments made by Bill Burke.[10] Like other captains, he saw himself not only as a performer but also as a designer. (In some brigades, there may be a greater division of responsibilities than is the case in Golden Crown.) "Had I known [when I was younger] what I know today, I would be directing or producing in New York; or I would be in production. I mean, I would be just fine in a chorus because I enjoy performing. . . . I love it. I like being the captain. But I also know that I like putting a show together. I enjoy that part of it—the production, [bringing] in all the people" (interview, 1995).

The creative process, as Bill explained it, begins with an idea about a theme that leads to a "story," and then to music, costumes, scenery, and a choreographed performance. Others may not have the same ability to develop an idea that will work as a four-and-a-half minute show, but for Bill and the other creative captains the idea requires a coordination of resources, the ability to excite others from the club about the concept, and an unusual talent for improvisation. The process begins with a not fully formed vision: "Yes, [I have a vision]. I see this [vision] and I see it in color, and nobody else [in the club] does. Watching a television program, I saw my opening this last year."

The creative experience that Bill describes is analogous to the fancy club member's idea for a finished piece of art or the comic's preparation of a skit; the fancy brigades present a string band production without the same emphasis on playing music. However, the brigades tend to be more reliant on one individual's creative vision; the classification of this play conforms to *agon* because each of these men is highly competitive and on mimicry because the intent is to create a fantasy world within the four-and-a-half minute framework.

Direct observations of Golden Crown's preparations for three parades showed the centrality of the captain's role. In larger clubs there may be more delegation of responsibilities, but television interviews included in parade coverage suggested that a "creative genius" drives the production, even if he or she assumes a more backstage role. Bill met with the scenery designers and the costumer and translated their ideas into the club's execution of the theme. Bill also led his brigade up the street, with a mixture of unflagging enthusiasm and fatherly concern.

Play and Structure: Innovation and Creativity in the Mummers Play

Play is a cultural universal. All societies at all times have played—singing, dancing, ornamenting the artifacts of everyday life, imagining, and pretending. As the accounts of the Mummers reveal, the play spirit is manifested in innumerable forms. Play has many faces. As the concrete manifestation of the play spirit, art constantly changes, because individuals have the capacity to create, to modify, to innovate. The relation between the individual and the life-world he or she inhabits is also reflected in play, since the definition of art and performance is based on shared definitions of the beautiful and the compelling. The Mummers create their folk art looking backward to traditions in the parade and inward to their own creative spirits. In the twist of a wire, a butterfly is revealed. Simmel (1971), in describing the "tragedy of culture," writes of the tension between "subjective life" and the contents of culture, which express—but also have the potential to suppress—the human spirit. But it seems that it is more accurate to describe potential tragedy; for the Mummers interviewed, there is no "tragedy" because, engaged in play, they exercise creativity and escape the boundaries of the ordinary world.

8   The Mummers Past and Future

The American population has lost discussion partners from both kin and outside the family. The largest losses, however, have come from the ties that bind us to community and neighborhood. . . . This may not be all bad, of course, since we know that weak ties expose us to a wider range of information than strong close ties. We also know that strong ties offer a wider range of support, both in normal times . . . and in emergencies. Only geographically local ties can offer some services and emotional support with ease.
—McPherson, Smith-Lowin, and Bradshaw (2006, 371–73)

A Google search for the phrase "loss of community" resulted in 153,000 entries.[1] The epigraph to this chapter appears in an article from the *American Sociological Review* that made headlines in national newspapers and news broadcasts. Robert Putnam's *Bowling Alone: The Collapse and Revival of American Community* (2000) stirred discussion beyond the academic community about the increasingly fragmented character of contemporary American life. The "loss of community" makes good headlines. But academic literature looks more deeply into this "social problem," and social scientists recognize the need to qualify their findings carefully. Alternative forms of community may be displacing the increasingly dispersed family, the residential community where everyone knows his or her next-door neighbor, the voluntary groups connected to churches, and traditional fraternal organizations. Humans are social animals, and they want and need connection to others, so it is logical that they will seek alternatives to what is "lost." The research reported in this book is a single example of community that is successful in a fragmented larger society.

The longevity of the Mummers Parade, produced and presented by a community with multiple, intersecting connections to one another may be anomalous or quaint. Or such communities may exist in places that social scientists have yet to discover and document. In keeping with the tradition of community studies, some of which are cited in the introduction to this study, it would be useful to seek out communities that form through play, because there is much to be learned about community formation in studying them.

The Mummers receive economic support from their city, but it is not vital to the survival of their tradition. Implicitly, however, the city, through this stipend, recognizes the importance of groups like the Mummers to the city's culture and in some cases to neighborhood stability. My research suggests that city support is more important symbolically than practically. Yet the Mummers Parade—playful, frivolous, irreverent, beautiful—brings thousands of Philadelphians together and generates through their interaction social capital, which L. J. Hanifan defines as

> those tangible substances [that] count for the most in the daily lives of people: namely, good will, fellowship, sympathy, and social intercourse among the individuals and families who make up a social unit. . . . The individual is helpless socially if left to himself. . . . If he comes into contact with his neighbors, there will be an accumulation of social capital which may immediately satisfy his social needs and which may bear a social potentiality sufficient to the substantial improvement of living conditions in the whole community. The community as a whole will benefit by the cooperation of all of its parts, while the individual will find in his associations the advantages of help, the sympathy and fellowship of his neighbors. (Quoted in Putnam 2000, 19)

The Mummers are distinctive because their bonds are formed and renewed through play, not forged by necessity or instrumentality. Huizinga (1955) has pointed out that not all groups formed around play become permanent. The Mummers' bonds are complex: they include a shared heritage encapsulated in their history, ethnic and family links, and neighborhood ties—but the rituals of the community that ensure continuity are all connected to the annual Mummers

Parade. Play generates and regenerates community. Over five years of personal interaction with the Mummers, I saw countless examples of clubs and individuals providing emotional support, nurturance, and practical assistance to those who were part of their community and to those outside it. The Mummers are a community of men and women, not a community of angels, and it does them a disservice to idealize what they have accomplished.

Within the Mummers' play community, competition pits the clubs against one another, and human relationships sometimes override the interests of the community as a whole. So it is with the Mummer "family." The tension within the community between cooperation and competition is often resolved through play and directed in healthy ways through the imposition of rules and norms that stress generosity and fairness. Ideally, these moral virtues guide individual conduct in areas of life that go beyond the experience of play.

Clearly, social capital such as that generated in the process of producing the Mummers Parade serves a positive function. Can the Mummers' success at generating social bonds serve a broader purpose in Philadelphia as a whole? This is possible if the Mummer community can be expanded to encompass other groups within the city. What the history of the parade reveals is that initially disparate groups of European immigrants in South Philadelphia came together by playing together. These groups were not integrated into the larger community, however, and the parade itself served as a vehicle through which they gained greater acceptance and respect. Blacks and women overcame barriers to complete membership within the community and participated fully in the parade itself.

Philadelphia in the twenty-first century is much more diverse culturally than South Philadelphia was in the eighteenth century. The city's neighborhoods are now home to a wide variety of Latinos and Asians, as well as traditional white ethnic groups and blacks. Though language presents barriers to communication, play is a cultural universal. And celebrations that fall broadly under the heading of carnival are found all around the world. The Mummers Parade is already a day-long extravaganza, but it need not be closed to other groups who want to join in celebrating every new year. It is in the Mummers' long-term interest to look for ways to expand participation in their parade, either through reaching out through the clubs or by encouraging other ethnic groups to come into the parade. This will be challenging.

Another challenge facing the Mummers, and one that will be aggravated should the city withdraw financial support, is the escalating cost of "going up the Street." With costs exceeding $50,000 each year, the clubs are scrambling to compete. Many have explored the option of commercial sponsorship to supplement neighborhood fund-raising. Rules against commercialization are enforced, to the extent that rental trucks have brown paper over their company names. Rules are subject to change, but a more important issue is whether the interdependency of the Mummers and their neighbors would be undercut by outside financing. This interdependency has been crucial to the cohesion of the Mummers because it reinforces the extended family spirit that is so much a part of their tradition. The Mummers "own" their parade, and outside sponsorship has the potential for bringing commercial influence into the tradition. It is difficult to know how business sponsorship can be brought into the parade while allowing the Mummers to retain their seditious spirit.

The Mummers Parade has shown remarkable resilience, maintaining membership (though the numbers are smaller) in the clubs despite the decision of individual families to move to nearby suburbs. Through the family emphasis, the Mummers have continued to attract young members, especially in the fancy brigades. They have continually updated their tradition by incorporating new trends in music and choreography. The most recent parades have had much larger attendance than those in the 1990s, an indication that the Mummers' hard work as entertainers is widely appreciated. All these trends point to a bright future for the Mummer community. Having come to know the Mummers, I have faith in their ability to keep up with the times and meet many of the changes that confront them. They celebrated their centennial in 2001, marching enthusiastically and optimistically toward a second century clad in their golden slippers.

To quote Bill Conners:

> *Wouldn't it be wonderful*
> *To just send out the call*
> *And have the whole world join us*
> *In "Goin' Round the Hall."*[2]

APPENDIX
Research Methods and Materials
The Ethnographic Challenge

In *The Sociological Imagination* C. Wright Mills proposed that "no social study which does not come back to the problems of biography, of history and of their intersections within a society has completed its intellectual journey" (1959, 6). Thus sociologists confront the challenge of placing the experiences of the individual in historical and cultural context; this is true of the present research. My research represents an attempt to understand the life-world that the Mummers of Philadelphia have created: its structure and essential components; its distinguishing features, as well as the characteristics that are common to communities; and the changes and transformations that this world has undergone over the 150-year history of the Philadelphia Mummers Parade. Equally important has been my goal of attempting to answer the questions Mills posed: "What varieties of men and women now prevail in this society [or in this case, life-world] and in this period? . . . In what ways are they selected and formed, liberated and repressed, made sensitive and blunted? What kinds of 'human nature' are revealed in the conduct and character we observe in this society [or life-world] in this period?"

In exploring these questions, which Mills identifies as the challenge of sociology, I used a variety of research methods, including participant observation, structured and unstructured interviews, textual analysis, and archival research. Whenever possible I have confirmed data gathered from one source by comparing it with another source or sources. Through this process the memories of individuals about the history of the parade could be checked against published histories and contemporaneous reports. Accounts did not always match in every particular, but discrepancies only reflected what social scientists have always known: reality is individually interpreted and socially constructed.

Overview of Methods

Taking the stance of "symbolic interaction," the ethnographic approach "commits the researcher to writing the theory of those studied. It assumes that persons in the social world already have a theory that guides and directs their behavior. [The task of ethnography] is to listen to that theory and write it. . . . There is no attempt to fit the theory that operates in the social world into an abstract scheme" (Denzin 1989, 177).

Participant Observation

To understand the worldview of the Mummers, I participated in getting ready for the parade and observed many different types of interaction that swirled around the parade itself. This required gaining entry into the Mummers' tight-knit community and establishing contact with the gatekeepers.

Denzin (1989, 165) identifies three stages in the "participant as observer" role. During the initial stages, the researcher is an outsider, "a stranger," and gains only superficial knowledge about the world. As with any other interaction, the members of the community the researcher approaches "place" him or her in a particular category. In this case, I introduced myself as a sociologist interested in the story of the parade and the Mummers' motivations for participating in this event. I maintained a low profile around the Mummers, and set about the process of "fitting in" in their world. Over time, as the Mummers understood my interest in their play and the extent to which I appreciated their efforts, we developed a reciprocal respect and trust of one another. I delayed asking some potentially sensitive questions until I knew them better, thus earning the status of "provisional" member of their community. During this stage I was socialized into their world. Denzin describes this as a second-stage relationship.

Because my direct observations of the community spanned five years, I became a "categorical" member of their community and found that the Mummers would, without prompting, suggest others whom I should interview because they had some special knowledge. During our interactions they volunteered information or told me things that they thought were relevant to my understanding of them. The first contacts I made were at the Mummers Museum in Philadelphia.

Building on the introductions provided by the museum's director and curator, I was able to interview a cross section of the Mummers through a snowball sample. This sampling method is not entirely satisfactory because it can prevent researchers from encountering alternative views of the community. So, to avoid too narrow a range of contacts, I continually looked for opportunities to interview other individuals who had important roles in Mummer organizations, as well as those whom other members identified as leaders. In addition, I made sure that I conducted interviews of Mummers from each division and talked with those outside the community to learn about how the Mummers fit into the larger community of Philadelphia.

At the early stage of asking questions and talking with the Mummers I encountered, I was told several times that to understand the parade experience it was absolutely necessary to go "up Broad Street" with a club. My experiences in the parade and in parade activities with the Golden Crown Fancy Brigade are discussed in detail in Chapter 4. Chapter 5 also relies on participation in the Mummers' world, as well as on other materials. My experience of "going up the Street" with Golden Crown established a basis for my subsequent contacts with Mummers in other clubs.

In the research process, I played a number of roles. In my historical exploration of the parade and the immigrant communities that produced it, I looked at a wide range of perspectives on the Mummers. Each historian—and there were many competent historians within the community itself—uses a distinctive lens in analyzing events and in assessing the motivations or views of those involved in those events.

In my discussions that were focused on understanding the competition between clubs and among divisions, I heard different accounts from each "side" in a controversy. My own accounts focus on the process of how disputes arose and how they were ultimately resolved. The Mummers understood that I was a neutral observer (to the extent humanly possible) of their internal conflicts.

One particularly difficult challenge arose in researching the conflict over the use of blackface within the parade. Because this controversy occurred thirty years ago, there were few individuals who could share firsthand experience with me. I thus relied on the work of contemporaries, though I was eventually able to speak with a member of one of the brass bands that had marched in the 1964 parade, at the height of the conflict. His recollections and those of a comic club leader are used extensively in Chapter 3. Of course, these two informants can only represent their own perspectives, so I was cautious about generalizing from their remarks about the community as a whole. At the same time, these accounts do reveal information about relations within the Mummer community between blacks and whites and, even more important, they reaffirm the ongoing participation of blacks in the parade.

Structured and Unstructured Interviews

In discussing the use of the biographical method, Denzin connects the use of this strategy to "symbolic interactionism": "The life history, life story, biographical method presents the experiences and definitions held by one person, one group, or one organization as this person, group or organization interprets these experiences. . . . Every human being, symbolic interactionism suggests, defines the world differently. If sociologists are to accurately explain these different definitions and relate them to action, they must penetrate this subject's world of concepts, experiences, and reactions" (1989, 182–83).

The meaning that play has for individuals and how that meaning affects their interactions is important in this research. My contact with the Mummers led to many interviews, both structured and formal, and unstructured (sometimes opportunistic) and informal. During the structured interviews, I obtained a life history of the individual, focusing particularly on the individual's involvement in the parade and his or her experiences as a member of the Mummer community. Through these interviews I came to understand Mummer definitions of the key terms used throughout this volume: tradition, play, family, and neighborhood; Denzin refers to this type of life history as "topical" (1989, 189). These sessions ranged over a broad spectrum of related areas and impressions the Mummers spontaneously shared.

Some Mummers I interviewed were known within the community as "historians" of the tradition, and they provided an informed and occasionally critical Mummers' "eye view" of the evolution of the parade. Many were able to trace the earliest roots of the tradition through their family's participation as Mummers. I interviewed club leaders as well as club members and sought out contacts with those who were involved in divisional and interdivisional activities to learn about the organizational structures of Mummery. The insights I gained through my contacts with the members of this community form the ethnographic core of this research.

Content Analysis

The Mummers are enthusiastic collectors, and they are public performers whose parade has been televised since 1947. Thus, throughout this research, I examined the clippings and photographs that the Mummers have collected and donated to the Mummers Museum. I also used tapes of past parades to trace the artistic changes in the tradition and to listen to the words of the Mummers from the past who are the "stars" of the vignettes the television production crews intersperse throughout their coverage of this event.

Through Mummers who have been commentators on the parade, I gained access to the information that the groups provide on their clubs and presentations; this is important to the present research because it reveals how the Mummers craft a public identity. In choosing to emphasize certain biographical details of their club leaders and particular aspects of their club histories—and in omitting others—they indirectly reveal values and norms that govern relations within the clubs.

Historical and Archival Methods

Mills asserts that biography and history intersect. Tuchman (1994, 306) similarly maintains that social science must incorporate a "theoretical use of historical information." In the case of an event such as the Mummers Parade, which grew out of the cultural and social traditions of many groups and represented a merging of these traditions as the newly arrived Europeans and already present African Americans sought a role in the culture of Philadelphia, history has a particular resonance between racial groups. In looking at the issues of inclusion and exclusion of different segments of Philadelphia's population, I made every effort to provide a historical framework, while maintaining a primary focus on the experience of those in the community.

Examining the way in which the Mummers appeared to the residents of Philadelphia through accounts of their earliest activities enriched my understanding of their drive to develop a tradition that reflected positively on their neighborhoods and their families. My findings are presented in Chapters 1, 2, and 3.

The Philadelphia Mummers Museum has an archive of historical material, including programs from past parades and scrapbooks of news clippings and magazine articles. One of the Mummers' historians has a personal collection of scrapbooks that include stories about the parade from the 1880s to the present. These historical texts provided a means of checking the personal recollections of the Mummers against the public accounts of the parade.

In addition, another collection of historical material was useful in this research. This resource included the club histories that the Mummers have written, including a recently published book on one of the string bands and several booklets on the lives of individual Mummers that are in the library collection.

The Mummers Museum archives also contain the tape-recorded interviews conducted by Andrea Ignatoff Rothberg, whose dissertation on the Mummers was completed in 1980. I listened to these interviews during the early stages of my research, and some of the information they contained is integrated with my own research.

"Going Native" and Other Challenges

Close involvement with any group over time increases the researcher's empathy with the individuals he or she encounters. Though I was predisposed to view the Mummers positively, I developed an admiration for their strengths as a community and for their considerable talents as performers and artists. I do not, however, believe that my portrait idealizes their life-world. Rather, I attempt to provide a balanced view of the satisfactions of play as well as the frustrations when play is co-opted, and to illuminate the ways in which individuals develop ties with one another and insights into how organizational competition divides players from one another.

My goal in writing about the Mummers' world is to render the complexity and richness of the play world and understand how potentially important play as a social form is in the formation of communities. I also hope that the Mummers who read this book will recognize themselves in the portrait I paint of their unique life-world.

NOTES

Introduction

1. These eighteen-inch baby dolls are elaborately dressed in costumes like those of string band performers, including headpieces and feathered backpieces.

2. Those who live on South Second Street proudly proclaim themselves "Two Streeters." Two Street is also known as Mummers Row.

3. This tradition was heavily influenced by the University of Chicago School of Sociology. Classic ethnographies include William F. Whyte's *Street Corner Society* (1943), Gerald D. Suttles's *The Social Order of the Slum: Ethnicity and Territory in the Inner City* (1968), and Elliot Liebow's *Talley's Corner* (1967). Contemporary ethnographies also focus on urban environments, notably Elijah J. Anderson's *Code of the Street* (1999) on Philadelphia, and Mitchell Duneier's *Sidewalk* (1999) on New York City.

4. Momus is the Greek god of mockery and censure, the patron of comics and clowns. The term "Mummery" is derived from his name.

5. Robert Putnam (2000, 19) uses L. J. Hanifan's definition of social capital: "those tangible substances that count for most in the daily lives of people: namely good will, fellowship, sympathy, and social intercourse among the individuals and families who make up a social unit." The social unit that is the focus of this book is the play community of Mummers.

6. The Appendix describes the methods that guided this research, including my role as a participant observer. I also discuss the kinds of texts that were available through the Mummers Museum and other sources, including the Mummers themselves.

7. The estimate of four to eight million dollars was provided by the Mummers Museum staff. Mummers familiar with the finances of the clubs reported that the production costs ranged from less than $100 for a small comic group to $75,000 for a string band or fancy brigade production. This figure seems high, and may include the city's prize money as well as costs for city services. It is unclear whether in the years from 1995 to 2000 these figures remained stable; the fancy club and string band presentations have gotten

more elaborate even as the parade itself has become smaller and shorter (owing to the city's insistence that the clubs stay on schedule).

8. Since 1947 the Mummers Parade has been televised. In the many hours of film I viewed of past parades, the "good working people" identification was practically synonymous with "the Mummers." Though the socioeconomic profile of the community presented in the Chapter 6, and my interviews, revealed a substantial middle-class membership as well as a smaller number of professionals who share in the fun, many individuals embrace the working-class label because it reflects how far they have traveled in relation to their immigrant grandparents who began the Mummers tradition.

9. After the disaster of Hurricane Katrina in 2005, there was a huge debate in New Orleans about whether to have Mardi Gras. Ultimately, a scaled-down version of the celebration occurred, but many small crewes and their members had neither the heart nor the resources to participate. When I casually asked the director of the Mummers Museum, Palma Lucas, whether the event would go on, she replied, "Of course, they'll have Mardi Gras. The Mummers would parade no matter what happened." Much of the commentary surrounding Mardi Gras focused on the need for the city to provide a distraction for residents. For the hotels and restaurants, Mardi Gras provided both jobs and dollars.

10. I had a tenuous connection to Philadelphia and the parade. I had "seen" my first parade as a two-year-old, when my family visited my grandmother in South Philadelphia. Footage of the string bands marching through falling snowflakes in 1947 is interspersed with birthday and holiday celebrations carefully filmed by my father.

11. Among those who have explored the definitions and experience of play whose work has been most influential in this study are Johan Huizinga (1955), Roger Caillois (1961), and Mihaly Csikszentmihalyi (1975, 1981, 1990).

Chapter 1

1. The term Shooters is used interchangeably with Mummers within the community. Both terms appear in early newspaper accounts of the parade, which I used extensively in my research. "Shooters" comes from the early tradition of shooting off guns or firecrackers to celebrate the New Year, a custom that was widely practiced in immigrant neighborhoods.

2. Through William Conners, a veteran of the parade and historian of the Mummers, I had access to his collection of clippings, as noted elsewhere in this book. I learned from him that many of the old newspaper clippings had been retrieved from people's homes when they replaced the kitchen floor linoleum, which had been laid on top of layers of newspapers. These articles were contributed to the Mummers Museum Library.

3. The Mummers' history, like that of other groups, can be examined through two lenses. The first is that used by historians and includes the dates

when different ethnic groups arrived in South Philadelphia, the conditions they encountered, and the sociocultural context within which their identity and traditions were formed. A second lens, equally important, is that of the Mummers themselves as they construct and interpret their past. This history is selective, sometimes choosing to emphasize some aspects of the group and gloss over others. The interpretive process forms the collective memory of the group. The Mummers' history comes from oral accounts shared across generations; their texts are scrapbooks and faded photographs that show the marks of age and handling as the Mummers recount "grandfather's story." Because press coverage was so often shaped by such shared memories, their official history reflects values and sentiments members of the community share. Thus their accounts are their heritage, rather than history in the conventional sense. As Kammen (1991) has noted, heritage reveals how a group wishes to be seen. There is, then, a mythical quality to the stories that Mummers tell, and often I heard a tall tale told with a wink, accompanied by a slight shrug. More frequently, though, the Mummers' accounts reflected pride in the very real accomplishments of their multigenerational community.

4. Though their early opposition was important to antislavery efforts before the Revolution, opposition to slavery by Quakers in Philadelphia was muted by the profitability of the slave trade in Pennsylvania and the centrality of slave labor to the economy. Pennsylvania was the first state to call for the outlawing of slavery in 1780, though emancipation was to be gradual rather than immediate (Horton and Horton 1997, 4–9).

5. Dennis Clark (1973a) makes a distinction between two waves of Irish immigrants. The Scots-Irish were the first group to arrive in South Philadelphia. They were Protestant, mostly Presbyterian, immigrants from the north of Ireland. After the cataclysmic famine of 1846–47, Irish Catholics came to Philadelphia in large numbers.

6. As Joseph Gusfield (1986) revealed, the temperance movement itself was as much about establishing the ascendancy of native-born Americans over immigrants as it was about promoting moderation or abstinence. Like their Boston counterparts, Philadelphia's temperance advocates disapproved of the Irish Catholic propensity to gather in saloons and drink heavily. Their concern was both moral and practical. Late nights spent in saloons compromised worker productivity, and drunkenness was also linked to family dissolution and domestic violence.

7. Susan Davis (1985) has written extensively about these disruptions. In addition, Bruce Laurie (1973, 71–87) identified two types of violence in South Philadelphia's neighborhoods: expressive and instrumental. Prior to the 1830s, fire brigades were made up of well-to-do young men who frequently displayed their equipment and uniforms in city processions. By the 1840s, however, the respectable members had been displaced by competing white gangs who feuded over "turf" in Southwark. Full-scale riots erupted with assaults on innocent bystanders, as these brigades raced to be the first to arrive at the fires.

Unfortunately, in the midst of this gang fighting, houses and businesses often burned to the ground. Ownership of the streets was—as it is for contemporary urban gangs—a proxy for power among the young men who expressed their animosities toward one another and their resentment of conventional society through such conflicts.

8. A three-volume history of Philadelphia, published in 1884, provides a partial listing of beneficial and welfare organizations, among them dozens of groups that served widows, orphans, the disabled, and other individuals who needed support in various forms. These groups usually served specific ethnic populations (Scharf and Westcott 1884, 2:1449–90).

9. Because the spokespersons for the Mummers are drawn primarily from leaders of the clubs, who are without exception descendants of the white ethnic groups associated with the early parade, the influence of black Philadelphians is rarely mentioned. This is consistent with the development of a Mummers heritage, discussed in note 3 above.

10. The 2004 Mummers Parade, for example, included a group of black high school students who marched with the comic division as the "Hip Hop Drill Team."

11. The meaning of minstrelsy in the context of a controversy surrounding the use of blackface that occurred in 1963 is explored at length in Chapter 3.

12. Golab (1973, 204) noted that the percentage of foreign-born residents in Philadelphia was the lowest of all the northern cities, including New York and Chicago, with 27 percent foreign born in 1870, 24 percent foreign born in 1880, and 26 percent foreign born in 1890.

13. Both Irish and Germans entered Philadelphia in large numbers between 1850 and 1880, but the Germans settled primarily in the area's southwestern and southeastern communities. This dispersion was consistent with the work opportunities for the two groups. Several of the authors in Hershberg (1981) emphasize that structural factors influence ethnic dispersion; Greenberg wrote that shared ethnicity was crucial in neighborhoods, but that, "in an era [when] communication beyond areas within walking distance was limited, it would be difficult to interact [regularly] with people living several miles away. If it were the case that neighborhoods formed within the context of accessibility to the work place, then the development of networks based on ethnicity would be undercut by the necessity of living among those with the same industrial affiliation but not necessarily the same cultural affiliation" (Greenberg 1981, 225). In South Philadelphia, for the Irish immigrants, shared ethnicity and common occupational skills seemed to have converged in the neighborhoods. As the Irish and other ethnic groups acquired more diverse skills, they left South Philadelphia. When they moved to other areas of the city, they formed play groups so that they could continue to celebrate as they had in their old neighborhoods. This change led to the dispersion of the Shooters and Mummers clubs throughout Philadelphia.

14. An important mechanism in the assimilation of immigrants into the community was their purchase of homes of their own. Philadelphia had, as Sutherland (1973, 178) wrote, many building and loan associations that enabled individuals with modest means to pool their resources and ultimately become homeowners. Clark (1973a, 137–39) also pointed out the importance of such institutions in stabilizing the situation of the Irish entering Philadelphia in the mid-1800s.

15. In nineteenth-century Philadelphia, Irish Catholics used their networks to great advantage, as did Italians in the late nineteenth and early twentieth centuries. Philadelphia—though to a lesser extent today than in the past because the old national distinctions have been largely superseded by white ethnicity as a broader affiliation—has long had Catholic parishes and schools that ministered to different groups. Dubin (1996) tracks the dispersion of Irish Catholics from South Philadelphia by the parishes they built; Italians, Poles, and Lithuanians, coming into Philadelphia in the latter part of the nineteenth century, built churches as their numbers grew. It is not unusual even today to hear South Philadelphians refer to "Irish" or "Italian" parishes. When I began my exploration of the Mummers' world, I found it helpful to share with those I interviewed my Philadelphia "lineage," through my mother. To "place" me, the Mummers asked which parish my mom grew up in. I told them—adding that I was baptized in her parish during World War II—to which they replied, correctly, "Oh, she was Irish."

16. Women did not belong officially to the clubs, though they did much of the sewing and other chores related to getting men and little boys (who marched as "juveniles") ready; women worked "backstage" until the mid-1970s, as discussed in Chapter 3. However, women did stand in for their men serving overseas in the 1940s, though they did not perform.

17. The number of groups participating in the celebrations throughout Philadelphia seemed to ebb and flow, for reasons that are difficult to discern. For example, the *Philadelphia Inquirer* (27 December 1899) published an article on a "dying tradition," citing financial strains caused by a decrease in prizes from the public as the reason for declining participation. The *Inquirer* reported that in 1888 211 permits were issued; in 1890, 145; in 1891, 108; in 1892, 101; in 1893, 55; in 1894, 69; in 1895, 54; in 1896, 46; in 1897, 55; in 1898, 47; and in 1899, 33. This article was not the first premature announcement of the Shooters' imminent disappearance, nor would it be the last. Contemporary newspapers, and the Mummers themselves, frequently complain about the rising costs and declining prize money, yet they always pull together to go up Broad Street. Given these statistics, however, it is accurate to say that the city's idea to move the neighborhood celebrations to a new venue in 1901 rejuvenated the Shooters.

18. The text of these rules was found on a parade permit in one of the Mummers Museum books of newspaper clippings, compiled by Tom DeNoti.

Chapter 2

1. Howard Becker (1984, 246) proposes that folk art be defined as "work done totally outside professional art worlds, work done by ordinary people in the course of their ordinary lives." He also distinguishes between the community of the folk artist and that of the canonical artist, noting that folk art originates within a community of family and neighbors. This definition applies to the Mummers, whose art was and is locally based.

2. Charles Welch's study of the folklore of Philadelphia Mummery (1991, 45–52) includes a detailed description of the 1929 parade. The description included in his book as well as in clippings from the Mummers Museum archives provided the information for this section.

3. Many Mummers began their careers as pages who carried the capes of club captains. These capes, lavishly decorated with embroidery (done by wives and daughters) and three-dimensional trim, were usually not worn but were attached to the lead float that the captain occupied. Over the years the capes became longer, posing a real challenge to pages on windy days. A very old satin cape in the Mummers Museum is beautifully trimmed with three-dimensional roses attached to a quilted background. One can only imagine the hours that were devoted to creating and producing such an extraordinary piece of needlework.

4. This kind of debate echoed the concerns of African American community leaders who deplored the "foolishness and wastefulness" of holiday parades and processions beginning in the nineteenth century (White 1994, 34).

5. Role reversal, including reversal of gender roles, is a staple of the carnival tradition, both African American and European American.

6. There was a rule against impersonating a policeman, but this did not appear to inhibit the 1929 comics.

7. Octavius V. Catto was a nineteenth-century civil rights leader and the victim of racist violence following the Civil War. As mentioned in Chapter 1, South Philadelphia was plagued by racist riots during the late nineteenth century. Catto was active in attempts to get newly enfranchised black men to the polls. The O. V. Catto group was later reconstituted as a brass band and marches with the fancy division noncompetitively to this day.

8. It is noteworthy that the individual performers are no longer judged at the City Hall judging stand but are diverted to other judging areas. This change has occurred because of time constraints.

9. One Mummer who had paraded for more than fifty years commented only half-jokingly that "it really would be more accurate to call them saxophone bands." He was a saxophone player.

10. The "pit" band is the core around which the "perimeter" band moves; though the Mummers placed instruments so that they were most acoustically complementary in the early years, when vertical and horizontal movement predominated, the complexity of the shows results in so much movement that they no longer do so. However, it is still the case that banjos and strings are

usually in the front of the formation, while saxophones and other reed instruments march behind them. Band members wearing the most elaborate costumes and those with backpieces tend to march on the perimeter (Conners, interview, 1998).

11. In 1999 the fancy brigades did not perform at City Hall, instead detouring to the Convention Center. Their performance was one element in a "package" that included face painting for children and the opportunity to watch the clubs create their floats. Though the other divisions were invited to join in this paid show, they declined the opportunity and decried the commercialism and loss of tradition that the new route signified. As a participant observer in 1999 with one of the brigades, I missed the opportunity of seeing the City Hall performance that had occurred in my previous marches up Broad Street with the brigade. The practice has continued, though after the successful 2004 Mummers Parade the brigades rejoined the Broad Street Parade, marching with only their hand-held props.

12. Costumers often work with many clubs, and in one of the years when I was conducting my research, one costumer did several string bands and five fancy brigades. In Chapter 4, I discuss my experience within a club and the extent to which the clubs themselves add embellishments to what may be a basic costume.

13. *Game* is a broad term that encompasses artistic performances by competing groups. Theorists, including Huizinga (1955), Caillois (1961), and Csikszentmihalyi (1975) emphasize the connection between rules and competitive play. The classification of the parade as a game does not minimize the rewards that Mummers gain through their creative efforts (as in the actual production of a fancy entry or envisioning of a brigade presentation), but recognition of artistry or skill by others within competitive settings validates the intrinsic satisfaction of creating something beautiful or unique. I would suggest that the artist "performs" for an audience even as he or she works in solitude. This is apparent in the accounts of play that nonperforming artists, especially those in the fancy clubs, gave when I interviewed them for this research. I explore this further in Chapter 7.

14. One of the most useful resources I used early in my research was a binder given to me by Charles Welch, who had served as a commentator for the local television station broadcasting the parade. It contained brief histories of the clubs, descriptions of their performances, and a full set of competition rules.

Chapter 3

1. Chapter 6 illustrates the importance of the Mummers' leaders and stars as role models.

2. These contributions are discussed in Chapter 1 and include one symbol of Mummery, the banjo.

3. Chapter 2 describes the Catto band's performance in 1929.

4. Elias Myers was with the city's Department of Recreation, which oversaw many of the logistical details of the annual parade. The city and the Mummers cooperate on decisions such as scheduling, but the department maintains licensing control for participation

5. More than twenty-seven thousand African Americans in New Orleans signed a petition to protest the Zulus' portrayal of blacks and urged city residents to boycott Mardi Gras. Initially the Zulus cancelled their plans to participate, but they changed course when the mayor, the chief of police, and local businesses persuaded them to parade as usual. They marched under heavy police protection in 1961 and experienced two difficult years as performers in 1962 and 1963. But, once the controversy settled down, they resumed their tradition as part of Mardi Gras (Welch 1991, 154–56). The full story of the Zulu controversy appears in an article, "The Zulus," by Calvin Trillin in *The New Yorker*, vol. 40, no. 25 (1964): 42. Welch excerpts portions of this article in his book.

6. In private, ethnic and minority groups may joke about the stereotypes outsiders hold of them. When this mockery occurs in public, it is seen as much more objectionable and tasteless.

7. This account is not intended to either defend or criticize the Mummers' actions during the controversy. Rather, it reflects my emphasis on the Mummers' interpretations. Conversations with the Mummers many years after the controversy revealed that they were still uncomfortable discussing this topic. It is difficult to engage in an open dialogue about race even retrospectively. Because of the sensitivity among Mummers even today, and because I agreed when the initial interview was conducted with the white comic club leader, I will not use their names. Using "white informant" and "black informant" makes the text a bit clumsy, but it honors a pledge made many years ago.

8. I understand that several bands participated, but it is reasonable to qualify this statement by allowing for the possibility that others did not.

9. His recollections of the date and timing of the controversy are erroneous.

Chapter 4

1. Bill Burke retired as captain of Golden Crown after the 2004 Mummers Parade.

2. Most of the string bands and fancy brigades go to a professional designer, who works with them in developing their costumes and in some cases their productions. This is a collaborative process that involves the theme committee. The design then goes to a costumer, who makes a basic suit. Trim and sequins are often added to the body suit and capes after they are delivered to the clubhouse. Relatively simple costumes, such as those worn by children, are made wholly within the club. At the beginning of this research, I was very much concerned with the co-optation of the parade by "professionals," but I learned that each club develops its own expertise on costume making, props,

music arranging, and other aspects of the production. The costume designer is more consultant than director, and the clubs limit their use of professional services, partly because of economic constraints but mostly because of their desire to retain creative control.

3. Golden Crown's women are members of the club in every respect, except that they are not required to pay club dues. Because there are many couples in the club, paying dues would create a double burden. Women do, however, in an "auxiliary" capacity, engage in various fund-raising activities, including T-shirt sales and selling hoagies, a favorite Philadelphia sandwich.

4. I was joined by my son and husband on New Year's Day. My son carried the captain's second backpiece, and my husband joined me in helping wherever anyone needed an extra set of hands. All three of us were marshals, whose role is to move scenery and help the show proceed up the street.

5. I sometimes discussed particular aspects about the performance of one division with club members from other divisions and found that few Mummers had a general sense of the broader history of their traditions. This does not mean that they were not interested in what other divisions did; rather, it suggests that at the club level members find little time to explore what others are doing. There were a few exceptions—for example, when a member started out as a comic and moved into another division because of personal ties, or saw other divisions as places where he or she could use and develop different skills.

Chapter 5

1. This poem is used with the permission of the author, William J. Conners, Ferko String Band.

2. Several Mummers added the detail that this group had consumed a quantity of beer and that the decision to visit the grave emerged from a kind of group dare.

3. This emphasis on the rule-governed nature of play is consistent with Huizinga's assertion that play is ritual. He writes in his chapter "The Nature and Significance of Play" that "the elements proper to play—order, tension, movement, change, solemnity, rhythm, and rapture," are all present in ritual (1955, 17). It is the elements of order, rhythm, and movement that make play aesthetically pleasing.

4. Sacrificial rites link in symbolic form the profane and the sacred; imitative rites focus on a concept of the ideal and are a means through which individuals, in emulating the ideal, are "spiritual and morally elevated"; piacular rites are "sad celebrations . . . whose object is to either met a calamity or deplore it" (Durkheim 1965, 434).

5. In the years prior to the Mass I observed, I learned that representatives from other religious denominations had joined in the religious celebrations. I was not able to discover when or why this practice was discontinued.

6. Max Raab's highly acclaimed documentary about the Mummers (*Strut!*) opened in Philadelphia in 2002 (Sidmax Productions, 2002). Within this documentary is some excellent footage of the string band Mass.

7. In 1999, for the first time, the fancy brigades did not parade the full distance to City Hall, instead choosing to perform at the Convention Center before a paying audience. This departure from tradition was roundly criticized by the other divisions, but the props used by the fancy brigades had become so large and complex that it was extremely difficult and time-consuming to move them up Broad Street and around City Hall. The brigades continued this practice through the 2004 parade.

Chapter 6

1. The "Show of Shows" is an annual string band performance that occurs after the parade. The clubs have performed in various venues, from the Convention Center to different sports stadiums. The event drew audiences for multiple shows scheduled over a couple of weeks in the past, but attendance had dwindled by the time I attended the annual show in the late 1990s to the point that only two performances were scheduled. This event has now moved to Wildwood, New Jersey, where many of the Mummers spend their vacations, and it occurs in the spring.

Chapter 7

1. Mummers consistently use the phrase "having fun" to describe their experiences of parading. This phrase captures the essential frivolity and fool-ishness of performing, but they are equally likely to label the times when they are engaged in the serious and sustained work of preparing for a performance as "having fun" because they are with others who share the anticipation of appearing in the parade. In using the terms "fun" and "having fun," I am echo-ing the Mummers.

2. One Mummer I interviewed recalled his grandmother thrusting a cake out the door and closing it quickly, because by the time the Shooters reached her home, they had consumed a great deal of holiday "cheer."

3. Play satisfies the imitative instinct of young children, and through play they learn. Adults release tension through play and satisfy the need to domi-nate others through competition. In this sense, then, play is instrumental.

4. Huizinga specifically distinguishes professional sports from the organ-ized games and matches of amateurs; as a translator's footnote points out, "It is probably significant that we no longer speak of 'games' but of 'sport.' Our author [Huizinga] may not have been sufficiently familiar with the develop-ment of 'sport' in the last ten or twenty years ... to stress the all important point that sport has become business, or to put it bluntly, a commercial racket" (1955, 197). Huizinga himself writes that "the spirit of the professional [com-

petitor] is no longer the true play-spirit; it is lacking in spontaneity and carelessness" (1955, 197).

5. Every year since I began this research, one of the comic clubs has challenged this rule by attempting to carry a case of beer up Broad Street. Only token efforts are made to conceal this flouting of the rules. What generally occurs is the discovery of the contraband beer by the police, who "arrest" the perpetrators (only briefly) and impose a fine. The event is a form of ritualized disobedience, with the participants challenging the city's authority over their parade and the authorities asserting the right to control public space. In this sense, the rowdy, seditious nature of the early Shooters' processions is celebrated.

6. The band to which he belonged has garnered nineteen first, second, and third prizes in the past thirty-two years.

7. Mr. Conners graciously gave me permission to use his article.

8. The line between professional and nonprofessional is not clear. As Palma stressed, many of those who now design suits and produce them began as nonprofessionals, making their own costumes and discovering that they had skills others were interested in purchasing. One of the most popular and successful designers is, however, a trained artist.

9. Frame suits and trio clowns are specific categories within the fancy brigade division. Frame suits, some of which weigh more than one hundred pounds, must be carried up the parade route; the addition of wheels is a recent modification to the tradition. Trio clowns are an older category of competition that has been combined with trio jockey into fancy trio. This category requires that three individuals dress in matching suits with a theme such as "galaxy" (a space theme) or "African nights."

10. I relied particularly on a tape of the 1997 Mummers Parade that featured coverage by Channel 17, with commentary by Robert Finnegan, formerly curator of the Mummers Museum and an experienced costume designer. These interviews, though brief, followed the content of my lengthy interview with Bill Burke that is quoted in this section.

Chapter 8

1. This search was done on 20 August 2006. Similar terms might have turned up equally large numbers of references.

2. The full text of this poem is given at the beginning of Chapter 5.

REFERENCES

A Note on Sources

I reconstructed the Mummers' history and heritage by consulting numerous sources. In addition to the newspaper articles listed below, I read many of Philadelphia's major newspapers from 1900 to the present, not only for their stories about the Mummers but also to learn about the context within which their traditions developed. These included the *Philadelphia Inquirer,* the *Philadelphia Daily News,* the *South Philadelphia Review,* and the *Philadelphia Bulletin.* I am grateful to the Mummers Museum Library for access to its collection of Mummer clippings. I also relied on Mr. William Conners's collection of scrapbooks, which contain articles from other area newspapers and club histories accumulated over the years.

The Mummers Museum also has a full set of films (tapes and videocassettes) of past parades and an extensive photo archive that helped me to see the evolution of the art of Mummery. In addition, information on how the Mummers wished to be seen is conveyed through the "Mummers Moments," short interviews featuring many individuals involved with the parade. Typically, these brief interviews are used to "fill in the gaps" in broadcasting the parade.

Finally, Mummers who are television commentators for the parade each year receive loose-leaf binders with background notes for the parading clubs, usually submitted to the Philadelphia Department of Recreation and then supplied to the television network broadcasting the event; I benefited from access to these materials as well. Through Professor Charles Welch Jr. and Mr. William Wayterra I received copies of 1992 and 1996 parade notebooks. These notebooks were extraordinarily useful in providing profiles of the clubs and confirming the extensive family relations that pervade this play community. Mr. Wayterra's notebook also contained material he had gathered on the comic club presentations by visiting clubhouses in the week before the 1996 parade.

References

Adler, Patricia A. 1993. *Wheeling and dealing: An ethnography of an upper-level drug dealing and smuggling community.* New York: Columbia University Press.

Alexander, John K. 1973. Poverty, fear, and continuity: An analysis of the poor in late eighteenth-century Philadelphia. In *The peoples of Philadelphia: A history of ethnic groups and lower-class life, 1790–1940,* ed. Allen F. Davis and Mark H. Haller, 13–36. Philadelphia: Temple University Press.

Anderson, Elijah J. 1999. *Code of the street: Decency, violence, and the moral life of the inner city.* New York: W. W. Norton and Company.

Atkinson, Paul, and Martin Hammersley. 1994. Ethnography and participant observation. In *Handbook of qualitative research,* ed. Norman K. Denzin and Yvonna S. Lincoln, 248–61. Thousand Oaks, Calif.: Sage Publications.

Aune, Michael F., and Valerie DeMarinis. 1996. *Religious and social ritual: Interdisciplinary explorations.* Albany: State University of New York Press.

Barrett, Joseph R. 1957. New Year's Shooters paraded in south Philadelphia. *Philadelphia Sunday Bulletin,* 29 December, 1.

Baur, Francis X., and Susan Baur. 1997. Interview by author. Tape recording. 15 July. Philadelphia.

Becker, Howard S. 1984. *Art worlds.* Berkeley and Los Angeles: University of California Press.

Bell, Catherine. 1992. *Ritual theory, ritual practice.* New York: Oxford University Press.

———. 1997. *Ritual perspectives and dimensions.* New York: Oxford University Press.

Bellah, Robert N., ed. 1973. *Emile Durkheim: On morality and society.* Chicago: University of Chicago Press.

Bender, Thomas. 1978. *Community and social change in America.* Baltimore: Johns Hopkins University Press.

Berger, Peter L., and Thomas Luckmann. 1966. *The social construction of reality: A treatise on the sociology of knowledge.* Garden City, N.Y.: Anchor Books.

Blumer, Herbert. 1986. *Symbolic interactionism: Perspective and method.* Berkeley and Los Angeles: University of California Press.

Bradshaw, Dave, and Tom Frangicetto. 1995. *Joe's Boys: The story of Joseph A. Ferko and the Ferko String Band.* Reading, Pa.: Exeter House Books.

Brandes, Stanley. 1988. *Power and persuasion: Fiestas and social control in rural Mexico.* Philadelphia: University of Pennsylvania Press.

Brandt, Frances Burke. 1930a. Philadelphia's Mummers Day wins world fame as survivor of Rome's glorious carnival of freedom and mad joy. *Philadelphia Evening Public Ledger,* 17 November, 1.

———. 1930b. Customs of Mummers Day traced back to first Swedish settlers in old Phila. *Philadelphia Evening Public Ledger,* 18 November, 1.

———. 1930c. Ancient English folk play seen as great contributor to Phila. Mummers Parade. *Philadelphia Evening Public Ledger,* 19 November, 1.

———. 1930d. Masked New Year's balls once forbidden in Penna. as "common nuisances." *Philadelphia Evening Public Ledger,* 20 November, 1.

———. 1930e. But growth of Mummery began in 1876 with birth of Silver Crown Association. *Philadelphia Evening Public Ledger,* 21 November, 1.

———. 1930f. New Year's feat recalls traditions and customs alive at city's founding. *Philadelphia Evening Public Ledger,* 22 November, 1.

Bright, Wendell. 2006. Interview by author. 24 August.

Burke, Walter. 1998. Interview by author. Tape recording. 6 March. Mummers Museum, Philadelphia.

Burke, Bill, Jr. 1995. Interview by author. Tape recording. 15 March. Philadelphia.

Burt, Struthers. 1945. *Philadelphia: Holy experiment.* Garden City, N.Y.: Doubleday, Duran, and Co.

Caillois, Roger. 1961. *Man, play, and games.* New York: Free Press.

Carey, Art. 1978. "Two Street" turns into Strutters lane. *Philadelphia Inquirer,* 30 January, 1.

Chicoine, Christine. 1993. Mummers begin New Year at Mass. *Catholic Standard and Times,* 7 January, 1, 10.

Clark, Dennis. 1973a. *Irish in Philadelphia: Ten generations of urban experience.* Philadelphia: Temple University Press.

———. 1973b. The Philadelphia Irish: Persistent presence. In *The peoples of Philadelphia: A history of ethnic groups and lower-class life, 1790–1940,* ed. Allen F. Davis and Mark H. Haller, 135–54. Philadelphia: Temple University Press.

Cloney, Tom. 1997. Interview by author. Tape recording. 11 October. Philadelphia.

Cohen, Abner. 1982. A polyethnic London carnival as a contested cultural performance. *Ethnic and Racial Studies* 5 (January): 23–41.

Coley, Mark. 1996. Interview by author. Tape recording. 11 July. Golden Crown Fancy Brigade Clubhouse, Philadelphia.

Collins, Randall. 1985. *Three sociological traditions.* New York: Oxford University Press.

Conner, Ed. 1997. Interview by author. Tape recording. 9 May. Mummers Museum, Philadelphia.

Conners, William J. 1978. Four minutes. Manuscript.

———. 1995. Interview by author. Tape recording. 5 January. Philadelphia.

———. 1998. Interview by author. 23 April. Philadelphia.

Creedon, Daniel F. 1997. Interview by author. Tape recording. 10 October. Philadelphia.

Creswell, John W. 1997. *Qualitative inquiry and research design: Choosing among five traditions.* Thousand Oaks, Calif.: Sage Publications.

Csikszentmihalyi, Mihaly. 1975. *Beyond boredom and anxiety: The experience of play in work and games*. San Francisco: Jossey-Bass.

———. 1981. Some paradoxes in the definition of play. In *Play as context: 1979 proceedings of the Association for the Anthropological Study of Play*, ed. Alyce Taylor Cheska, 14–36. West Point, N.Y.: Leisure Press.

———. 1990. *Flow: The psychology of optimal experience*. New York: Harper-Perennial.

Davis, Allen F., and Mark H. Haller., eds. 1973. *The peoples of Philadelphia: A history of ethnic groups and lower-class life, 1790–1940*. Philadelphia: Temple University Press.

Davis, Susan G. 1985. *Parades and power: Street theatre in nineteenth-century Philadelphia*. Philadelphia: Temple University Press.

Denzin, Norman K. 1982. The paradoxes of play. In *The paradoxes of play: Proceedings of the eighth annual meeting of the Association for the Anthropological Study of Play*, ed. John W. Loy, 13–24. West Point, N.Y.: Leisure Press.

———. 1989. *The research act: A theoretical introduction to sociological methods*. Englewood Cliffs, N.J.: Prentice-Hall.

Denzin, Norman K., and Yvonna S. Lincoln, eds. 1994. *Handbook of qualitative research*. Thousand Oaks, Calif.: Sage Publications.

Donio, James. 1976. *Alfred Fink*. Lifetime Mummer series, vol. 1, no. 1. Philadelphia: JSL, Inc.

Dougherty, Frank. 1992. The Northeast strut: Mummer clubs make their homes from Fishtown to Mayfair. *Philadelphia Daily News*, 24 September, NE 3, 19.

Driver, Tom F. 1991. *Magic of ritual*. San Francisco: Harper.

Dubin, Murray. 1996. *South Philadelphia: Mummers, memories, and the Melrose Diner*. Philadelphia: Temple University Press.

Duneier, Mitchell. 1999. *Sidewalk*. New York: Farrar, Straus and Giroux.

Durkheim, Emile. 1965. *The elementary forms of the religious life*. Trans. Joseph Ward Swain. New York: Free Press.

———. 1984. *The division of labor in society*. Trans. W. D. Halls, with an introduction by Lewis Coser. New York: Free Press.

Falassi, Alessandro. 1987. Festival: Definition and morphology. In *Time out of time: Essays on the festival*, ed. Alessandro Falassi, 1–10. Albuquerque: University of New Mexico Press.

Falk, Sally, and Barbara G. Myerhoff, eds. 1975. *Symbol and politics in communal ideology: Cases and questions*. Ithaca, N.Y.: Cornell University Press.

Fancy Brigade Association. 1988. *Rhythm in motion: 1988 yearbook*. Philadelphia: Fancy Brigade Association.

———. 1998. *Twentieth anniversary: 1978–1998*. Philadelphia: Fancy Brigade Association.

Fischer, Claude S. 1976. *The urban experience*. New York: Harcourt Brace Jovanovich.

————. 1982. *To dwell among friends: Personal networks in town and city.* Chicago: University of Chicago Press.

Fontana, Andrea, and James H. Frey. 1994. Interviewing: The art of science. In *Qualitative research methods,* ed. Norman K. Denzin and Yvonna S. Lincoln, 361–76. Thousand Oaks, Calif.: Sage Publications.

Galvin, James J. 1964. *Saint John Neumann: Fourth bishop of Philadelphia.* Baltimore: Helicon Press.

Gerth, H. H., and C. Wright Mills, eds. 1958. *From Max Weber: Essays in sociology.* New York: Oxford University Press.

Giancaterino, Randy. 1996. A soft spot in Mummers hearts. *South Philadelphia Review,* 18 December.

————. 1997. Interview by author. Tape recording. 14 April. Mummers Museum, Philadelphia.

Gilje, Paul A. 1987. *The road to mobocracy: Popular disorder in New York City.* Chapel Hill: University of North Carolina Press.

Glassie, Henry. 1975. *All silver and no brass: An Irish Christmas mumming.* Philadelphia: University of Pennsylvania Press.

Goffman, Erving. 1963. *Behavior in public places: Notes on the social organization of gatherings.* New York: Free Press.

————. 1967. *Interaction rituals.* New York: Doubleday.

————. 1974. *Frame analysis: An essay on the organization of experience.* New York: Harper & Row.

Golab, Carolina. 1973. The immigrant and the city: Poles, Italians, and Jews in Philadelphia. In *The peoples of Philadelphia: A history of ethnic groups and lower-class life, 1790–1940,* ed. Allen F. Davis and Mark H. Haller, 203–30. Philadelphia: Temple University Press.

Goldwyn, Ron. 1984a. On a strut down Mummery lane. *Philadelphia Daily News,* 25 April, 26.

————. 1984b. City opens parade to new Mummers. *Philadelphia Daily News,* 22 May, 3.

————. 1984c. Mummers lottery a comic solution. *Philadelphia Daily News,* 6 June, 5.

Gradante, William J. 1986. The message in the mask: Costuming in the festival context. In *The many faces of play: Proceedings of the ninth annual meeting of the Association for the Anthropological Study of Play,* ed. Kendall Blanchard, 172–86. Champaign, Ill.: Human Kinetics Publishers.

Greenberg, Nancy, and Marci Shatzman. 1974. All-male parade stirs envy. *Philadelphia Sunday Bulletin,* 6 January.

Greenberg, Stephanie W. 1981. Industrial location and ethnic residential patterns in an industrializing city, Philadelphia. In *Philadelphia: Work, space, family, and group experience in the nineteenth century,* ed. Theodore Hershberg, 204–32. New York: Oxford University Press.

Gusfield, Joseph R. 1986. *Symbolic crusade: Status politics and the American temperance crusade.* 2d ed. Urbana: University of Illinois Press.

Harris, Janet C. 1981. Beyond Huizinga: Relationships between play and culture. In *Play as context: 1979 proceedings of the Association for the Anthropological Study of Play*, ed. Alyce Taylor Cheska, 26–36. West Point, N.Y.: Leisure Press.

Hart, Jake. 1982. Oh, dem golden wing tips. *The Shingle* 45 (winter): 16–21, 41–45.

———. 1990. Down the aisle, down the hall. Manuscript.

Heller, Al. 1996. Interview by author. Tape recording. 9 July. Philadelphia.

Hershberg, Theodore. 1973. Free blacks in antebellum Philadelphia. In *The peoples of Philadelphia: A history of ethnic groups and lower-class life, 1790–1940*, ed. Allen F. Davis and Mark H. Haller, 111–34. Philadelphia: Temple University Press.

———, ed. 1981. *Philadelphia: Work, space, family, and group experience in the nineteenth century.* New York: Oxford University Press.

Hershberg, Theodore, Harold E. Cox, Dale Light Jr., and Richard Greenfield. 1981. The journey to work. In *Philadelphia: Work, space, family, and group experience in the nineteenth century*, ed. Theodore Hershberg, 128–73. New York: Oxford University Press.

Hobsbawm, Eric. 1982. Introduction: Inventing tradition. In *The invention of tradition*, ed. Eric Hobsbawm and Terence Ranger, 1–14. New York: Cambridge University Press.

Hollman, Laurie. 1992. Two worlds join on Broad Street. *Philadelphia Inquirer,* 31 December, B1, B4.

Horton, James Oliver, and Lois E. Horton. 1997. *In hope of liberty: Culture, community, and protest among northern free blacks, 1700–1860.* New York: Oxford University Press.

Huizinga, Johan. 1955. *Homo ludens: A study of the play-element in culture.* Boston: Beacon Press.

Hundzynski, William. 1996. Interview by author. Tape recording. 9 July. Mummers Museum, Philadelphia.

Johnson, David R. 1973. Crime patterns in Philadelphia, 1840–1870. In *The peoples of Philadelphia: A history of ethnic groups and lower-class life, 1790–1940*, ed. Allen F. Davis and Mark H. Haller, 89–110. Philadelphia: Temple University Press.

Kammen, Michael. 1991. *Mystic chords of memory.* New York: Random House.

Kasinitz, Philip. 1992. *Caribbean New York: Black immigrants and the politics of race.* Ithaca: Cornell University Press.

Kenney, James F. 1996. Interview by author. Tape recording. 20 June. Philadelphia.

Knorr, Jack. 1979. Patty wants to show 'em. *Philadelphia Journal,* 27 November, 40.

Koresco, Alice. 1997. Interview by author. Tape recording. 13 June. Mummers Museum, Philadelphia.

Laurie, Bruce. 1973. Fire companies and gangs in Southwark: 1840–1870. In *The peoples of Philadelphia: A history of ethnic groups and lower-class life,*

1790–1940, ed. Allen F. Davis and Mark H. Haller, 71–88. Philadelphia: Temple University Press.

Liebow, Elliot. 1967. *Tally's corner: A study of Negro streetcorner men*. New York: Little, Brown.

———. 1993. *Tell them who I am: The lives of homeless women*. New York: Penguin Books.

Lorber, Judith. 1993. Believing is seeing: Biology as ideology. *Gender and Society* 7, no. 4: 568–81.

Lott, Eric. 1993. *Love and theft: Blackface minstrelsy and the American working class*. New York: Oxford University Press.

Lowery, Patricia. 1997. Interview by author. Tape recording. 10 October. Hegeman String Band Clubhouse, Philadelphia.

Lucas, Palma. 1994. Interview by author. Tape recording. 10 January. Golden Sunrise Fancy Clubhouse, Philadelphia.

———. 1995. Interview by author. 24 February.

MacAloon, John J. 1984. *Rite, drama, festival, spectacle: Rehearsals toward a theory of cultural performance*. Philadelphia: Institute for the Study of Human Issues.

Magendra, S. P. 1971. *The concept of ritual in modern sociological theory*. New Delhi: Academic Journals of India.

Manning, Frank E. 1983. The scholar as clown: An approach to play. In *The world of play: Proceedings of the seventh annual meeting of the Association for the Anthropological Study of Play*, ed. Frank. E. Manning, 11–21. West Point, N.Y.: Leisure Press.

Mastroianni, Debbie. 1996. Interview by author. Tape recording. 7 January. Golden Crown Fancy Brigade Clubhouse, Philadelphia.

Mathias, Elizabeth. 1981. Italian-American culture and games: The Minnesota Iron Range and south Philadelphia. In *Play as context: 1979 proceedings of the Association for the Anthropological Study of Play*, ed. Alyce Taylor Cheska, 73–92. West Point, N.Y.: Leisure Press.

Max L. Raab Productions, in association with Jones Film. 2002. *Strut!* DVD. Produced and directed by Max L. Raab. Sidmax Productions, LLC.

Mayer, John E. 1972. *Q.C.S.B.: 1931–1971*. Philadelphia: Quaker City String Band.

———. 1981. *Quaker City String Band: Celebrating 50 wonderful years, 1931–81*. Philadelphia: Quaker City String Band.

McCord, Frederick A. 1956. The Mummers Parade: From ancient times comes a unique Philadelphia festival. *Philadelphia Sunday Bulletin*, 1 January, 1, 4.

McGrath, Donald. 1998. Interview by author. Tape recording. 6 March. Mummers Museum, Philadelphia.

McHale, Sonja. 1997. Interview by author. Tape recording. 8 May. Mummers Museum, Philadelphia.

McPherson, Miller, Lynn Smith-Lovin, and Matthew L. Bradshaw. 2006. Social isolation in America: Changes in core discussion networks over two decades. *American Sociological Review* 71 (June): 353–75.

Mead, George Herbert. 1934. *Mind, self, and society.* Chicago: University of Chicago Press.

Mills, C. Wright. 1959. *The sociological imagination.* New York: Oxford University Press.

Mitchell, Reid. 1995. *All on a Mardi Gras day: Episodes in the history of New Orleans carnival.* Cambridge: Harvard University Press.

Murray Comic Club. 1996. *Murray Comic Club: 60th anniversary, 1936–1996.* Philadelphia: Murray Comic Club.

Naedele, Walter F. 1975. Two teenage girls (girls?) march with string band. *Philadelphia Evening Bulletin,* 2 January, 2.

Nisbet, Robert. 1974. *The sociology of Emile Durkheim.* New York: Oxford University Press.

Olick, Jeffrey K., and Daniel Levy. 1997. Collective memory and cultural constraint: Holocaust myth and rationality in German politics. *American Sociological Review* 62 (December): 921–36.

Pegg, Bob. 1981. *Rites and riots: Folk customs of Britain and Europe.* Poole, U.K.: Blandford Press.

Philadelphia Daily News. 1955. Little Mummers' parade on Second. 1 January, 1.

———. 2004. Comeback of the year. 2 January, 2, 7, 16.

Philadelphia Evening Bulletin. 1932a. Klein, Ferko and League Island win Mummers Parade. 2 January, 1, 13.

———. 1932b. Mummers ready to please through gay carnival. 2 January, 3.

———. 1932c. Two hundred female impersonators seen in elaborate gowns. 2 January, 2.

———. 1964. Mummers reaction to ban. 4 January, 5.

———. N.d. Women's ears: They must be protected at all hazards. 33:226, 1.

Philadelphia Evening Item. 1900. Plans for glorious celebration and birth of twentieth century: Councils committed. 11 December, 1.

Philadelphia Evening Public Ledger. 1934. Neighborhoods enjoy Mummers frolic despite lack of prizes from City. 1 January, 1, 17.

Philadelphia Inquirer. 1900a. Giant reception planned by mayor: The cost would be small. 1 December, 1.

———. 1900b. A night parade of the Mummers: What Chairman Seeds suggests for twentieth century demonstration. 4 December, 1.

———. 1900c. Committee named for big jubilee . . . Shooters to volunteer. 7 December, 1.

———. 1900d. Gay Mummers by the thousands: One of the features of the city's welcome to the New Year. 14 December, 1.

———. 1900e. Celebration will be a rouser. 20 December, 1.

———. 1934. Mummers frolic before neighbors in rain for fun. 2 January, 1.

———. 1935. Fragment of an article on "judging." 2 February, 4.

———. 1955. Kensington businessman's parade. 15 January.

———. 1984. The glory that is Mummery must grow in brotherhood (editorial). 30 April, A10.

Philadelphia Mummers String Band Association, Inc. 1994. *1994 Show of Shows spectacular.* Philadelphia: String Band Association.

———. 1995. *1995 Show of Shows Souvenir Program.* Philadelphia: String Band Association.

Philadelphia New Year Shooters and Mummers Association. 1963–73. *Mummers Magazine,* issues for 1963, 1964, 1965, 1966, 1967, 1968, 1971, 1972, and 1973. Philadelphia: PNYSMA.

———. 1977. *Mummers Souvenir Book.* Philadelphia: PNYSMA.

Philadelphia Record. 1900. Ready for the next century. 30 December, 1.

———. 1916. Fragment of a story on "Negro participation." 2 January.

Philadelphia Times. 1893. Honoring the New Year: Its birth to be celebrated with old-time customs. 31 December.

Pierson, William D. 1993. *Black legacy: America's hidden heritage.* Amherst: University of Massachusetts Press.

Pignotti, John. 1997. Interview by author. Tape recording. 7 May. Hegeman String Band Clubhouse, Philadelphia.

Pilla, Sandra. 1992. Women Mummers growing in number. *South Philadelphia Review,* 31 December, 1, 10.

Porco, Rich. 1997. Interview by author. Tape recording. 26 April. Philadelphia.

Preston, Jennifer. 1983a. Mummers strike note of discord. *Philadelphia Daily News,* 16 March, 14.

———. 1983b. Hegeman bandsmen feel like unsung heroes. 23 June, 4.

Putnam, Robert D. 1993. The prosperous community. *American Prospect* 13 (spring): 35–42.

———. 2000. *Bowling alone: The collapse and revival of American community.* New York: Simon and Schuster/Touchstone.

Regan, Edward J. 1996. *Back to the schoolyard: A biographical essay of the Fralinger String Band.* Philadelphia: Fralinger String Band.

Richman, Alan. 1974. All in the family: Four generations of Joseph Tylers in one parade. *Philadelphia Sunday Bulletin Discover Magazine,* 29 December, 7–8.

Roediger, David R. 1996. *The wages of whiteness: Race and the making of the American working class.* New York: Verso.

Rothberg, Andrea Ignatoff. 1980. Philadelphia Mummery: Individual rewards and social interaction. Ph.D. diss., University of Wisconsin.

Rubin, Lillian B. 1994. *Families on the fault line: America's working class speaks about the family, the economy, race, and ethnicity.* New York: Harper-Perennial.

Scharf, J. Thomas, and Thompson Westcott. 1884. *History of Philadelphia, 1609–1884.* 3 vols. Philadelphia: L. H. Everts.

Schutz, Alfred. 1970. *On phenomenology and social relations.* Ed. Helmut R. Wagner. Chicago: University of Chicago Press.

Sexton, James. 1996. Interview by author. Tape recording. 9 July. Philadelphia.

Shuey, Joseph. 1998. Interview by author. Tape recording. 6 March. Mummers Museum, Philadelphia.

Shuler, Evelyn. 1930a. New Year's Shooters quaintly clad and ringing cowbells, toured homes in "the Neck" to kiss girls. *Philadelphia Evening Public Ledger,* 15 November, 1.

————. 1930b. New Year's Shooters toil twelve long months to become "kings for a day" on Broad Street. *Philadelphia Evening Public Ledger,* 24 November, 1.

————. 1930c. Change to fancy costumes, fine bands, and prizes increased Shooters' fame. *Philadelphia Evening Public Ledger,* 26 November, 1.

————. 1930d. Shooters vie to keep their costumes secret until very last minute of parade starting time. *Philadelphia Evening Public Ledger,* 27 November, 1.

————. 1930e. Shooters paraded to neighborhoods for century before fame soared afar. *Philadelphia Evening Public Ledger,* 28 November, 1.

————. 1930f. New Year Shooters made first city-wide showing in greeting 20th century. *Philadelphia Evening Public Ledger,* 29 November, 1.

————. 1930g. Silver Crown Club, granddaddy of New Year's Shooters, will celebrate its 54th birthday in parade of 1931. *Philadelphia Evening Public Ledger,* 1 December, 1.

————. 1930h. George B. McClernand, Jr., became youngest captain after being spanked for turning Shooter at age of 6. *Philadelphia Evening Public Ledger,* 2 December, 1.

————. 1930i. Clements Club, first headed by William S. Vare, existed in gay old nineties when parade often ended in battle. *Philadelphia Evening Public Ledger,* 3 December, 1.

————. 1930j. David W. Crawford, head of Funston Club, typifies ardent Shooter spirit of annual New Year's parade. *Philadelphia Evening Public Ledger,* 4 December, 1.

————. 1930k. Lobster New Year Association, founded in saloon, makes 23rd appearance this year as Shooters' club. *Philadelphia Evening Public Ledger,* 5 December, 1.

————. 1930l. Charles Dumont, drummer in '93, led clowns in 1903; Jack Himes, "old timers," got into parade line in 1913. *Philadelphia Evening Public Ledger,* 6 December, 1.

————. 1930m. Frank A. Collins Shooter Association has made history in New Year parade. *Philadelphia Evening Public Ledger,* 8 December, 1.

————. 1930n. Charles Roberts, leader of League Island Comic Club, first marches with Shooters when only 6 years old. *Philadelphia Evening Public Ledger,* 9 December, 1.

————. 1930o. B. E. Stevens Club wins $75 when forced into Shooters parade by policeman. *Philadelphia Evening Public Ledger,* 10 December, 1.

————. 1930p. Shooters' string bands trace origin back to Trilby, formed 30 years ago. *Philadelphia Evening Public Ledger,* 11 December, 1.

————. 1930q. This string band hangs up great record by winning challenge cup for Shooters. *Philadelphia Evening Public Ledger,* 12 December, 1.

————. 1930r. Shooters parade doomed, says McHugh, unless civic backing is increased. *Philadelphia Evening Public Ledger,* 13 December, 3.

Simmel, Georg. 1971. *On individuality and social forms.* Ed. Donald N. Levine. Chicago: University of Chicago Press.

Slough, Rebecca J. 1996. "Let every tongue, by art refined, mingle its softest notes with mine": An exploration of hymn-singing events and dimensions of knowing. In *Religious and social ritual: Interdisciplinary explorations,* ed. Michael B. Aune and Valerine D. Marinas, 175–205. Albany: State University of New York Press.

Smart, James. 1965. Want to know about the Mummers? Don't ask a Mummer. *Philadelphia Sunday Bulletin Magazine,* 29 December, 4–5.

Stake, Robert W. 1994. Case studies. In *Handbook of qualitative research,* ed. Norman K. Denzin and Yvonna S. Lincoln, 236–47. Thousand Oaks, Calif.: Sage Publications.

Stermel, Frank. N.d. Interview, *Mummers Magazine.*

Stermel, Michael. 1996. Interview by author. Tape recording. 15 March. Mummers Museum, Philadelphia.

Sutherland, John F. 1973. Housing the poor in the city of homes: Philadelphia at the turn of the century. In *The peoples of Philadelphia: A history of ethnic groups and lower-class life, 1790–1940,* ed. Allen F. Davis and Mark H. Haller. Philadelphia: Temple University Press.

Suttles, Gerald. 1972. *The social construction of communities.* Chicago: University of Chicago Press.

Tallant, Robert. 1948. *Mardi Gras.* Garden City, N.Y.: Doubleday.

Thomas, W. I. 1996. *W. I. Thomas on social disorganization and social personality.* Ed. Morris Janowitz. Chicago: University of Chicago Press.

Toll, Robert C. 1974. *Blacking up: The minstrel show in nineteenth-century America.* New York: Oxford University Press.

Trillin, Calvin. 1964. The Zulus. *The New Yorker* 40 (no. 25, June).

Tuchman, Gaye. 1994. Historical social science: Methodologies, methods, and meanings. In *Handbook of Qualitative Research,* ed. Norman K. Denzin and Yvonna S. Lincoln, 306–23. Thousand Oaks, Calif.: Sage Publications.

Tumulo, Irene. Interview by Suzy Seriff. 19 November 1975.

Turner, Jonathan H. 1991. *The structure of sociological theory.* Belmont, Calif.: Wadsworth Publishing.

Turner, Stephen P., ed. 1993. *Emile Durkheim: Sociologist and moralist.* London: Routledge.

Turner, Victor. 1969. *The ritual process.* Chicago: Aldine Publishing.

————, ed. 1982. *Celebration: Studies in festivity and ritual.* Washington, D.C.: Smithsonian Institution Press.

————. 1983. Play and the horns of a dilemma. In *The world of play: Proceedings of the seventh annual meeting of the Association of the Anthropological Study of Play,* ed. Frank E. Manning, 217–24. West Point, N.Y.: Leisure Press.

Van Maanen, John. 1988. *Tales of the field: On writing ethnography*. Chicago: University of Chicago Press.

Vittolino, Sal, and Frank Conforti. 1976. Who really came in first? *South Philadelphia Chronicle*, 8 January, 1, 4.

———. 1977. "Outsider" Harrowgate wins again. *South Philadelphia Review*, 6 January, 1, 12.

Vogel, Morris J. 1991. *Cultural connections: Museums and libraries of Philadelphia and the Delaware Valley*. Philadelphia: Temple University Press.

Wagner, Helmut R. 1970. Introduction: The phenomenological approach to sociology. In Alfred Schutz, *On phenomenology and social relations*, ed. Helmut R. Wagner, 1–50. Chicago: University of Chicago Press.

Walsh, Jack. 1996. Interview by author. Tape recording. 27 December. Mummers Museum, Philadelphia.

Wayterra, William. 1996. Interview by author. Tape recording. 18 June. Philadelphia.

Weighley, Russell F. 1973. A peaceful city: Public order in Philadelphia from consolidation through the Civil War. In *The peoples of Philadelphia: A history of ethnic groups and lower-class life, 1790–1940*, ed. Allen F. Davis and Mark H. Haller, 155–73. Philadelphia: Temple University Press.

Welch, Charles E., Jr. 1968. The Philadelphia Mummers parade: A study in folklore and popular tradition. Ph.D. diss., University of Pennsylvania.

———. 1991. *Oh! Dem golden slippers: The story of the Philadelphia Mummers*. Philadelphia: Book Street Press.

White, Shane. 1994. "It was a proud day": African-Americans, festivals, and parades in the North, 1741–1834." *Journal of American History* 81, no. 1 (June): 13–50.

Whyte, William Foote. 1955. *Street corner society*. 2d ed. Chicago: University of Chicago Press.

Williams, Edgar. 1977. All plumed and sequined, the Mummers are ready to strut their stuff. *Philadelphia Inquirer*, 30 December, 23.

———. 1979. Mummers Parade: Broad Street is where these angels want to tread. *Philadelphia Inquirer*, 21 December, C1–C2.

Yow, Valerie Raleigh. 1994. *Recording oral history: A practical guide for social scientists*. Thousand Oaks, Calif.: Sage Publications.

INDEX

Note: Information in endnotes is indicated by "n." Page numbers in *italics* refer to illustrations.

PATRICIA ANNE MASTERS is Term Assistant Professor of Sociology and Director of the Undergraduate Program in the Department of Sociology and Anthropology, George Mason University.